The "Belleville"

Pocket Dictionary

1.0

Prague Manifesto

The Prague Manifesto was elaborated in 1996, during the international esperanto congress in Prague. There lie the main goals which the esperanto movement gave itself. The Quebec Esperanto Society subscribes to these goals, and promotes Esperanto for the achievement of those.

*W*e, members of the worldwide movement for the promotion of Esperanto, address this Manifesto to all governments, international organizations and people of good will; declare our unshakeable commitment to the objectives set out here; and call on all organizations and individuals to join us in working for these goals.

For more than a century Esperanto, which was

2

launched in 1887 as a project for an auxiliary language for international communication and quickly developed into a rich living language in its own right, has functioned as a means of bringing people together across the barriers of language and culture. The aims that inspire the users of Esperanto are still as important and relevant as ever. Neither the worldwide use of a few national languages, nor advances in communications technology, nor the development of new methods of language teaching is likely to result in a fair and effective language order based on the following principles, which we hold to be essential.

1 DEMOCRACY

Any system of communication which confers lifelong privileges on some while requiring others to devote years of effort to achieving a lesser degree of competence is fundamentally antidemocratic. While Esperanto, like any language, is not perfect, it far outstrips other languages as a means of egalitarian communication on a world scale.

We maintain that language inequality gives rise to

3

communicative inequality at all levels, including the international level. We are a movement for democratic communication.

2 GLOBAL EDUCATION

All ethnic languages are bound to certain cultures and nations. For example, the child who learns English learns about the culture, geography and political systems of the English-speaking world, primarily the United States and the United Kingdom. The child who learns Esperanto learns about a world without borders, where every country is home.

We maintain that education in any language is bound to a certain view of the world. We are a movement for global education.

3 EFFECTIVE EDUCATION

Only a small percentage of foreign-language students attain fluency in the target language. In Esperanto, fluency is attainable even through home study. Various studies have shown that Esperanto is useful as a preparation for learning other languages. It has also been recommended as a core element in courses in language awareness.

We maintain that the difficulties in learning ethnic languages will always be a barrier for many students who would benefit from knowing a second language. We are a movement for effective language learning.

4 MULTILINGUALISM

The Esperanto community is almost unique as a worldwide community whose members are universally bilingual or multilingual. Every member of the community has made the effort to learn at least one foreign language to a communicative level. In many cases this leads to a love and knowledge of several languages and to broader personal horizons in general.

We maintain that the speakers of all languages, large and small, should have a real chance of learning a second language to a high communicative level. We are a movement for providing that opportunity to all.

5 LANGUAGE RIGHTS

The unequal distribution of power between languages is a recipe for permanent language insecurity, or outright language oppression, for a large part of the world's population. In the Esperanto community the speakers of languages large and small, official and unofficial meet on equal terms through a mutual willingness to compromise. This balance of language rights and responsibilities provides a benchmark for developing and judging other solutions to language inequality and conflict.

We maintain that the wide variations in power among languages undermine the guarantees, expressed in many international instruments, of equal treatment regardless of language. We are a movement for language rights.

6 LANGUAGE DIVERSITY

National governments tend to treat the great diversity of languages in the world as a barrier to communication and development. In the Esperanto community, however, language diversity is experienced as a constant and indispensable source of enrichment. Consequently every language, like every biological species, is inherently valuable and worthy of protection and support.

We maintain that communication and development policies which are not based on respect and support for all languages amount to a death sentence for the majority of languages in the world. We are a movement for language diversity.

7 HUMAN EMANCIPATION

Every language both liberates and imprisons its users, giving them the ability to communicate among themselves but barring them from communication with others. Designed as a universally accessible means of communication, Esperanto is one of the great functional projects for the emancipation of humankind -- one which aims to let every individual citizen participate fully in the human community, securely rooted in his or her local cultural and language identity yet not limited by it.

We maintain that exclusive reliance on national languages inevitably puts up barriers to the freedoms of expression, communication and association. We are a movement for human emancipation.

Prague, July 1996

Rules of Esperanto

1. There is no **indefinite article** (English *a, an*); there is only a **definite article** *la*, alike for all genders, cases and numbers (English *the*). The use of the article is as in other languages. People for whom use of the article offers difficulties {e.g. speakers of Russian, Chinese, etc.) may at first elect not to use it at all.

2. Nouns have the ending *-o*. To form the **plural**, add the ending *-j*. There are only two **cases**: nominative and accusative; the latter can be obtained from the nominative by adding the ending *-n*. The other cases are expressed with the aid of prepositions (genitive by *de* (English *of*), dative by *al* (English *to*), ablative by *per* (English *by means of*) or other prepositions, according to meaning).

3. Adjectives end in *-a*. Cases and numbers are as for nouns. The **comparative** is made with the word *pli* (English *more*),
the **superlative** with *plej* (English *most*); for the

comparative the conjunction *ol* (English *than*) is used.

4. The basic **numerals** (not declined) are: *unu, du, tri, kvar, kvin, ses, sep, ok, naŭ, dek, cent, mil* (English *one, two, three, four, five, six, seven, eight, nine, ten, hundred, thousand*). Tens and hundreds are formed by simple juxtaposition of the numerals. To show ordinal numbers we add the adjective ending; for multiples, the suffix *-obl*; for fractions (actually, reciprocals), *-on*; for collectives, *-op*; for divisionals, the word (particle) *po*. Noun and adverb numerals can also be used.

5. Personal **pronouns**: *mi, vi, li, ŝi, ĝi* (for an object or animal), *si, ni, vi, ili, oni* (English *I, you, he, she, it, oneself, we, you, they, they-one-people*); the possessive pronouns are formed by addition of the adjective ending. Declension is as for nouns.

6. The **verb** does not change for person or number. Forms of the verb: present time takes the ending *-as*; past time, *-is*; future time, *-os*; conditional mood, *-us*; command mood, *-u*;

9

infinitive mood, *-i*. Participles (with adjectival or adverbial meaning): present active, *-ant*; past active, *-int*; future active, *-ont*; present passive, *-at*; past passive, *-it*; future passive, *-ot*. All forms of the passive are formed with the aid of the corresponding form of the verb *esti* (English *to be*) and the passive participle of the required verb; the preposition with the passive is *de* (English *by*).

7. Adverbs can be formed from adjectives by changing the *-a* ending to an *-e* ending (like English *-ly*).

8. All **prepositions** take the nominative.

9. Every word is read as it is written.

10. The **accent** always falls on the next-to-last syllable (vowel).

11. Compound words are formed by simple juxtaposition of words (the main word stands at the end); the grammatical endings are also viewed as independent words.

12. When another **negative** word is present, the word *ne* (English *no, not*) is omitted.

13. To show **direction**, words take the accusative ending.

14. Every preposition has a definite and permanent meaning, but if we have to use a preposition and the direct meaning doesn't tell us what preposition we should take, then we use the preposition **je**, which has no independent meaning. Instead of *je* the accusative without a preposition may be used.

15. The so-called **foreign words**, i.e. those taken by the majority of languages from one source, are used in Esperanto without change, taking on only the orthography of this language; but for different words from a single root it is better to use without change only the basic word, and form the rest from this latter according to the rules of Esperanto.

16. The **final vowel** of the noun and the article may be dropped and replaced by an apostrophe (without effect on stress).

Prefixes

bo'—denotes relationship resulting from marriage:

> *patro*, father, *bo'patro*, father-in-law.
>
> *patrino*, mother, *bo'patrino*, mother-in-law.

dis'—denotes division, separation, dissemination:

> *semi*, to sow, *dis'semi*, to scatter.
>
> *ŝiri*, to tear, *dis'ŝiri*, to tear in pieces.

ek'—denotes an action just begun, also short duration of an action:

> *kanti*, to sing, *ek'kanti*, to begin to sing.
>
> *ridi*, to laugh, *ek'ridi*, to burst out laughing.

ge'—denotes persons of both sexes taken together:

> *mastro*, master, *ge'mastroj*, master and mistress.
>
> *edzo*, husband, *ge'edzoj*, husband and wife.

mal'—denotes contraries, opposition of idea:

> *estimi*, to esteem, *mal'estimi*, to despise.
>
> *varma*, warm, *mal'varma*, cold.
>
> *amiko*, friend, *mal'amiko*, enemy.

re'—denotes the repetition of an act; it corresponds to the English "re," *back* or *again*:

>*doni*, to give, *re'doni*, to give back; *iri*, to go, *re'iri*, to go again.
>
>*diri*, to say, *re'diri*, to repeat; *veni*, to come, *re'veni*, to return.

Suffixes

'ad'—denotes duration or continuation of an action:

>*spiri*, to breathe, *spir'ad'o*, breathing.
>
>*pafi*, to fire (a gun, etc.), *paf'ad'o*, a fusilade.

'aĵ'—denotes a thing having a certain quality, something made from a certain matter:

>*mola*, soft, *mol'aĵ'o*, a soft thing or substance.
>
>*ovo*, egg, *ov'aĵ'o*, omelet; *bovo*, ox, *bov'aĵ'o*, beef.

'an'—denotes an inhabitant, partisan, member of:

>*Londono*, London, *London'an'o*, a Londoner.
>
>*Kristo*, Christ, *Krist'an'o*, a Christian.

'ar'—denotes a collection or reunion of certain things:

> *vorto*, a word, *vort'ar'o*, a dictionary.
>
> *homo*, a man, *hom'ar'o*, mankind.

'ĉj'—inserted between 1-5 letters of a masculine name denotes a term of endearment:

> *Johano*, John, *Jo'ĉj'o*, Jack, Johnnie.
>
> *Ernesto*, Ernest, *Erne'ĉj'o*, Ernie.

'ebl'—denotes possibility, something likely to happen:

> *legi*, to read, *leg'ebl'a*, legible.
>
> *kredi*, to believe, *kred'ebl'a*, credible.

'ec'—denotes an abstract quality (similar to the English suffix *ness*):

> *bona*, good, *bon'ec'o*, goodness.
>
> *pura*, clean, *pur'ec'o*, cleanliness.

'eg'—denotes augmentation, intensity of degree:

> *granda*, great, *grand'eg'a*, enormous.
>
> *pafilo*, gun, *pafil'eg'o*, cannon.

'ej'—denotes the place specially used for or allotted to:

14

dormi, to sleep, *dorm'ej'o*, a dormitory.

lerni, to learn, *lern'ej'o*, a school.

'em'—denotes propensity, inclination, disposition:

timi, to fear, *tim'em'a*, timorous.

amo, love, *am'em'a*, lovable.

'er'—denotes one of many objects of the same kind, the smallest fragment:

sablo, sand, *sabl'er'o*, a grain of sand.

mono, money, *mon'er'o*, a coin.

'estr'—denotes a chief, a leader, a ruler, the head of:

imperio, an empire, *imperi'estr'o*, an emperor.

ŝipo, a ship, *ŝip'estr'o*, captain (of a ship).

'et'—denotes diminution of degree:

ridi, to laugh, *rid'et'i*, to smile.

monto, a mountain, *mont'et'o*, a hill.

'id'—denotes the young of, offspring, descendant:

kato, a cat, *kat'id'o*, a kitten.

Izraelo, Israel, *Izrael'id'o*, an Israelite.

'ig'—denotes causing to be in a certain state or condition:

15

morti, to die, *mort'ig'i*, to kill (to *cause* to die).

pura, clean, *pur'ig'i*, to clean (to make clean).

'iĝ'—denotes to become, to be made to:

ruĝa, red, *ruĝ'iĝ'i*, to become red (to blush).

riĉa, rich, *riĉ'iĝ'i*, to become (or to grow) rich.

'il'—denotes an instrument or tool:

kombi, to comb, *komb'il'o*, a comb.

razi, to shave, *raz'il'o*, a razor.

'in'—denotes feminines:

frato, brother, *frat'in'o*, sister.

leono, lion, *leon'in'o*, lioness.

'ind'—denotes worthiness, to be "worthy of," "deserving of":

laŭdi, to praise, *laŭd'ind'a*, praiseworthy, worthy of praise.

estimi, to esteem, *estim'ind'a*, estimable, worthy of esteem.

'ing'—denotes a holder (thing), that which is used for holding *one* object:

cigaro, a cigar, *cigar'ing'o*, a cigar holder.

kandelo, a candle, *kandel'ing'o*, a candlestick.

16

'ist'—denotes profession, trade, occupation, etc.:

> *drogo*, a drug, *drog'ist'o*, druggist.
>
> *maro*, the sea, *mar'ist'o*, a sailor.

'nj'—has the same force as the suffix *ĉj*, but is used for feminine names only.

'uj'—denotes that which contains, produces, encloses or bears:

> *pomo*, apple, *pom'uj'o*, apple-tree; *mono*,
> money, *mon'uj'o*, a purse.
>
> *Anglo*, Englishman, *Angl'uj'o*,
> England; *cigaro*, a cigar, *cigar'uj'o*, a cigar-
> case.

> "Tree" may also be expressed
> by *arbo*, *pomarbo*, an apple tree.
> Names of countries may also be
> denoted by *lando*, as *Anglolando*,
> England, *Francolando*,
> France, *Irlando*, Ireland.

'ul'—denotes a person or being characterised by the idea contained in a root-word:

timo, fear, *tim'ul'o*, a coward, a poltroon.

avara, miserly, *avar'ul'o*, a miserly person (a miser).

moŝto—this word denotes a general title of respect or politeness:

reĝo, a king, *via reĝa moŝto*, your Majesty.

via moŝto, your highness, your eminence, your worship.

How to Use the Prefixes and Suffixes

	Esperanto.	Free Translation.
	Lern'	root word.
I	Lerni	to learn.
Ad	Lernadi	" study.
Eg	Lernegi	" cram.
Ig	Lernigi	" cause to learn.
Iĝ	Lerniĝi	" learn intuitively.
Et	Lerneti	" dabble in learning.
dis	Dislerni	" learn in a desultory manner.
Ek	Eklerni	" begin to learn.
El	Ellerni	" learn thoroughly.
mal	Mallerni	" unlearn.
Re	Relerni	" learn again.

18

ant	Lernanto	a pupil, a learner (mas.).
"	Lernantino	a pupil, a learner (fem.).
An	Lernejano	a schoolboy.
"	Lernejanino	a schoolgirl.
Ge	Gelernantoj	pupils (mas. and fem.).
Ist	Lernejisto	a school teacher.
estr	Lernejestro	a school master.
ant	Lernantaro	a class.
Ej	Lernejo	a school.
Et	Lernejeto	an elementary school.
Ar	Lernejaro	an university.
Ul	Lernulo	a learned man, a savant.
"	Lernulino	a learned woman, a "blue stocking."
Aĵ	Lernaĵo	knowledge.
Il	Lernilo	intelligence (the).
ind	Lerninda	worth learning.
O	Lerno	act or action of learning.
ebl	Lernebla	learnable.
Ec	Lerneco	learnedness.
Em	Lernema	studious.
Er	Lernero	a subject of a curriculum.
Ar	Lernaro	a curriculum.
A	Lerna	learned.

E   Lerne   learnedly.

ABBREVIATIONS.

Adj.	Adjective.	Math.	Mathematics.
Adv.	Adverb.	Med.	Medical.
Anat.	Anatomy.	Milit.	Military.
Arith.	Arithmetic.	Mus.	Music.
Bot.	Botany.	N.	Noun.
Conj.	Conjunction.	Phil.	Philosophy.
Fem. F.	Feminine.	Plur.	Plural.
Fig.	Figurative.	Polit.	Politics.
Geog.	Geography.	Prep.	Preposition.
Gram.	Grammar.	Prof.	Profession.
Inter.	Interjection.	Relig.	Religion.
Intrans.	Intransitive.	Sing. S.	Singular.
Jud.	Judicial.	Trans.	Transitive.
Lit.	Literary.	V.	Verb.
Mas. M.	Masculine.	Zool.	Zoology.

<u>English-Esperanto</u>

A

A, indefinite article, not used in Esperanto.

Aback, to take, surprizi.

Abaft, posta parto.

Abandon, forlasi.

Abase, humiligi.

Abash, hontigi.

Abate (lower), mallevi.

Abate (speed), malakceli.

Abbey, abatejo.

Abbot, abato.

Abbreviate, mallongigi.

Abdicate, demeti la reĝecon.

Abdomen, ventro.

Abduct, forrabi.

Abduction, forrabo.

Abed, lite.

Aberration, spiritvagado.

Abet, kunhelpi.

Abhor, malamegi.

Abhorrence, malamego.

Abide, loĝi (resti).

Ability, lerteco.

Ability, XXXalent.

Abject, humilega.

Abjure, malkonfesi, forĵuri.

Ablative, ablativo.

Able, to be, povi.

Able (skilful), lerta.

Abnegation, memforgeso.

Aboard, en ŝipo.

Abode, loĝejo.

Abolish, neniigi.

Abominable, abomena.

Abomination, abomeno.

Abound, sufiĉegi.

About (prep.), ĉirkaŭ.

About (adv.), ĉirkaŭe.

Above (prep.), super.

Above (adv.), supre.

Above all, precipe.

Abreast, flanko ĉe flanko.

Abridge, mallongigi.

Abridgement, resumo.

Abroad, eksterlande.

Abrupt, subita.

Abscess, absceso.

Abscond, sin forkaŝi.

Absent, to be, foresti.

Absence, foresto—ado.

Absolute, absoluta.

Absolutely, absolute.

Absolution, senkulpigo.

Absolution (from sin), senpekigo.

Absolve, senkulpigi.

Absolve (from sin), senpekigi.

Absorb, sorbi.

Absorption, sorbo.

Abstain, deteni sin.

Abstemious, sobrema.

Abstinence, deteno.

Abstinent, detenema.

Abstract (abridgement), resumo.

Abstract, abstrakti.

Abstracted, abstrakta.

Abstruse, tre malklara.

Absurd, absurda.

Absurdity, absurdo.

Abundance, sufiĉego.

Abuse, trouzi.

Abuse, trouzo.

Abyss, profundegaĵo.
Acacia, akacio.
Academic, akademia.
Academy, akademio.
Accede, konsenti.
Accelerate, akceli.
Accent (sign, mark),
signo.
Accent, akcenti.
Accent, akcento.
Accentuate, akcentegi.
Accept, akcepti.
Acceptable,
akceptebla.
Acceptance, akceptaĵo.
Acceptation, akcepto.
Access, aliro.
Accession, plimultigo.
Accessory,
kunhelpanto.
Accident (chance),
okazo.
Accident (injury),
malfeliĉo.
Acclamation,
aplaŭdego.
Acclimatize,
alklimatigi.
Acclivity, supreniro.
Accommodate, alfari.
Accompany, akompani.
Accomplice,
kunkulpulo.
Accomplish, plenumi.
Accomplished (of
things), elfarita.
Accomplishment,
talento.
Accord (music),
akordo.
Accord, konsento.
According to, laŭ.
Accouchement, akuŝo.

Account (bill), kalkulo.
Account, rakonto.
Accountable, to be,
respondi pri.
Accountant (profn.),
kalkulisto.
Account (current),
konto kuranta.
Accounts, kalkularo.
Account (rendered),
raporto.
Accoutre (milit.), armi.
Accrue, kreskiĝi.
Accumulate, amasigi.
Accumulation, amaso.
Accuracy, akurateco.
Accurate, akurata.
Accursed, malbena.
Accusation, kulpigo.
Accusative, akuzativo.
Accuse, kulpigi.
Accustomed, to be,
kutimi.
Ace, aso.
Acerbity, acideco.
Acetous, acida.
Ache, doloro.
Achieve, plenumi.
Achievement, elfaro.
Acid, acida.
Acid, acido.
Acidity, acideco.
Acidulous, acideta.
Acknowledge, konfesi.
Acknowledge (letters,
etc.), avizi.
Acknowledgement (lett
ers, etc.), avizo.
Acknowledgment,
konfeso.
Aconite, akonito.
Acorn, glano.
Acoustics, akustiko.

23

Acquaint, sciigi.
Acquaintance, konato.
Acquainted, to be, konatiĝi.
Acquiesce, konsenti.
Acquire, akiri.
Acquirement, akiro.
Acquisition, akiraĵo.
Acquit (debt), kvitanci.
Acquit (blame), senkulpigi.
Acrid, acida.
Acrimonious, akretema.
Acrobat, ekvilibristo.
Across, trans.
Act, agi.
Act (statute), regulo, leĝo.
Act (drama), akto.
Action, to bring an, procesi.
Active, aktiva.
Activity, aktiveco.
Actor, aktoro.
Actor (drama), komediisto.
Actual (time), nuna.
Actual, reala.
Actuality, nuneco, realeco.
Actuated, incitita.
Acumen, sagaceco.
Acute, akra.
Acuteness, sagaceco.
Adage, proverbo.
Adapt, alfari.
Adaptation, alfarado.
Add up, sumigi.
Add together, kunmeti.
Add to, aldoni.
Addendum, aldono.
Adder, kolubro.

Addicted, to be, kutimi.
Addition, aldono.
Additional, aldona.
Addled, senfrukta.
Address, adresi.
Adduce, prezenti.
Adept, adepto.
Adequate, sufiĉa.
Adhere, aliĝi.
Adherent, aliĝulo.
Adhesion, aliĝo.
Adhesive, glua.
Adieu, adiaŭ.
Adjacent, apuda.
Adjective, adjektivo.
Adjoining, apuda.
Adjourn, prokrasti.
Adjudge, aljuĝi.
Adjure, petegi.
Adjust, aranĝi, almezuri.
Administer, administri.
Administration, administracio.
Admirable, admirinda.
Admiral, admiralo.
Admiration, admiro.
Admire, admiri.
Admission, allaso.
Admissible, permesebla.
Admit, allasi.
Admonish, admoni.
Admonition, admono.
Adolescence, juneco.
Adolescent, junulo.
Adopt, alpreni.
Adopt (child), filigi.
Adore, adori.
Adorn, ornami.
Adroit, lerta.
Adroitness, lerteco.
Adulation, adulacio,

flato.
Adult, plenkreskulo.
Adult, plenkreska.
Adulterate, falsi.
Adultery, adulto.
Adultery, to commit,
adulti.
Advance, antaŭeniri.
Advancement,
progreso.
Advantage, utilo,
profito.
Advantageous, utila,
profita.
Advent, advento.
Adverb, adverbo.
Adversary, kontraŭulo.
Adverse, kontraŭa.
Adversity, kontraŭeco.
Advert to (to), aludi
(al).
Advertise, anonci.
Advertisement, anonco.
Advice, konsilo.
Advise, konsili.
Advocate, defendi.
Aerial, aera.
Aerolite, aerolito.
Aeronaut,
aerveturanto.
Afar, malproksime.
Affable, afabla.
Affability, afableco.
Affair, afero.
Affected (manner),
afekta.
Affected, to be, afekti.
Affecting (touching),
kortuŝanta.
Affection, afekteco.
Affection (love), amo.
Affectionate, aminda.
Affectionately, aminde.

Affinity (relationship),
parenceco.
Affiliate, aligi, anigi.
Affiliated, to become,
aliĝi, aniĝi.
Affirm (attest), atesti.
Affirm (assure), certigi.
Affirmation, atesto.
Affirmation, certigo,
jeso.
Affirmative, jesa.
Affix, afikso.
Afflict, malĝojigi.
Affluence, riĉeco.
Affluent, riĉega.
Afford, to give, doni.
Affray, batiĝo.
Affright, timigi.
Affront, insulto.
Afloat, flose, naĝe.
Afraid, timigita.
Aft, posta parto.
After, post.
Aftermath, postfojno.
Afternoon,
posttagmezo.
Afterwards, poste.
Again, ree.
Against, kontraŭ.
Agate, agato.
Age, aĝo.
Aged, maljuna.
Agency, agenteco.
Agenda, memorlibro.
Agent, agento.
Aggrandize,
pligrandigi.
Aggrandisement,
pligrandigo.
Aggravate,
plimalbonigi.
Aggression, atako.
Aggressor, atakanto.

Aghast, terurega.
Agile, facilmova.
Agitate, agiti.
Ago, antaŭ.
Agonize, agonii.
Agony, agonio.
Agree, konsenti.
Agreeable, agrabla.
Agreement (deed), kontrakto.
Agreement, interkonsento.
Agriculture, terkulturo.
Agriculturist, terkulturisto.
Agronomy, agronomio.
Ague, febreto.
Ah! ha!
Ahead, antaŭe.
Aid, helpo.
Aide-de-Camp, adjutanto.
Ail, malsani.
Ailment, malsano.
Aim (purpose), celo.
Air (appearance), mieno.
Air (music), ario.
Air, aerumi.
Air (atmosphere), aero.
Airball (toy), pilkego.
Airballoon, aerostato.
Airhole, fenestreto.
Airpump, aeropumpilo.
Aisle, flankaĵo.
Ajar, duonfermita.
Akin, parenca.
Alabaster, alabastro.
Alacrity, rapideco.
Alarm, maltrankviligi.
Alarum (clock), vekhorloĝo.
Alas! ho ve!

Albeit, kvankam.
Album, albumo.
Albumen, albumeno.
Alchemy, alĥemio.
Alcohol, alkoholo.
Alcoholic, alkohola.
Alcoholism, alkoholismo.
Alcove, alkovo.
Alder (tree), alno.
Ale, biero.
Alert, vigla.
Algebra, algebro.
Alias, alie.
Alien, alilandulo.
Alike, simila.
Aliment, manĝaĵo.
Alimony, nutramono.
Alive, viva.
Alkali, alkalio.
All (every one), ĉiu, ĉiuj (plur.).
Allay, trankviligi, kvietigi.
Allege, pretendi.
Allegiance, fideleco.
Allegory, alegorio.
Alleviate, dolĉigi.
Alley, aleo, strateto.
Alliance, interligo.
Allocution, paroladeto.
Allot, lotumi.
Allotment, lotaĵo.
Allow, permesi.
Allowance (a/c), dekalkulo.
Allowance (share), porcio.
All-powerful, ĉiopova.
Allude, aludi.
Allure, logi.
Allurement, logo.
Allusion, aludo.

Alluvial, akvemetita.
Ally, interligi.
Almanac, almanako.
Almighty, ĉiopova.
Almost, preskaŭ.
Almond, migdalo.
Alms, almozo.
Almshouse,
maljunulejo.
Aloes, aloo.
Aloft, supre.
Alone, sola (adj.), sole
(adv.).
Along with, kune kun.
Aloof, to keep, eviti.
Aloud, laŭte.
Alphabet, alfabeto.
Alps, Alpoj.
Already, jam.
Also, ankaŭ.
Altar, altaro.
Alter, aliigi.
Alteration, aliigo.
Altercation, malpaco.
Alternate, alterni.
Alternative, elekteco.
Althea, alteo.
Although, kvankam.
Altitude, alto.
Alto, aldo.
Altogether, tute.
Alum, aluno.
Always, ĉiam.
Amalgam, amalgamo.
Amalgamate, unuigi.
Amalgamation,
unuigo.
Amanuensis, skribisto.
Amass, amasigi.
Amateur, nemetiisto.
Amaze, miregigi.
Amazed, to be,
miregiĝi.

Amazement, mirego.
Amazing, miriga.
Amazon, rajdantino.
Ambassador,
ambasadoro.
Amber, sukceno.
Ambiguous, dusenca.
Ambition, ambicio.
Ambitious, ambicia.
Amble, troteti.
Ambrosia, ambrozio.
Ambulance (place),
malsanulejo.
Ambuscade, embusko.
Ambush, embuski.
Ameliorate, plibonigi.
Amend, reformi.
Amends, to make,
rekompenci.
America, Ameriko.
American, Amerikano.
Amiability, amindeco.
Amiable, afabla,
aminda.
Amicably, pace.
Amid, meze.
Amidst, meze.
Amity, amikeco.
Ammonia, amoniako.
Among, inter.
Amongst, inter.
Amorous, amema.
Amount, sumo.
Amphibious, amfibia.
Amphitheatre,
amfiteatro.
Amphora, amforo.
Ample, sufiĉa.
Amplify, grandigi.
Amplitude, amplekso.
Amputate, detranĉi.
Amulet, talismano.
Amuse, amuzi.

Anagram, anagramo.
Analogy, analogio.
Analysis, analizo.
Analyze, analizi.
Anarchy, anarĥio.
Anatomy, anatomio.
Ancestors, praavoj,
prapatroj.
Anchor, ankro.
Anchorite, dezertulo.
Ancient, antikva.
And, kaj.
Anecdote, rakonteto.
Anew, ankoraŭ, ree.
Angel, anĝelo.
Angelic, anĝela.
Anger, kolero.
Anger, kolerigi.
Angle (corner), angulo.
Angling, fiŝkaptado.
Angle (fish), fiŝkapti.
Angler, fiŝkaptisto.
Angry, to be, koleri.
Anguish, dolorego.
Angular, angula.
Animal, besto.
Animate, vivigi.
Animated, vivigita.
Animating, viviga.
Animation, viveco.
Animosity,
malamikeco.
Aniseed, anizo.
Anisette, anizlikvoro.
Ankle, maleolo.
Annals, historio.
Annex, kunigi.
Annexation, kunigo.
Annihilate, neniigi.
Anniversary,
datreveno.
Annotate, noti.
Announce, anonci.

Announcement,
anonco.
Annoy, ĉagreni.
Annoyance, ĉagreno,
enuo.
Annual (publication),
jarlibro.
Annual (yearly),
ĉiujara.
Annuity, jarpago.
Annul, nuligi.
Annular, ringforma.
Annunciation,
anunciacio.
Anoint, ŝmiri.
Anointing, ŝmiro, ado.
Anomaly, anomalio.
Anonymous, anonima.
Answer, respondi.
Answer (affirmatively),
jesi.
Answerable for, to be,
respondi pri.
Ant, formiko.
Antagonist,
kontraŭulo.
Antarctic, antarktika.
Antecedents, antaŭaĵo.
Antechamber,
antaŭĉambro.
Antedate, antaŭdatumi.
Antelope, antilopo.
Anterior, antaŭa.
Anteroom,
antaŭĉambro.
Anthem, antemo,
himnego.
Ant-hill, formikejo.
Anthropology,
antropologio.
Antichrist, antikristo.
Anticipate, antaŭvidi.
Antidote,

kontraŭveneno.
Antimony, antimono.
Antipathy, antipatio.
Antipodes, antipodoj.
Antiquary, antikvisto.
Antiquated, antikva.
Antique, antikva.
Antique (noun),
antikvaĵo.
Antiquity, antikveco.
Antler, kornbranĉo.
Anvil, amboso.
Anxiety,
maltrankvileco.
Anxious, maltrankvila.
Any, ia.
Anybody, iu.
Anyhow, iel.
Anyone, iu.
Anyone's, ies.
Any quantity, iom.
Anything, io.
Anywhere, ie.
Aorta, aorto.
Apace, rapide.
Apart, aparte.
Apartment, ĉambro.
Apathetic, apatia.
Apathy, apatio.
Ape, simio.
Ape (verb), imiti.
Aperient, laksileto.
Aperture, malfermaĵo.
Apex, pinto,
suprapinto.
Apiary, abelejo.
Apish, simia.
Apocryphal, apokrifa.
Apogee, apogeo.
Apologise, pardonon
peti.
Apologue, apologo.
Apology, apologio.

Apoplexy, apopleksio.
Apostle, apostolo.
Apostolic, apostola.
Apostrophe, apostrofo.
Apostrophize, alparoli.
Apothecary,
apotekisto.
Apothecary's, apoteko.
Apotheosis, apoteozo.
Appal, terurigi.
Apparatus, aparato.
Apparel, vesto.
Apparent, videbla.
Apparition, apero.
Apparitor (beadle),
pedelo.
Appeal, alvoki.
Appear (come in
sight), aperi.
Appear, ŝajni.
Appearance (aspect),
vidiĝo, mieno.
*Appearance, to put in
an*, ĉeesti.
Appease, pacigi.
Append, aldoni.
Appendage, aldonaĵo.
Appendix, aldono.
Appetising, apetitdona.
Appetite, apetito.
Applaud, aplaŭdi.
Applause, aplaŭdo—
ado.
Apple, pomo.
Apple tree, pomarbo,
pomujo.
Appliance, aparato.
Application, atento.
Apply (to put on),
almeti.
Apply to, sin turni (al).
Appoint (nominate),
nomi.

29

Appointment, elekto.
Apportion, lotumi, dividi.
Appraise, taksi.
Appreciate, ŝati.
Apprehend (seize), ekkapti.
Apprehend (understand), kompreni.
Apprehension (fear), timo.
Apprentice, lernanto.
Apprenticeship, lernado.
Apprise, sciigi, informi.
Approach, proksimiĝi.
Approaching (time), baldaŭa.
Approbation, aprobo.
Appropriate, to be, difinita por.
Appropriate (take, keep), proprigi.
Approval, aprobo.
Approve, aprobi.
Approximate (time), baldaŭa.
Apricot, abrikoto.
April, Aprilo.
Apron, antaŭtuko.
Apt, kapabla.
Aptitude, kapableco.
Aptly, kapable.
Aquatic, akva.
Aqueduct, akvokonduko.
Aqueous, akva.
Arab, Arabo.
Arable, plugebla.
Arbitrary, arbitra.
Arbitrate, arbitracii.
Arbitration, arbitracio.

Arbitrator (profn.), arbitraciisto.
Arbour, laŭbo.
Arc, arko.
Arcade, arkado.
Arch, arko.
Arch, arkefleksi.
Archangel, ĉefanĝelo.
Archæology, arĥeologio.
Archbishop, ĉefepiskopo.
Archduke, arĥiduko.
Archer, pafarkisto.
Archipelago, insularo.
Architect, arĥitekturisto.
Architecture, arĥitekturo.
Archives, arĥivo.
Arctic, arktika.
Ardent, fervora.
Ardour, fervoro.
Arduous, laborega.
Arena, areno.
Areopagus, Aeropago.
Argue, argumenti.
Argument, argumento.
Arid, seka.
Aright, bone.
Arise, leviĝi.
Aristocracy, aristokrataro.
Aristocrat, aristokrato.
Arithmetic, aritmetiko.
Ark, ŝipego.
Arm (milit.), armi.
Arm (of the body), brako.
Armament, armilaro.
Armchair, seĝego.
Armistice, interpaco.
Armlet, ĉirkaŭbrako.

Armorials, insigno.
Armour, armaĵo.
Armourer, armilfaristo.
Armoury, armilejo.
Armpit, subbrako.
Arms (weapons),
armiloj, bataliloj.
Army (military),
militistaro.
Army (non-military),
armeo.
Army-corps, korpuso.
Arnica, arniko.
Aroma, aromo.
Aromatic, aroma.
Around (prep.), ĉirkaŭ.
Around (adv.), ĉirkaŭe.
Arouse, veki.
Arpeggio, arpeĝo.
Arraign, kulpigi.
Arrange, aranĝi.
Arrant, fama.
Array (deck out),
ornami.
Arrears, in, malantaŭe.
Arrest, aresti.
Arrival, alveno.
Arrive (on foot),
alveni.
Arrive (by vehicle),
alveturi.
Arrogance,
aroganteco.
Arrogant, aroganta.
Arrow, sago.
Arsenal, armilejo.
Arsenic, arseniko.
Arson, brulkrimo.
Art, arto.
Artery, arterio.
Artful, ruza.
Arthritic, artritulo.
Artichoke, artiŝoko.

Article, artikolo.
Article (commerce),
komercaĵo.
Articulate, elparoli.
Articulation (anat.),
artiko.
Artifice, artifiko.
Artificial, artefarita.
Artillery, artilerio.
Artisan, metiisto.
Artist, artisto.
Artless, simplanima,
naiva.
Artlessness, naiveco.
As, kiel.
As—as, tiel—kiel.
Ascend, supreniri.
Ascension (feast of),
Ĉieliro.
Ascension,
suprenirado.
Ascent, supreniro.
Ascertain, certiĝi.
Ascribe, aligi al.
Ashamed, to be, honti.
Ashes, cindro.
Ashpan, cindrujo.
Asia, Azio.
Asiatic, Aziano.
Aside, aparte.
As if, kvazaŭ.
Ask, demandi.
Ask (beg), peti.
Asleep, dormanta
(adj.), dormante (adv.).
As long as, tiel longe
kiel.
As many, tiom.
As much, tiom.
As many as, tiom,
kiom.
As much as, tiom,
kiom.

Asp, aspido.
Asparagus, asparago.
Aspect, vidiĝo.
Aspect (phase), fazo.
Aspen, tremolo.
Asperse, kalumnii.
Asphalte, asfalto.
Asphyxia, asfiksio.
Aspirate, elspiri.
Aspirant, aspiranto.
Aspiration (breathing), elspiro—ado.
Aspiration (aim, intention), celo.
Aspire, celi.
Ass, azeno.
Assail, ataki.
Assailant, atakanto.
Assassin, mortiganto.
Assault, atako.
Assay, provo.
Assemble, kunveni, kunvoki.
Assembly, kunveno, aŭditorio.
Assent, konsenti, jesi.
Assert, certigi.
Assess, taksi.
Assessment, takso.
Assiduous, diligenta.
Assign, asigni.
Assignment, asigno.
Assimilate, similigi.
Assist, helpi.
Assist (at), ĉeesti (ĉe).
Assistance, helpo.
Assistant, helpanto.
Assistant-master, submajstro.
Associate, kunulo.
Association, societo.
Assort, dece kunmeti.
Assuage, dolĉigi.

Assume, supozi.
Assurance, self, memfido.
Assure, certigi.
Assure (life etc.), asekuri.
Asterisk, steleto.
Asthma, malfacila spirado.
Astonish, mirigi.
Astonished, to be, miri.
Astonishing, mira.
Astonishment, miro.
Astound, miregi.
Astral, astra.
Astray, to go, erariĝi.
Astringent, kuntira.
Astrologer, astrologiisto.
Astrology, astrologio.
Astronomer, astronomiisto.
Astronomy, astronomio.
Astute, ruza.
Asunder, aparte.
Asylum, rifuĝejo.
At, ĉe, je.
At (house of), ĉe.
At all events, kio ajn okazos.
At any time, iam.
Atheist, ateisto.
Atheism, ateismo.
Athletic, atleta.
Athlete, atleto.
Atlas, landkartaro.
Atmosphere, atmosfero.
Atom, atomo.
Atomism, atomismo.
At once, tuj.
Atone, rebonigi.

Atonement, rebonigo.
Atrocious, kruelega.
Atrocity, kruelego.
Atrophy, atrofio.
Attach, alligi.
Attachment, alligo.
Attack, atako.
Attack, ataki.
Attain, atingi.
Attain (to), trafi, atingi (al).
Attainment, akiro.
Attempt, atenci.
Attempt, atenco.
Attendants (retinue), sekvantaro.
Attend (on), servi.
Attention, to call (to), atentigi (al).
Attention, to pay, atenti.
Attention, atento.
Attentive, atenta.
Attest (a document), subskribi.
Attest, atesti.
Attestation, atesto.
Attic, tegmentĉambro.
Attire, vestaĵo.
Attitude, sintenado.
Attorney, advokato.
Attract, altiri.
Attract (entice), logi.
Attraction, logaĵo.
Attractive, ĉarma.
Attribute (v.), aligi al.
Attribute (quality), eco.
Auction, aŭkcia vendo.
Audacious, maltimega.
Audacity, maltimego.
Audible (adj.), aŭdebla.
Audience (interview), aŭdienco.

Audience (congregation), aŭditorio.
Audit, kontekzameni.
Auditorium, aŭskultejo.
Auger, borilego.
Aught (anything), io.
Augment, plimultigi, pliigi.
August (month), Aŭgusto.
August, nobla.
Aunt, onklino.
Aureola, aŭreolo.
Au revoir, ĝis revido.
Auriferous, orhava.
Auscultate, subaŭskulti.
Auspices, aŭspicioj.
Auspicious, favora.
Austere, severmora.
Austerely, severmore.
Austerity, severmoreco.
Australia, Aŭstralio.
Austrian, Aŭstro.
Authentic, vera, verega.
Authenticate, verigi.
Author, aŭtoro.
Authorise (permit), permesi.
Authorities (of town, etc.), estraro.
Authority, aŭtoritato.
Autocrat, aŭtokrato.
Automatic, aŭtomata.
Automobile, aŭtomobilo.
Autumn, aŭtuno.
Auxiliary, helpanto (noun), helpa (adj.).
Avalanche, lavango.

Avarice, avareco.
Avaricious, avara.
Avaunt, for de tie ĉi!
Avenge, venĝi.
Avenue, aleo.
Average (n.),
mezonombro. meza
kvanto.
Averse, antipatia,
kontraŭa.
Aversion, antipatio,
kontraŭo.
Avert, deturni.
Avidity, avideco.
Avid, avida.
Avoid, eviti.
Avow, konfesi.
Avowal, konfeso.
Await, atendi.
Awake, veki.
Awake (intrans.),
vekiĝi.
Awaken, veki.
Award, aljuĝi.
Aware, to be, scii.
Away!, for!
Away, malproksime.
Awe, teruro, timego.
Awful, terura.
Awkward, mallerta,
malgracia.
Awl, borileto.
Awning, sunŝirmilego.
Awry, malrekta.
Axe, hakilo.
Axis, akso.
Axle, akso.
Axle-tree, akso.
Axiom, aksiomo.
Ay (yes), jes.
Aye (always), ĉiam.
Azote, azoto.
Azure, lazuro.

B

Babble, babili.
Babe, infaneto.
Baboon, paviano.
Baby, infaneto.
Bachelor, fraŭlo.
Back (of body), dorso.
Back (reverse side),
posta flanko.
Back (behind), poste.
Backbite, kalumnii.
Backbone, spino.
Backslider, rekulpulo.
Backward (slow),
mallerta.
Bacon, lardo.
Bad, ly, malbona, e.
Badge, simbolo.
Badger, melo.
Bag, sako.
Bagatelle (trifle),
bagatelo.
Baggage, pakaĵo.
Bail, garantiaĵo.
Bailiff (legal), juĝa
persekutisto.
Bait, allogaĵo.
Bake, baki.
Baker, panisto,
bakisto.
Balance (scales),
pesilo.
Balance (poise),
balanci.
Balance of a/c,
restaĵo.
Balance-sheet,
bilanco.
Balcony, balkono.
Bald, senhara.
Baldness, senhareco.

34

Bale, pakego.
Baleful, pereiga.
Balk, malhelpi.
Ball (globe), globo.
Ball (playing), pilko.
Ball (party), balo.
Ball (bullet), kuglo.
Ballad, balado.
Ballast, balasto.
Ballet, baleto.
Balloon, aerostato.
Balloon (plaything), aerpilkego.
Ballot, voĉdoni.
Balm, balzamo.
Balm-mint, meliso.
Balsam, balzamo.
Balustrade, balustrado.
Bamboo, bambuo.
Banana, banano.
Band (strap), ligilo.
Band (gang, troop), bando.
Bandage, bandaĝi.
Bandit, malbonulo, rabulo.
Bane, pereigo.
Baneful, pereiga.
Banish (exile), ekzili.
Banish (send away), forpeli.
Bank (money), banko.
Bank (river), bordo.
Bank (sand), sablaĵo.
Bank (note), banka bileto.
Banker, bankiero.
Bankrupt, bankroto.
Bankrupt, to become, bankroti.
Banner, flago, standardo.

Banns, edziĝanonco.
Banquet, festeno.
Banter, moki.
Baptism, bapto.
Baptize, bapti.
Bar, bari.
Barbarian, barbaro.
Barbarism, barbarismo.
Barber, barbiro.
Bard, bardo.
Bare, nuda.
Barefoot, nudpiede.
Bargain, marĉandi.
Barge, ŝarĝbarko.
Bark (ship), barko.
Bark (of dog), hundobleko, bojo.
Bark (of tree), ŝelo.
Bark (a tree), senŝeligi.
Barley, hordeo.
Barm, feĉo.
Barn, garbejo.
Barometer, barometro.
Baron, barono.
Barrack, soldatejo.
Barrel, barelo.
Barrel-organ, gurdo.
Barren, senfrukta.
Barrenness, senfrukteco.
Barricade, barikado.
Barrier, barilo.
Barrister, advokato.
Barrow, puŝveturilo.
Barter, interŝanĝi.
Barytone, baritono.
Basalt, bazalto.
Base, fundamento.
Base (mean), malnobla.

Basely, perfide.
Baseless,
senfundamenta.
Basement, subetaĝo.
Baseness, perfideco.
Bashful, modesta.
Basin, pelvo.
Basis, fundamento.
Basket, korbo.
Bass (music), baso.
Bastard, bastardo.
Baste, surverŝi.
Bastion, bastiono.
Bat (animal),
vesperto.
Bath, banilo.
Bathe, bani sin.
Baths (place), banejo.
Battalion, bataliono.
Battery (milit.),
baterio.
Battle, batalo.
Battle, fight a, batali.
Battledore, pilkraketo.
Bauble, bagatelo.
Bawl, kriegi.
Bay (geog.), golfeto.
Bay (bark),
hundobleki, boji.
Bay, to keep at,
repuŝi.
Bayonet, bajoneto.
Bazaar, bazaro.
Be, esti.
Be, able to, povi.
Be, obliged to, devi.
Be, willing to, voli.
Beach, marbordo.
Beacon, lumturo.
Bead, globeto.
Beadle, pedelo.
Beak, beko.
Beam (timber), trabo.

Beam (light), radio.
Beam (of scales),
vekto.
Bean, fabo.
Bear (animal), urso.
Bear, give birth to,
naski.
Bear with, suferi.
Bearable, tolerebla.
Beard, barbo.
Beardless, senbarba.
Bearer, alportanto.
Beast (animal), besto.
Beast (brute), bruto.
Beastly, bruta.
Beat, bati.
Beat (with a rod),
vergi.
Beatitude, feliĉegeco.
Beau, koketulo.
Beautiful, bela.
Beauty, beleco.
Bearer, kastoro.
Because, ĉar, tial ke.
Beckon, signodoni.
Become, iĝi, fariĝi.
Becoming, konvena,
deca.
Bed, lito.
Bed (horse), pajlaĵo.
Bed (garden), bedo.
Bed (river), kuŝujo.
Bedding, litaĵo.
Bedroom,
dormoĉambro.
Bedstead, kuŝejo.
Bee, abelo.
Beehive, abelujo.
Beech-tree, fago.
Beef, bovaĵo.
Beer, biero.
Beet (root), beto.
Beetle, skarabo.

Befall, okazi.
Befitting, deca.
Before (prep.), antaŭ.
Before (adv.), antaŭe.
Before (conj.), antaŭ ol.
Beforehand, antaŭe.
Beg (entreat), peti.
Beg (alms), almozon peti.
Beggar, almozulo.
Beggary, almozpeto.
Begin, ek, komenci.
Beginning (origin), deveno.
Begone! for de tie ĉi!
Beguile (deceive), trompi.
Beguile, amuzi.
Behalf, parto.
Behave, konduti.
Behaviour, konduto.
Behead, senkapigi.
Behind (prep.), post.
Behind (adv.), poste.
Behold, rigardi.
Beholder, rigardanto.
Behoof, profito.
Being, estaĵo.
Belabour, bategi.
Belch, rukti.
Belfry, sonorilejo.
Belgian, Belgo.
Belgium, Belgujo.
Belie, kalumnii.
Belief, kredo.
Believe, kredi.
Bell, sonorilo.
Bell (door, etc.), sonorileto.
Bell (ornament), tintilo.
Bell ringer, sonorigisto.
Belladonna, beladono.
Belle, belulino.
Bellow, blekegi.
Bellows, blovilo.
Belly, ventro.
Belong, aparteni.
Below (adv.), sube, malsupre.
Below (prep.), sub.
Belt, zono.
Bench (seat), benko.
Bench (work), stablo.
Bench (of judges), juĝistaro.
Bend, fleksi.
Beneath, sub.
Benediction, beno.
Benefactor, bonfaristo.
Beneficial, profita.
Benefit, profito.
Benevolence, bonfaro.
Bent, kurba.
Benumb, rigidigi.
Bequeath, testamenti.
Bequest, heredaĵo.
Bereave (of), senigi (je).
Berry, bero.
Berth (ship), kuŝejo.
Beseech, petegi.
Beset, ĉirkaŭi.
Beside, apud.
Besides, krom.
Besiege, sieĝi.
Besot, bestiĝi.
Besprinkle, ŝprucigi sur.
Best (adj.), la plej bona.
Best (adv.), la plej bone.

Bestial, besta.
Bestir, one's self, sin movetadi, vigliĝi.
Bestow, donaci.
Bet, veti.
Bet, veto.
Betimes, frue.
Betray, perfidi.
Betroth, fianĉigi.
Betrothing, fianĉiĝo.
Better (adj.), pli bona.
Better (adv.), pli bone.
Between, inter.
Bevel, tranĉi oblikve.
Beverage, trinkaĵo.
Bewail, ploregi.
Bewilder, konfuzi.
Bewitch, ensorĉi.
Bewitchment, ensorĉo.
Beyond, preter.
Beyond (across), trans.
Biassed, partia.
Bible, Biblio.
Biblical, Biblia.
Bicker, disputi.
Bicycle, biciklo.
Bid (good day, etc.), diri.
Bid (at auction), pliproponi.
Bid (order), ordoni.
Bidding, invito.
Bide, atendi.
Bifurcation, disduiĝo.
Big, granda.
Bigamy, bigamio.
Bigot, fanatikulo.
Bigotry, fanatikeco.
Bilberry, mirtelo.
Bile, galo.
Bilious, gala.
Bill (a/c), kalkulo.

Bill (of exchange), kambio.
Bill (beak), beko.
Bill (posted up), afiŝo.
Bill-poster, afiŝisto.
Billhook, branĉhakileto.
Billet (note), letereto.
Billet (wood), ŝtipo.
Billiard-ball, globo.
Billiards, bilardo.
Billow, ondego.
Bin, grenkesto.
Bind, ligi.
Bind (books), bindi.
Bind (together), kunligi.
Bind (wounds), bandaĝi.
Bind-weed, liano.
Biography, biografio.
Biology, biologio.
Biped, dupiedulo.
Birch (tree), betulo.
Bird, birdo.
Birth, naskiĝo.
Birthday, naskotago.
Biscuit, biskvito.
Bisect, bisekcii.
Bishop, episkopo.
Bismuth, bismuto.
Bit (piece), peco.
Bit (horse), enbuŝaĵo.
Bite, mordi.
Bitter, akra—ema.
Bitters, vermuto.
Bitumen, terpeĉo.
Bivouac, bivako.
Blab, babili.
Black, nigra.
Blackboard, nigra tabulo.
Black-currant, nigra

38

ribo.
Black pudding,
sangokolbaso.
Blackbird, merlo.
Blacken, nigrigi.
Blackguard,
sentaŭgulo.
Blacking, ciro.
Blackish, dubenigra.
Blacksmith, forĝisto.
Bladder, veziko.
Blade (grass),
trunketo.
Blade (knife),
tranĉanto.
Blamable,
mallaŭdinda.
Blame, mallaŭdi.
Blanch, paliĝi.
Bland, afabla.
Blanket, lankovrilo.
Blaspheme, blasfemi.
Blast, blovego.
Blaze, flamegi.
Bleach, blankigi.
Bleat, bleki.
Bleed (trans.),
sangeltiri.
Bleed (intrans.),
sangadi.
Blemish, makulo.
Blend, miksi.
Bless, beni.
Blessing, beno—ado.
Blight, velkigi.
Blind, blinda.
Blind, window,
rulkurteno.
Blindness, blindeco.
Blind-alley, senelirejo.
Bliss, feliĉegeco.
Blister, veziko.
Blister (plaster),

vezikigilo.
Blithe, gaja.
Bloat, ŝveli.
Block (pulley),
rulbloko.
Block (log), ŝtipo.
Blockade, blokado.
Blockhead, malsaĝulo.
Blond, blonda.
Blood, sango.
Bloodshed,
sangverŝo—ado.
Bloodvessel,
sangvejno.
Bloom, flori.
Blossom, flori.
Blot, makulo.
Blotch, skabio.
Blotting paper, sorba
papero.
Blow (stroke), bato.
Blow, blovi.
Blouse, kitelo.
Blow (of flowers),
ekflori.
Bludgeon, bastonego.
Blue, blua.
Bluish, dubeblua.
Blunder, erarego.
Blunt, malakra.
Blunt (mannered),
malafabla.
Blur, malpurigi.
Blush, ruĝiĝi.
Bluster, fanfaroni.
Boa, boao.
Boar, porkviro.
Board (food),
nutrado—aĵo.
Board (plank), tabulo.
Board, loĝi.
Boarder (house),
loĝanto.

Boarder (school),
edukato.
Boarding school,
edukejo.
Boarding-house,
loĝantejo.
Boast, fanfaroni.
Boast, fanfarono.
Boaster, fanfaronulo.
Boat, boato.
Boatman, boatisto.
Boat-hook, hokstango.
Boat-race, ŝipkurado.
Boat (rowing),
remboato.
Bobbin, bobeno.
Body, korpo.
Bog, marĉego.
Bohemian, Bohemo.
Boil (blain), furunko.
Boil, boli.
Boiler (saucepan),
bolpoto.
Boiler, bolegilo.
Boisterous, perforta.
Bold, maltima.
Boldness, maltimo.
Bolster, kapkuseno.
Bolt, rigli.
Bolt, riglilo.
Bomb, bombo.
Bombard, bombardi.
Bonbon, bombono.
Bond (finance),
obligacio.
Bondage, servuto.
Bondman, vasalo.
Bondservant,
servutulo.
Bondsman (surety),
garantianto.
Bone, osto.
Bonnet, ĉapo.

Bonny, beleta.
Bonus, liberdonaco.
Booby, simplanimulo.
Book, libro.
Book-keeper,
librotenisto.
Book (copy-book),
kajero.
Bookseller, libristo.
Boom, soni.
Booming, sonado.
Boon, bonfaro, gajno.
Boorish, maldelikata.
Boot, boto.
Booth, budo.
Bootless, neprofita.
Bootmaker, botisto.
Booty, akiraĵo.
Borax, borakso.
Border (edge),
randaĵo.
Border, to put a,
borderi.
Bore (a hole), bori.
Bore (of a gun),
kalibro.
Borer (tool), borilo.
Born, to be, naskiĝi.
Born again, renaskiĝi.
Borne, portita.
Borough, urba
distrikto.
Borrow, prunto preni.
Bosom, brusto.
Botany, botaniko.
Botch (spoil),
malbonigi.
Both, ambaŭ.
Bother, enui.
Bottle, botelo.
Bottom, fundo.
Bottom, malsupro.
Bough, branĉo.

Bouillon, buljono.
Boulder, ŝtonego.
Bounce, salti.
Bound, salti.
Bound, salto.
Boundary, limo.
Bounden, deviga.
Bountiful, malavara.
Bounty, helpa mono.
Bouquet, bukedo.
Bourn, limo.
Bout (contest),
konkurso.
Bow, saluti.
Bow, saluto.
Bow, pafarko.
Bow (violin), arĉo.
Bow (ribbons), banto.
Bowels, internaĵo.
Bower, laŭbo.
Bowl, pelvo.
Box (small), skatolo.
Box, kesto.
Box, money,
monoskatoleto.
Box (shrub), bukso.
Box (theatre), loĝio.
Box, pugnebati.
Boy, knabo.
Brace, paro.
Bracelet, ĉirkaŭmano.
Braces, ŝelko.
Bracket, tableto.
Brackish, saleta.
Bray, fanfaroni.
Braggart, fanfaronulo.
Brain, cerbo.
Brake (fern), filiko.
Brake (for wheels),
haltigilo.
Bran, brano.
Branch (of tree),
branĉo.

Branch (of roads,
etc.), disvojo.
Brand (fire), brulaĵo.
Brandish, svingi.
Brandy, brando.
Brasier, fajrujo.
Brass, flava kupro.
Brave, brava.
Brave, bravulo.
Brave, kontraŭstari al.
Bravery, braveco.
Bravo! brave!
Brawl, malpacego.
Brawny, muskola.
Bray (ass), bleki.
Bray (to pound), pisti.
Brazen, bronza.
Breach, breĉo.
Bread, pano.
Bread (unleavened),
maco.
Breadth, larĝeco.
Break, rompi.
Break off, disrompi.
Break, to pieces,
frakasi.
Breakfast,
matenmanĝi.
Bream, bramo.
Breast, brusto.
Breast, mamo.
Breath, elspiraĵo.
Breathe, spiri.
Breathe (heavily),
stertori.
Breathing, spirado.
Breech (of gun),
ŝargujo.
Breeches, pantalono.
Breed (race), raso.
Breeze, venteto.
Brevity, mallongeco.
Brew, bierfari.

41

Brewer, bierfaristo.
Brewery, bierfarejo.
Bribe, subaĉeti.
Brick, briko.
Brick (fire), fajrŝtono.
Bride, novedzino.
Bridge, ponto.
Bridle, brido.
Brief, mallonga.
Brier, rozo sovaĝa.
Brigade, brigado.
Brigand, rabisto.
Brigandage, rabado.
Bright (clear), hela.
Bright, to get, heliĝi.
Brighten, briligi.
Brighten (polish), poluri.
Brightness, brilo.
Brilliant, brila.
Brilliant (jewel), brilianto.
Brimful, plenpota.
Brine, peklakvo.
Bring, alkonduki.
Bring back, rekonduki.
Bring down (of prices), rabati.
Bring forth (a child), naski.
Bring up (a child), elnutri.
Brink, rando.
Briny, sala.
Brisk (lively), vigla.
Brisk (quick), rapida.
Briskness, rapideco.
Bristle, harego.
Brittle, facilrompa.
Broach, trapiki.
Broad, larĝa.
Brochure, broŝuro.

Broil, rosti.
Broker, makleristo.
Broker, to act as, makleri.
Brokerage, maklero.
Bromine, bromo.
Bronchitis, bronkito.
Bronchial, bronka.
Brooch, broĉo.
Brood (fowl), kovi.
Brook, rivereto.
Broth, buljono.
Broom (sweeping), balailo.
Broom (shrub), ŝtipo.
Brother, frato.
Brotherhood, frateco.
Brotherly, frata.
Brougham, kaleŝo.
Brown, bruna.
Brownish, dubebruna.
Browse, sin paŝti.
Bruise (crush), pisti.
Bruise, kontuzi.
Bruit, bruego.
Brush, broso.
Brutal, bruta.
Brute, bruto.
Buccaneer, marrabisto.
Bucket, sitelo.
Buckle, buko.
Buckler, ŝildo.
Buckwheat, poligono.
Bud, burĝono.
Budget (finance), budĝeto.
Buffalo, bubalo.
Buffer, ŝtopilo.
Buffet, frapi.
Buffet (restaurant), bufedo.
Buffoon, ŝercemulo.

Bug, cimo.
Build, konstrui.
Building, a,
konstruaĵo.
Bulb, bulbo.
Bulgarian, Bulgaro.
Bulk, dikeco.
Bulky, multdika.
Bull, bovoviro.
Bullet, kuglo.
Bulletin, noto, karteto.
Bullfinch, pirolo.
Bullion (ingot),
fandaĵo.
Bullock, juna
bovoviro.
Bulwark, remparo.
Bump, ĝibeto.
Bumper, plenglaso.
Bun, bulko.
Bunch (cluster), aro.
Bundle, fasko.
Bung, ŝtopilo.
Bungle, fuŝi.
Buoy, naĝbarelo.
Buoyant, naĝema.
Burden, ŝarĝo.
Burden (refrain),
rekantaĵo.
Burden, ŝargi.
Burdensome,
multepeza.
Bureau (office),
oficejo.
Burgess, burgo.
Burglar, domorabisto.
Burial, enteriĝo.
Buried, to be, enteriĝi.
Burn (trans.), bruligi.
Burn (intrans.), bruli.
Burner (gas),
flamingo.
Burnish, poluri.

Burrow, kavigi.
Bury (something),
enfosi.
Bury (inter.), enterigi.
Bush, arbetaĵo.
Bushel, buŝelo.
Buskin, duonboto.
Business (profession),
profesio.
Business (in general),
afero.
Business-man,
aferisto.
Bust, busto.
Bustle, movo,—ado.
Busy, okupa.
But, sed.
But (prep.), krom.
Butcher, buĉisto.
Butler, kelisto.
Butt (end of gun),
kapo de la pafilo.
Butter, butero.
Butterfly, papilio.
Button (verb),
butonumi.
Button-hook,
butonumilo.
Button, butono.
Button-hole,
butontruo.
Buy, aĉeti.
By means of, per.

C

Cab, fiakro.
Cabal, kabalo.
Cabbage, brasiko.
Cabin, kajuto,
ĉambreto.
Cabinet (room),
ĉambreto.

Cabinet (ministry), kabineto.
Cabinet-maker, meblisto.
Cabinet-making, meblofarado.
Cable, ŝnurego.
Cackle, pepegi.
Cacophony, malbonsoneco.
Cadence, kadenco.
Cadet, kadeto.
Café (coffee house), kafejo.
Cage, kaĝo.
Cajoler, delogisto.
Cake, kuko.
Calcine, pulvorigi.
Calculate, kalkuli.
Calculation, kalkulo.
Caldron, kaldrono.
Calendar, kalendaro.
Calf, bovido.
Calf (of leg), tibiviando.
Calibre, kalibro.
Calico, kalikoto.
Calk, kalfatri.
Call, voki.
Call on (visit), viziti.
Call (a meeting), kunvoki.
Call, voko.
Call (visit), vizito.
Caller (visitor), vizitanto.
Calling, profesio.
Callous, kala.
Callosity, kalo.
Calm, kvietigi.
Calm, kvieta.
Calm, trankvila.
Calmness, kvieteco.

Calumniate, kalumnii.
Calumny, kalumnio.
Camel, kamelo.
Camelia, kamelio.
Camisole, kamizolo.
Camomile, kamomilo.
Camp, tendaro.
Campaign, militiro.
Camphor, kamforo.
Can (vb.), povas.
Canal, kanalo.
Canary, kanario.
Cancel (erase), surstreki.
Cancel (nullify), nuligi.
Candelabrum, kandelabro.
Candid, simplanima.
Candid, naiva.
Candidate (political), kandidato.
Candidate, aspiranto.
Candidature, kandidateco.
Candle, kandelo.
Candlestick, kandelingo.
Candour, verdiremo, sincereco.
Candy, kando.
Cane, kano.
Cane (walking stick), bastono.
Cane, vergi.
Canine, huna.
Canker, mordeti.
Cannibal, hommanĝulo.
Cannon, pafilego.
Cannon (at billiards, etc.), karamboli.
Cannonade,

44

pafilegado,
bombardado.
Canon, kanono.
Canopy, baldakeno.
Cant, hipokrito.
Canteen, drinkejo.
Canter, galopeti.
Canticle, himno.
Canto, versaro.
Canton, kantono.
Canvas, kanvaso.
Canvass, subpostuli.
Cap, ĉapo.
Cap (military), kepo.
Capability, kapableco.
Capable, kapabla.
Capacious, vasta.
Capacity, enhavebleco.
Cape, promontoro.
Capital (city), ĉefurbo.
Capital (money),
kapitalo.
Capital letter, granda
litero.
Capital (of a column),
kapitelo.
Capitalist, kapitalisto.
Capitulate, kapitulaci.
Capitulation,
kapitulaco.
Capon, kapono.
Caprice, kaprico.
Capsize, renversiĝi.
Captain (ship),
ŝipestro.
Captain (milit.),
kapitano.
Captive, malliberulo.
Captive, mallibera.
Captivate (charm),
ĉarmegi.
Captivity, mallibereco.
Capture, preno.

Capuche, kapuĉo.
Car, ĉaro.
Car (of balloon),
korbego.
Carabine, karabeno.
Carafe, karafo.
Carat, karato.
Caravan, karavano.
Carbon, karbono.
Carbuncle,
karbunkolo.
Card, karto.
Card (playing),
ludkarto.
Card (visiting),
karteto.
Cardboard, kartono.
Cardinal, Kardinalo.
Cardinal (adj.), ĉefa.
Care, zorgo.
Care of, take, zorgi pri.
Careful, zorga.
Careless, senzorga.
Caress, karesi.
Caress, kareso.
Cargo, ŝarĝo.
Carman, veturigisto.
Carmine, karmino.
Carnage, buĉado.
Carnation (flower),
dianto.
Carnation (color),
flavroza.
Carnival, karnavalo.
Carnivorous,
viandomanĝanta.
Caricature, karikaturi.
Carousal, karuselo.
Carp, karpo.
Carpenter, ĉarpentisto.
Carpentering, to do,
ĉarpenti.
Carpet, tapiŝo.

Carriage, veturilo.
Carriage (railway),
vagono.
Carriage (cost),
transsenda pago.
Carriage (of goods),
transporto.
Carrion, mortintaĵo.
Carrot, karoto.
Carry, porti.
Carry away, forporti.
Carry back, reporti.
Carry off (by force),
rabi, forrabi.
Carry (by vehicle),
veturigi.
Cart, veturigi.
Cart, ŝarĝoveturilo.
Carter, veturigisto.
Cartilage, kartilago.
Cartridge, kartoĉo.
Cartridge-box,
kartoĉujo.
Cartwright,
veturilfaristo.
Carve (sculpture),
skulpti.
Carve (cut), tranĉi,
detranĉi.
Cascade, kaskado.
Case (gram.), kazo.
Case (cover), ingo.
Case (in court),
proceso.
Casement, kazemato.
Cash, mono.
Cash (ready),
kontanto.
Cashier, kasisto.
Cask, barelo.
Casket, skatoleto.
Cassock, pastra vesto.
Cast (throw), ĵeti.

Cast (iron, etc.), fandi.
Cast (skin, etc.), ŝanĝi
felon.
Cast out, elĵeti.
Cast lots, loti.
Castaway, forĵetulo.
Castellan, kastelestro.
Caster, radeto.
Casting, fandaĵo.
Castigate (with a rod),
vergi.
Cast-iron, ferfandaĵo.
Castle, kastelo.
Castrate, kastri.
Castration, kastro.
Casual, okaza.
Casually, okaze.
Casuality, okazeco.
Cat, kato.
Catacombs, subteraj
galerioj.
Catafalque, katafalko.
Catalepsy, katalepsio.
Catalogue, katalogo.
Cataract (eyes),
katarakto.
Catarrh, kataro.
Catch, kapti.
Catechise, kateĥizi.
Catechism, kateĥismo.
Catechist, kateĥisto.
Category, kategorio.
Cater, provizi.
Caterpillar, raŭpo.
Cathedral, katedro.
Catholic, Katoliko.
Catholicism,
Katolikismo.
Cattle, bestaro.
Cattle-pen, bestejo.
Caudal, vosta.
Cauldron, kaldrono.
Cauliflower,

florbrasiko.
Cause, kaŭzo.
Cause, kaŭzi.
Cause, igi.
Cauterize, kaŭterizi.
Caution, averti.
Caution, singardemo.
Cautious, singardema.
Cavalcade, rajdantaro.
Cavalier, rajdanto.
Cavalry, kavalerio.
Cave, kaverno.
Caviare, kaviaro.
Cavil, ĉikani.
Cavity, kavo, kavaĵo.
Cease, ĉesi.
Cedar, cedro.
Cede, cedi.
Ceiling, plafono.
Celebrate (feast), festi.
Celebrate (solemnize),
solenigi.
Celebrated, fama.
Celerity, rapideco.
Celery, celerio.
Celestial, ĉiela.
Celibacy, fraŭleco.
Cell (of honeycomb),
ĉelo.
Cellar, kelo.
Cellular, ĉela.
Cement, cemento.
Cemetery, tombejo.
Censer,
bonodorfumilo.
Censor, cenzuristo.
Censorious, cenzura.
Censure, cenzuri.
Censure (blame),
riproĉo.
Census (take a),
sumigi.
Cent, cendo.

Centenarian,
centjarulo.
Centenary, centjara
festo.
Centigramme,
centigramo.
Centime, centimo.
Centimeter,
centimetro.
Central, meza, centra.
Centralize, alcentrigi.
Centre, centro.
Centre-bit, turnborilo.
Centrifugal,
decentrokura.
Centripetal,
alcentrokura.
Century, centjaro.
Ceremonious,
ceremonia.
Ceremony, ceremonio.
Certain (some), kelkaj.
Certain (sure), certa.
Certainly, certe, nepre.
Certainty, certeco.
Certify, certigi.
Certify, atesti.
Certitude, certeco.
Cessation (of
hostilities), interpaco.
Cessation, ĉesado.
Cession, cedo.
Cetaceous, balena.
Chaff (ridicule), moki.
Chaff, pajlrestaĵo.
Chaffinch, fringo.
Chagrin, ĉagreno.
Chain, ĉeno.
Chain of mountains,
montaro.
Chair, seĝo.
Chairman, prezidanto.
Chaise, veturileto.

Chalice, kaliko.
Chalk, kreto.
Chalky, kreteca.
Challenge, to, ekciti, al.
Chamber, ĉambro.
Chambermaid, ĉambristino.
Chamberlain, ĉambelano.
Chameleon, kameleono.
Chamois, ĉamo.
Chamois-leather, ŝamo.
Champagne, ĉampano.
Champion, probatalanto.
Chance, hazardo.
Chance (to happen), okazi.
Chancel, ĥorejo.
Chancellor, kanceliero.
Chandelier, lustro.
Change, ŝanĝi.
Changeable, ŝanĝebla.
Channel, kanalo.
Chant, kantado.
Chaos, ĥaoso.
Chaotic, ĥaosa.
Chapel, kapelo.
Chaplain, ekleziulo.
Chapter, ĉapitro.
Char, bruleti.
Character, karaktero.
Character (theatre), rolo.
Characterize, karakterizi.
Charge (attack), atakegi.
Charge (price), kosto.

Chariot, ĉaro.
Charitable, bonfarada.
Charity, bonfarado.
Charity (alms), almozo.
Charlatan, ĉarlatano.
Charm, ĉarmi.
Charm, ĉarmo.
Charm, talismano.
Charming, ĉarma.
Charnel house, karnejo.
Chart (geog.), karto geografia.
Chase, ĉasi.
Chase, ĉaso.
Chaste, ĉasta.
Chasten, korekti.
Chastise, puni.
Chastisement, puno.
Chastity, ĉasteco.
Chasuble, mesvesto.
Chat, interparoleti.
Chattels, bieno.
Chatter, babili.
Cheap, malkara.
Cheat, trompi.
Cheat (trick), trompo.
Cheat (deceiver), trompanto.
Check (restrain), haltigi.
Check, kontraŭmarki.
Cheek, vango.
Cheekbone, vangosto.
Cheer, aplaŭdegi.
Cheer, konsoli.
Cheerful, gaja.
Cheerfulness, gajeco.
Cheer up, rekuraĝigi.
Cheese, fromaĝo.
Chemise, ĉemizo.
Chemist, apotekisto.

Chemist-shop,
apoteko.
Chemistry, ĥemio.
Cheque, ĉeko.
Cherry, ĉerizo.
Cherub, kerubo.
Chess-pieces, ŝakoj.
Chess-board, ŝaka
tabulo.
Chest of drawers,
komodo.
Chest (box), kesto.
Chest, brusto.
Chestnut (edible),
kaŝtano.
Chevalier, kavaliro.
Chew, maĉi.
Chicane, ĉikani.
Chicken, kokido.
Chicken-house,
kokejo.
Chicory, cikorio.
Chide, riproĉi.
Chief, ĉefo.
Chief, ĉefa.
Chiffonier, ĉifonujo.
Chignon, harligaĵo.
Chilblain,
frostabsceso.
Child, infano.
Childhood, infaneco.
Childish, infana.
Childishness, infanaĵo.
Chill, malvarmigi.
Chill, malvarmo.
Chime, sonorilado.
Chimera, ĥimero.
Chimney, kamentubo.
Chimney-sweep,
kamentubisto.
Chin, mentono.
China, Ĥinujo,
Ĥinlando.

China, porcelano.
Chinese (man), Ĥino.
Chink, tinti.
Chink (crack), fendaĵo.
Chirp, pepi.
Chisel, ĉizi.
Chisel, ĉizilo.
Chivalrous, kavalira.
Chivalry, kavalireco.
Chocolate, ĉokolado.
Choice, elekto.
Choir, ĥoro.
Choke, sufoki.
Choke up, obstrukci.
Choler, kolero.
Cholera, ĥolero.
Choleric, kolera.
Choose, elekti.
Chop, haki.
Chop down, dehaki.
Chopper, hakilo.
Choral, ĥora.
Chorister, ĥoristo.
Chorus, ĥoraro.
Chrism, sankta oleo.
Christ, Kristo.
Christen, bapti.
Christendom,
Kristanaro.
Christian, Kristano.
Christian-name,
baptonomo.
Christianity,
Kristanismo.
Christmas, Kristnasko.
Christmas-box,
Kristnaskdono.
Chronicle, kroniko.
Chronology,
kronologio.
Chrysanthemum,
krizantemo.
Church, preĝejo.

Church-yard,
preĝejkorto.
Churl, malĝentilulo.
Churn, buterilo.
Churn, buterfari.
Cider, pomvino.
Cigar, cigaro.
Cigar-holder,
cigaringo.
Cigarette, cigaredo.
Cinder, cindro.
Cinnabar, cinabro.
Cinnamon, cinamo.
Cipher, cifero.
Cipher, nulo.
Circle, rondo.
Circlet, rondeto.
Circuit, ĉirkaŭo.
Circular, cirkulero.
Circulate, ĉirkaŭiri.
Circumference,
ĉirkaŭo.
Circumlocution,
ĉirkaŭfrazo.
Circumscribe,
ĉirkaŭskribi.
Circumspect,
singardema.
Circumstance,
cirkonstanco.
Circus, cirko.
Cistern, akvujo.
Citadel, fortikaĵo.
Citation, citaĵo.
Cite, citi.
Citizen, urbano.
Citron, citrono.
City, urbo.
Civic, urba.
Civil, civila.
Civil (polite), ĝentila.
Civilian, nemilita.
Civility, ĝentileco.

Civilization,
civilizacio.
Civilize, civilizi.
Claim, pretendo.
Claimant, pretendanto.
Clamber, suprenrampi.
Clammy, glua.
Clamour, bruego.
Clan, gento.
Clandestine, sekreta.
Clank, resoni.
Clap, manfrapi.
Clarify, klarigi.
Clarion, milita
trumpeto.
Clarionet, klarneto.
Clasp (buckle), buko.
Clasp, preno.
Clasp, preni.
Class, klaso.
Class, ordigi.
Classify, ordigi.
Clatter, bruegado.
Claw, ungego.
Clay, argilo.
Clean, purigi.
Clean, pura.
Clean (boots, etc.),
senkotigi.
Cleanliness, pureco.
Cleanse, purigi.
Clear, klara.
Clear (mental),
malkonfuza.
Clearness, klareco.
Cleave (split), fendi.
Cleaver, fendilo.
Cleft, fendo.
Clemency,
malsevereco.
Clement, malsevera.
Clergy, pastraro.
Clergyman, pastro.

Clerk (commercial), komizo.
Clerk (ecclesiastic), ekleziulo.
Clever, lerta.
Cleverness, lerteco.
Client, kliento.
Cliff, krutaĵo.
Climate, klimato.
Climb, suprenrampi.
Clinical, klinika.
Clink, tinti.
Clip (shear), tondi.
Clip off, detranĉi.
Clipper, tondisto.
Clique, fermita societo, kliko.
Cloak, mantelo.
Cloak-room, pakaĵejo.
Clock, horloĝo.
Clock-maker, horloĝisto.
Clod, bulo—aĵo.
Close (finish), fini.
Close, fermi.
Closet (w.c.), necesejo.
Cloth, a, drapo.
Cloth (material), tuko.
Clothe, vesti.
Clothes, vestaĵo.
Cloud, nubo.
Cloudy (not clear), malklara.
Clove, kariofilo.
Clover, trifolio.
Clown, ŝercemulo.
Cloy, satigi.
Club (thick stick), bastonego.
Club (cards), trefo.
Club (society), klubo.
Clue, postsigno.
Clump (tuft), tufo.

Clumsy, mallerta.
Cluster (of berries), beraro.
Clutch, kapti, ekkaptigi.
Clyster, klistero.
Clyster-pipe, tubeto.
Coach, veturilo.
Coach-maker, veturilfaristo.
Coachman, veturigisto.
Coal, karbo.
Coalesce, kuniĝi.
Coalition, kuniĝo.
Coarse (manner), vulgara.
Coast, marbordo.
Coat, vesto.
Coat of arms, blazono.
Coat (walls, etc.), ŝmiri.
Coax, logi.
Cobalt, kobalto.
Cobweb, araneaĵo.
Cock (trigger), ĉano.
Cock (tap), krano.
Cock (rooster), koko.
Cockerel, kokido.
Cock's comb, kresto.
Cocoa, kakao.
Cocoa-nut, kokoso.
Cod, gado.
Code, leĝaro.
Codicil, kodicilo.
Coddle, dorloti.
Coerce, devigi.
Coercion, devigo.
Coffee, kafo.
Coffee-house, kafejo.
Coffee pot, kafkruĉo.
Coffee tin or box, kafujo.
Coffer, kesto.

Coffin, ĉerko.
Cogent, videbla.
Cognomen, alnomo.
Coherence, kunligo.
Coil, rulaĵo. volvaĵo.
Coin, monero.
Coincide, koincidi.
Coincident, samtempa.
Coke, koakso.
Colander, kribrilo.
Cold, malvarmo.
Cold in the head,
nazkataro.
Cold, catch a,
malvarmumi.
Coldness, malvarmeco.
Colic, koliko.
Collaborate,
kunlabori.
Collaboration,
kunlaborado.
Collar, kolumo.
Collation, manĝeto.
Colleague, kolego.
Collect, kolekti.
Collection, kolekto.
Collector (of taxes,
etc.), kolektisto.
Collector (of stamps,
etc.), kolektanto.
Collective, opa.
College, kolegio.
Collier, karbfosisto.
Colliery, karbejo.
Collision, interfrapo.
Colon, dupunkto.
Colonel, kolonelo.
Colonial, koloniano.
Colonist, koloniisto.
Colonize, koloniigi.
Colonnade, kolonaro.
Colony, kolonio.
Colossal, kolosa.

Color, koloro.
Color, kolori.
Color (complexion),
vizaĝokoloro.
Colorless, senkolora.
Colt, ĉevalido.
Column, kolono.
Comb, kombi.
Comb, kombilo.
Combat, batalo.
Combat, batali.
Combatant, batalanto.
Combine, kombini.
Combustible, brulebla.
Combustion, brulado.
Come, veni.
Come (after), postveni.
Come (back), reveni.
Comedian,
komedianto.
Comedy, komedio.
Comely, gracia, beleta.
Comet, kometo.
Comfort, komforti.
Comfort, komforto.
Comic, komika,
ridinda.
Coming, veno.
Comma, komo.
Command (milit.),
komandi.
Command, ordoni.
Commandant,
komandanto.
Commander,
komandoro.
Commandment,
ordono.
Commemorate,
memorigi.
Commence, komenci.
Commend, laŭdi.
Commendation, laŭdo.

Comment, komentarii.
Commentary, komentario.
Commerce, komerco.
Commercial man, komercisto.
Commission, komisii.
Commission, komisio.
Commission (brokerage), maklero.
Commission agent, makleristo.
Commissioner, komisario.
Commit, fari.
Commit (to prison), aresti.
Committee, komitato.
Commodity, komercaĵo.
Common, komuna.
Common (vulgar), vulgara.
Commoner, malnobelo, burĝo.
Commonly, ordinare.
Commonwealth, respubliko.
Commotion, konfuzo.
Commune, mempensi.
Commune, komunumo.
Communicant, komuniiĝanto.
Communicate, komuniki.
Communicative, komunikema.
Communism, komunismo.
Communist, komunisto.
Community, komunumaro.

Community of interests, solidareco.
Compact, kontrakto.
Compact, densa.
Companion, kunulo.
Companion (travelling), kunvojaĝanto.
Company, kompanio.
Company (society), societo.
Company (theatrical), trupo.
Company (military), roto.
Company (troop), anaro.
Comparative, kompara.
Compare, kompari.
Compartment, fako.
Compartment (train), fakego, kupeo.
Compass, kompaso.
Compassion, kompato.
Compassionate, to be, kompati.
Compatriot, samlandano.
Compel, devigi.
Compend, resumo.
Compend, resumo.
Compensate, kompensi.
Compete, konkuri.
Competent, kompetenta.
Competition, konkurso.
Competitor, konkuranto.
Compile, redakti.
Complacency, komplezo, servemo.

Complainant, plendanto.
Complaint, plendo.
Complaisance, komplezo.
Complement, plennombro.
Complement (gram.), komplemento.
Complete, plenigi.
Completely, plene.
Complex, malsimpla.
Complexion, vizaĝkoloro.
Compliant, ceda—ema.
Complicate, malsimpligi.
Complication, malsimpleco.
Complicity, kunkulpeco.
Compliment, komplimenti.
Comply, cedi.
Compose, verki.
Compose (soothe), trankviligi.
Compose one's self, kvietiĝi.
Composer, verkisto.
Composition (music), kompozicio.
Composition (mixture), kunmeto.
Compositor (printer), kompostisto.
Compound, kunmeti.
Comprehend, kompreni.
Comprehensible, komprenebla.
Comprehension,

kompreneco.
Compress, kunpremi.
Compressible, kunpremebla.
Comprise, enhavi.
Compromise, kompromiti.
Compromise, kompromiso.
Compulsion, devigo.
Compunction, memriproĉo.
Computation, kalkulo.
Compute, kalkuli.
Comrade, kamarado.
Concave, kaveta.
Conceal, kaŝi.
Consecutive, intersekva.
Concede, cedi.
Conceit, malmodesteco.
Conceited, malmodesta.
Conceive, gravediĝi.
Concentrate, koncentrigi.
Concentric, koncentra.
Conception (idea), elpenso.
Concern, koncerni.
Concern (anxiety), zorgemo, malkvieto.
Concerning, pri.
Concert, koncerto.
Concession, cedo, cedemo.
Conciliate, pacigi.
Conciliating, pacema.
Concise, mallonga.
Conclude (infer), konkludi.
Conclude (finish), fini.

Conclusion (inference)
, konkludo.
Concord, konsento.
Concordant, unuvoĉa.
Concordat, kontrakto.
Concourse, konkurso.
Concrete, konkreta.
Concubine,
kromvirino.
Concur, konsenti.
Concussion, skuego.
Condemn, kondamni.
Condemnation,
kondamno.
Condense, densigi.
Condensed, mallonga,
mallongigita.
Condescend, bonvoli.
Condition, kondiĉo.
Conditionally,
kondiĉe.
Condole, simpatii,
kondolenci.
Condolence,
kondolenco.
Conduct, one's self,
konduti.
Conduct, konduki.
Conduct, behaviour,
konduto.
Conductor,
kondukisto.
Conduit, tubo.
Cone, konuso.
Confectioner,
konfitisto.
Confederate,
konfederi.
Confederation,
konfederacio.
Confer (holy orders),
ordoni.
Conference,

konferenco.
Confess, konfesi.
Confession, konfeso.
Confide, konfidi.
Confidence,
konfidencio.
Confident, konfidema.
Confine, enfermi.
Confirm, certigi.
Confirm (religious),
konfirmi.
Confirmation, certigo.
Confiscate, konfisiki.
Conflagration,
brulado.
Conflict, konflikto.
Confluence, kunfluiĝo.
Conform, konformi.
Conformable,
konforma.
Conformity,
konformeco.
Confound, konfuzegi.
Confrère, kunfrato.
Confront,
kontraŭstarigi.
Confuse, konfuzi.
Confusion, konfuzo—
ado.
Confute, rifuti.
Congeal, firmigi.
Congestion,
sangalfluo.
Congratulate, gratuli.
Congratulation,
gratulo.
Congregate, kolekti.
Congregation,
aŭdantaro.
Congress, kongreso.
Conical, konusa.
Conjecture, konjekti.
Conjoin, kuni.

Conjointly, kune.
Conjugate, konjugacii.
Conjunction, konjunkcio.
Conjunction (joining), kunigo.
Conjure, petegi.
Conjure, ĵongli.
Conjurer, ĵonglisto.
Connect, kunigi.
Connection, kunigo.
Connections, parencaro.
Connoisseur, virtuozo.
Conquer, venki.
Conqueror, venkanto.
Conquest, venko.
Consanguineous, samsanga.
Conscience, konscienco.
Conscientious, konscienca.
Consecrate, dediĉi.
Consecutive, intersekva.
Consent, konsenti.
Consequence, sekvo.
Consequently, sekve.
Consequential, malmodesta.
Conserve (preserve), konservi.
Conservative, Konservativulo.
Consider, pripensi, konsideri.
Considerable, grandega.
Consideration, konsidero.
Consign, sendi.
Consignment, sendo.

Consist (of), konsisti (el).
Consistent, unuforma.
Consistory, konsistorio.
Console, konsoli.
Consolation, konsolo.
Consolidate, fortigi.
Consonant (letter), konsonanto.
Consonant, unuforma.
Consort, kunulo.
Conspicuous, videgebla.
Conspiracy, konspiro.
Conspire, konspiri.
Constant, konstanta.
Constellation, stelaro.
Consternation, konsterno.
Constipation, mallakso.
Constitution, konstitucio.
Constitutional, konstitucia.
Constraint, devigo.
Construct, konstrui.
Construction (building), konstruaĵo.
Consul, konsulo.
Consulate, konsulejo.
Consult, konsiliĝi kun.
Consultation, konsiliĝo.
Consume, konsumi.
Consumer, konsumanto.
Consummate, plenigi.
Consummation, plenigo.
Consumption (phthisis), ftizo.

Consumption,
konsumiĝo.
Contact, kontakto.
Contagious,
komunikebla.
Contain, enhavi.
Contaminate,
malpurigi.
Contemn, malestimi.
Contemplate,
rigardadi.
Contemporary,
samtempa.
Contempt, malestimo.
Contemptible,
malestima.
Contend, batali.
Content, kontentigi.
Contentedness,
kontenteco.
Contention,
kontraŭstaro.
Contentious,
malpacula.
Contentment,
kontenteco.
Contents, enhavo.
Contest, disputi.
Contest, disputo.
Continence,
sindetenemo.
Continent (geog.),
kontinento.
Contingent (milit.),
kontingento.
Contiguity, apudeco.
Contiguous, apuda.
Continue (to last),
daŭri.
Continue (go on),
daŭrigi.
Contortion (of face),
grimaco.

Contour, konturo.
Contraband,
kontrabando.
Contract, kontrakto.
Contract, make a,
kontrakti.
Contract, kuntiriĝi.
Contractor,
entreprenisto.
Contradict,
kontraŭdiri.
Contrariwise,
kontraŭe.
Contrary, kontraŭa.
Contrary, on the, male,
kontraŭe.
Contrast, kontrasti.
Contrast, kontrasto.
Contravention,
malobeo.
Contribution, depago.
Contrite, penta.
Contrition, pento—
eco.
Contrivance,
elpensaĵo.
Contrive, elpensi.
Control, kontroli.
Controversy,
disputado.
Contumacious,
obstinema.
Contumacy, obstineco.
Contumely, malestimo.
Contuse, kontuzi.
Convalescence,
resaniĝo.
Convalescent (man),
resaniĝanto.
Convene, kunvoki.
Convenience,
oportuneco.
Convenient, oportuna.

Convent, monaĥinejo.
Conventional, kutima.
Converge, konvergi.
Conversation,
konversacio.
Converse,
interparoladi.
Converse, mala.
Conversely, male.
Conversion (of one's
self), konvertiĝo.
Conversion (of some
one else), konverto.
Convert (relig.),
konverti.
Convex, malkaveta.
Convey, alporti.
Convey (by vehicle),
veturigi.
Conveyance, veturilo.
Convict (man),
kondamnulo.
Convict, kondamnato.
Conviction, kondamno.
Convince, konvinki.
Convocation, kunvoko.
Convolution,
konvolvado—aĵo.
Convolvulus,
konvolvulo.
Convoy, veturilaro.
Convulse, konvulsii.
Convulsion, kunvulsio.
Cook, kuiri.
Cook (man), kuiristo.
Cookery, kuirado.
Cool, malvarmetigi.
Cool, malvarmeta.
Coolness, malvarmeto.
Coop, kaĝego.
Coop, kaĝigi.
Cooper, barelisto.
Co-operation,

kunhelpo—ado.
Copeck, kopeko.
Copier, kopiisto.
Copious, plena,
plenega.
Copper (boiler),
kaldronego.
Copper (metal), kupro.
Copse, arbetaro.
Copy, kopii.
Copy, ekzemplero.
Copybook, kajero.
Copy (a corrected),
neto.
Copyist, skribisto.
Coquet, koketi.
Coquetry, koketeco.
Coquette, koketulino.
Coral, koralo.
Cord, ŝnuro.
Cordage, ŝnuraĵo.
Cordial, kora.
Core, internaĵo.
Co-religionist,
samreligiano.
Cork, korko.
Cork, ŝtopi.
Corkscrew, korktirilo.
Corn (on foot, etc.),
kalo.
Corn, greno.
Corned, salita.
Corner, angulo.
Cornice, kornico.
Corolla, kroneto.
Coronation, kronado.
Corporal, korporalo.
Corporal, korpa.
Corporation,
korporacio.
Corpse, malvivulo.
Corpulent, vastkorpa.
Correct, korekta.

58

Correction, korekto.
Correctness, korekteco.
Correspond, korespondi.
Correspondence, korespondado.
Corridor, koridoro.
Corrode, mordeti.
Corrupt, putrigi.
Corrupt (bribe), subaĉeti.
Corrupt (vicious), malvirta.
Corruption, putro.
Corsage, korsaĵo.
Corsair, korsaro.
Corse, malvivulo.
Corset, korseto.
Cortege, sekvantaro.
Cossack, Kozako.
Cosmopolite, kosmopolita.
Cosmography, kosmografio.
Cost, kosto.
Costiveness, mallakso.
Costly, multekosta.
Costume, kostumo.
Cosy, komforta.
Cot, liteto.
Cottage, dometo.
Cotton (raw), kotono.
Cotton (manufactured), katuno.
Cotton plant, kotonujo.
Couch, kuŝejo.
Cough, tusi.
Counsel, konsili.
Counsel, advokato.
Counsel, konsilo.
Counsel, to take, konsiliĝi kun.

Counsellor, konsilanto.
Count, kalkuli.
Count upon, konfidi al.
Count (title), grafo.
Countenance, vizaĝo.
Counter (token), ludmarko.
Counteract, malhelpi.
Counter-bass, kontrabaso.
Counterfeit, imiti.
Counterfeit, falsi.
Counterfeit, falsaĵo.
Countermand (an order), kontraŭmendi.
Counterpane, litkovrilo.
Counterpart, kontraŭparto.
Counting-house, kontoro.
Country, lando.
Country (rural), kamparo.
Countryman, kamparano.
Countryman, fellow, samlandano.
Country-house, kampodomo.
Country-seat, somerloĝo.
County, graflando.
Couple, paro.
Couple, kunigi.
Couplet, strofo.
Courage, kuraĝo.
Courageous, to be, kuraĝi.
Courier, kuriero.
Course (race), kuro.
Course (of lessons), kurso.

Course (of course), kompreneble.
Court (royal), kortego.
Court (justice), juĝejo.
Court (yard), korto.
Court, amindumi.
Courteous, ĝentila.
Courtesy, ĝentileco.
Courtier, kortegulo.
Cousin (masc.), kuzo.
Covenant, kondiĉi.
Covenant, interkonsento.
Cover, kovri.
Cover (the head), surmeti.
Cover (roof), tegi.
Cover, kovrilo.
Covet, avidi.
Covetousness, avideco.
Covey, kovitaro.
Cow, bovino.
Coward, malkuraĝulo.
Cowardice, malkuraĝeco.
Cowherd, bovgardisto.
Cow shed, bovinejo.
Cowl, kapuĉo.
Cowslip, verprimolo.
Coxcomb, dando.
Coy, rezerva.
Coyness, rezerveco.
Cozen, trompi.
Crab, kankro.
Crack (split), fendi.
Crack (noise), kraki.
Crackle, kraketi.
Cradle, lulilo.
Craft, ruzo.
Craft (vessel), ŝipeto.
Crafty, to be, ruzi.
Crafty, ruza.
Cram (of food), supersatigi.
Cram, plenegigi.
Cramp (metal), krampo.
Crane (bird), gruo.
Crane, ŝarĝlevilo.
Crape, krepo.
Crater, kratero.
Cravat, kravato.
Crave, petegi.
Crawl, rampi.
Crayon, krajono.
Crazy, freneza.
Cream, kremo.
Create, krei.
Creation, kreitaĵo.
Creator, kreinto.
Creature, estaĵo.
Credence, kredo.
Credible, kredebla.
Credit, kredito.
Creditor, kreditoro.
Credulity, kredemo.
Creed, kredo.
Creep, rampi.
Creole, Kreolo.
Crest, tufo.
Crevice, fendo—aĵo.
Crew, maristaro.
Cricket (insect), grilo.
Crime, krimo.
Criminal, krimulo.
Criminally, kriminale.
Crimson, ruĝega.
Cripple, kripligi.
Cripple, kriplulo.
Crippled, kripla.
Crisis, krizo.
Crisp, friza.
Critic, kritikisto.
Criticism, kritiko.
Croak, bleki.
Crockery, fajenco.

Crocodile, krokodilo.
Crooked, hoka,
malrekta.
Crop (harvest), rikolto.
Crosier, episkopa
bastono.
Cross, kruco.
Cross, krucigi.
Cross (manner),
malafabla.
Cross-over, transiri.
Cross-out, streki.
Crossing, krucigo.
Crotchet, kvarona
noto.
Croup, krupo.
Crow, korniko.
Crow, bleki.
Crow-bar, levilo.
Crowd, amaso.
Crown, krono.
Crown, kroni.
Crown (of head),
verto.
Crucifix, krucifikso.
Crucifixion, krucumo.
Crucify, krucumi.
Crude, kruda.
Cruel, kruela.
Cruelty, kruelo—eco.
Cruet, oleujo.
Cruise, krozi.
Cruiser, krozŝipo.
Crumb (bread),
panmolaĵo.
Crumble, elfali.
Crumple, ĉifi.
Crupper, postaĵo.
Crush, premegi.
Crust, krusto.
Crustaceous,
kankrogenta.
Crutch, lambastono.

Cry (call out), krii.
Cry (weep), plori.
Cry out, ekkrii.
Cry (of animals, etc.),
bleki.
Crypt, subteraĵo.
Crystal, kristalo.
Crystallise, kristaligi.
Cub (of lion), leonido.
Cube, kubo.
Cuckoo, kukolo.
Cucumber, kukumo.
Cudgel, bastonego.
Cuff, manumo.
Cuirass, kiraso.
Cull, kolekti.
Cullender, kribrilo.
Culpable, kulpa.
Culprit, kulpulo.
Cultivate, kulturi.
Culture, kulturo.
Cunning, ruzo.
Cunning, ruza.
Cup, taso.
Cupboard, ŝranko.
Cupidity, avideco.
Cupola, kupolo.
Curable, kuracebla.
Curacy, paroĥo.
Curate, vikaro.
Curator, kuratoro,
gardisto.
Curb, haltigi.
Cure (act of curing),
kuraco.
Cure (remedy),
kuracilo.
Cure (a malady),
kuraci.
Curious (inquisitive),
sciama.
Curious (strange),
stranga.

Curiosity, kuriozaĵo.
Curl, buklo.
Currant, ribo.
Current, fluo.
Currier, ledpretigisto.
Curse, malbeni.
Curt, mallonga.
Curtail, mallongigi.
Curtain, kurteno.
Curve, kurbigi.
Curve, kurbeco.
Cushion, kuseno.
Custard, flanaĵo.
Custom, kutimo.
Customary, kutima.
Customer, kliento.
Cut (with knife),
tranĉi.
Cut (with scissors),
tondi.
Cut off, detranĉi.
Cutaneous, haŭta.
Cute, ruza.
Cutlass, tranĉilego.
Cutlet, kotleto.
Cutter (blade),
tranĉanto.
Cutting (under-
ground), subtervojo.
Cycle, ciklo.
Cyclone, ciklono.
Cylinder, cilindro.
Cymbal, cimbalo.
Cypress, cipreso.
Czar, Caro.

D

Dab, bateto.
Daffodil, narciso.
Dagger, ponardo.
Dahlia, dalio.
Daily, ĉiutage,

ĉiutaga.
Dainty, frandaĵo.
Dainty, frandema.
Dairy, laktovendejo.
Daisy, lekanto.
Dale, valeto.
Dally, malfrui.
Dam, bestopatrino.
Dam, akvoŝtopilo,
digo.
Damage, difekti.
Damage, difektaĵo.
Damask, damasko.
Dame, sinjorino,
patrino.
Damn, kondamni.
Damp, malseka.
Damsel, fraŭlino.
Dance, danci.
Dancing (the art of),
dancarto.
Dandle, luleti.
Dandy, dando.
Dane, Dano.
Dandelion, leontodo.
Danger, danĝero.
Dangle, pendeti.
Dare, kuraĝi.
Daring, kuraĝa,
maltima.
Dark (colour),
malpala.
Dark, malluma.
Dark (to become),
mallumiĝi.
Darken, mallumigi.
Darkness,
mallumeco.
Darling, karegulo.
Darn, fliki.
Darning, flikado.
Dart, sago, pikilo.
Date (time), dato.

Date (fruit), daktilo.
Date, dati.
Dative, dativo.
Daub, fuŝi.
Daubing, fuŝo—ado.
Daughter, filino.
Daughter-in-law,
bofilino.
Daunt, timigi.
Dauntless, sentima.
Dawn, tagiĝo.
Day, tago.
Day (a, per), laŭtage.
Day (before
yesterday),
antaŭhieraŭ.
Daybreak, tagiĝo.
Daybook, taglibro.
Daydream, revo.
Day laborer,
taglaboristo.
Daze, duonesvenigi.
Dazzle, blindigi.
Deacon, diakono.
Dead (lifeless),
senviva.
Deadly, pereiga.
Deadhouse,
mortintejo.
Deaf, surda.
Deafen, surdigi.
Deafmute,
surdamutulo.
Deafness, surdeco.
Deal (sell), komerci.
Deal out, disdoni.
Dealer, komercisto.
Dean, fakultestro.
Dear, kara.
Dear (person),
karulo.
Dear (price),
multekosta.

Dearth, seneco.
Death, morto.
Deathless, senmorta.
Debar, eksigi.
Debase, malnobligi.
Debate, disputo.
Debauch, diboĉigi.
Debauch, diboĉo.
Debility, malforteco.
Debit, debito.
Debris, rubo—aĵo.
Debt, to get into,
ŝuldiĝi.
Debt, ŝuldo.
Debtor, ŝuldanto.
Debut, komenco.
Decadence,
kadukeco.
Decalogue, dekalogo.
Decant, transverŝi.
Decanter, karafo.
Decapitate,
senkapigi.
Decay, kadukeco.
Decaying, kaduka.
Decease (v.), morti.
Deceit, artifiko—eco.
Deceive, trompi.
Deceived, to be,
trompiĝi.
December,
Decembro.
Decent, deca.
Deception, trompo.
Decide, decidi.
Decided, decida.
Decimal, decimalo.
Decipher, deĉifri.
Decisive, decidiga.
Deck (adorn),
ornami.
Deck (ship), ferdeko.
Declaim, deklami.

Declaration,
deklaracio.
Declaration (of
love), amesprimo.
Declare, sciigi,
anonci.
Declension,
deklinacio.
Decline, ekfiniĝo.
Decline (health),
ekmalfortiĝi.
Decline (refuse),
rifuzi.
Decline (grammar),
deklinacii.
Decline (in price),
malplikariĝo.
Declivity, deklivo.
Decompose, dismeti.
Decorate, ornami.
Decorator,
ornamisto.
Decorum, dececo.
Decorous, bonmora.
Decoy, trompi,
delogi.
Decoy, kaptilo.
Decrease, malkreski.
Decree, dekreto.
Dedicate, dediĉi.
Dedication, dediĉo.
Deduce, depreni.
Deduct, depreni.
Deduction, depreno.
Deed, faro.
Deem, pensi.
Deep (sound), basa.
Deep, profunda.
Deer, cervo.
Deface, forigi,
surstreki.
Defame, kalumnii.
Defeat, venki.

Defeat (n.),
malvenko—ego.
Defect, difekto—aĵo.
Defend, defendi.
Defer, prokrasti.
Deference,
respektego.
Deficiency, deficito.
Defile (n.),
intermonto.
Defile (soil),
malpurigi.
Define, difini.
Definite, difinita.
Definitive, definitiva.
Deform,
malbonformigi.
Deformed,
malbelforma.
Defraud, trompi.
Defray, elpagi.
Defunct, mortinto.
Defy, kontraŭstari.
Degenerate,
degeneri.
Degrade, degradi.
Degree, grado.
Deign, bonvoli.
Deism, diismo.
Deist, diisto.
Deity, diaĵo.
Deject, senkuraĝi.
Dejection,
malĝojeco.
Delay (trans.),
prokrasti.
Delay (intrans.),
malfrui, tromalfrui.
Delay, prokrasto.
Delegate, delegi.
Delegate, delegito.
Delegation,
delegacio.

Deliberate,
prikonsiliĝi.
Deliberation,
prikonsiliĝo.
Delicacy, frandaĵo.
Delicate, delikata.
Delightful, rava,
ĉarmega.
Delinquent, kulpulo.
Delirium, deliro.
Deliver (save), savi.
Deliver (liberate),
liberigi.
Deliver (goods),
liveri.
Delivery (childbirth),
nasko.
Dell, valeto.
Delude, trompi.
Deluge, superakvego.
Delusion, trompo.
Demagogue,
demagogo.
Demand, postulo.
Demean, humili.
Demeanour, konduto.
Demesne, bieno—
aĵo.
Demise, morto.
Democrat,
demokrato.
Democracy,
demokrataro.
Demolish, detruegi.
Demon, demono.
Demoniac,
demoniako.
Demonstrate, pruvi.
Demonstrative,
montra.
Demoralized, to
become, malkuraĝiĝi.
Demur, ŝanceliĝi.

Demure, modesta.
Den (animals, etc.),
nestego.
Denial, neo.
Deniable, neigebla.
Denote, montri.
Denounce, denunci.
Dense, densa.
Density, denseco.
Dental, denta.
Dentist, dentisto.
Denude, senkovrigi.
Denunciation,
denunco—ado.
Deny, nei.
Depart, foriri.
Depart (life), morti.
Department, fako,
departemento.
Departure, foriro.
Depend, dependi.
Dependence,
dependeco.
Depict, priskribi.
Deplore, bedaŭregi.
Deponent, atestanto.
Depopulate,
senhomigi.
Depopulated,
senhoma.
Deportment,
konduto.
Depose (give
evidence), atesti.
Depose, eksiĝi,
detroni.
Deposit, enmeti.
Depot, tenejo.
Deprave, malvirtigi.
Depravity, malvirto.
Depreciate,
maltaksigi.
Depredation, rabado.

Depress, malleveti.
Deprivation, senigo.
Depth, profundo—aĵo.
Depute, deputi.
Deputy, deputato.
Derail, elreliĝi.
Derange, malordigi.
Deride, moki, mokegi.
Derive, deveni.
Derivation, devenigado.
Descend, malsupreniri.
Descendant, ido, posteulo.
Describe, priskribi.
Desecration, malpiegaĵo.
Desert, forlasi.
Desert (place), dezerto.
Deserter, forkurinto.
Deserve, meriti.
Design (draw), desegni.
Design (intend), intenci.
Design (intention), intenco.
Designate, montri, nomi.
Designing, ruza.
Desire, deziri.
Desist, ĉesi, ĉesigi.
Desk, skribtablo.
Desolate, ruinigi.
Despair, malesperi.
Despatch, ekspedi.
Desperate, furioza.
Despicable, malnobla.

Despise, malestimi.
Despond, malesperi.
Despot, tirano.
Despotism, tiraneco.
Dessert, deserto.
Destine, for, difini (por).
Destiny, sorto.
Destitute, malriĉega.
Destroy, detrui.
Destruction, detruo.
Detach, apartigi.
Detachment (milit.), taĉmento.
Detail, detalo.
Details (minutes), detaleto.
Detain, malhelpi, deteni.
Detect, eltrovi.
Deter, malhelpi.
Deteriorate, difekti.
Determine, decidi.
Determination, decideco.
Determined, decida.
Detest, malami.
Dethrone, detroni.
Detonation, eksplodbruo.
Detract, kalumnii.
Detriment, malprofito, perdo.
Detrimental, malhelpa.
Devastate, dezertigi, ruinigi.
Develope, vastigi.
Development, vastigo.
Deviate, malrektiĝi.
Deviation, malrektiĝo.

Device, devizo.
Devil, diablo.
Devine, diveni.
Devious, malrekta.
Devise (invent),
elpensi.
Devoid, senenhava.
Devote one's self, sin
doni.
Devoted, sindona.
Devotion, sindono.
Devotee, religiulo.
Devoid, religia.
Devour, manĝegi.
Dew, roso.
Dexterity, lerteco.
Diadem, diademo.
Diagonal, diagonalo.
Diagram, diagramo.
Dial, ciferplato.
Dialect, dialekto.
Dialogue, dialogo.
Diameter, diametro.
Diamond, diamanto.
Diarrhœa, lakso.
Dice, ludkuboj.
Dictate, dikti.
Dictation, diktato.
Dictator, diktatoro.
Dictionary, vortaro.
Die, morti.
Die, presilo.
Diet, dieto.
Differ, diferenci.
Difference (dispute),
malpaco.
Difficulty,
malfacileco.
Diffusion, vastigo.
Dig, fosi.
Digest, digesti.
Digit, fingro, cifero.
Dignify, indigi.

Dignitary, rangulo.
Dignity, indeco.
Dignity (rank), rango.
Dilapidate, ruinigi.
Dilate, plilarĝigi.
Dilatory,
prokrastema.
Diligence, diligento.
Diligent, diligenta.
Dim, dubeluma.
Diminish (length),
mallongigi.
Diminish (price),
rabati.
Diminutive,
malgranda—eta.
Din, bruegado.
Dine (midday),
meztagmanĝi.
Dine (evening),
vespermanĝi.
Dining-room,
manĝoĉambro.
Dining-
room (public),
restoracio.
Dinner-service,
manĝilaro.
Dip, trempi.
Dip (in water),
subakvigi.
Diphthong, diftongo.
Diploma, diplomo.
Diplomacy,
diplomatio.
Diphtheria, difterio.
Dire, terura.
Direct (govern),
direkti.
Direct (command),
ordoni.
Direct (straight),
rekta.

Directly (time), tuj.
Directly, rekte.
Director, direktoro.
Directory, adresaro.
Dirge, funebra kanto.
Dirt (soil), malpurigi.
Dirt, malpurajô.
Dirt (mud), koto.
Dirtiness, malpureco.
Dirty, malpura.
Disable, kripli.
Disadvantage,
malutilo.
Disagree,
malkonsenti.
Disagreement,
malkonsento.
Disappear, malaperi.
Disappoint,
malkontentigi.
Disappointment,
malkontentigo.
Disapprove,
malaprobi.
Disarm, senarmigi.
Disarray, konfuzego.
Disarrange,
malordigi.
Disaster,
malfeliĉego.
Disastrous, ruiniga.
Disavow, malkonfesi.
Disband, disigi.
Disbelieve, malkredi.
Disburse, elspezi.
Disbursement,
elspezo.
Disc, disko.
Discard, forigi,
forĵeti.
Discern, distingi.
Discernment,
sagaceco.

Discharge, eligi.
Discharge (dismiss),
eksigi.
Discharge (a debt),
elpagi.
Disciple, aliĝanto.
Discipline,
disciplino.
Disclaim,
malkonfesi.
Disclose, malkaŝi.
Discolour,
senkolorigi.
Discomfit,
malvenkigi.
Discompose,
malkvietigi.
Disconcert, konfuzi.
Disconnect, disigi.
Disconsolate,
ĉagrenega.
Discontented,
malkontenta.
Discontinuance,
interrompo.
Discord, malpaco.
Discord (music),
malakordo.
Discordant, malpaca,
malakordo.
Discount, diskonto.
Discourage,
senkuraĝigi.
Discouragement,
senkuraĝeco.
Discourse, parolado.
Discourteous,
malĝentila.
Discover, eltrovi.
Discovery, eltrovo.
Discredit,
senkreditigi.
Discreet, diskreta.

Discretion,
singardemo, diskreto.
Discriminate,
distingi.
Discursive, tro
skribema.
Discuss, diskuti.
Discussion,
diskutado.
Disdain, malŝati.
Disease, malsano—
ego.
Disembark, elŝipiĝi.
Disengage, liberigi.
Disentangle, liberigi.
Disfavour,
malfavoro.
Disgrace, malhonori.
Disguise, alivesti.
Disgust, naŭzi.
Dish, plado.
Dishcloth, telertuko.
Dishearten,
malkuraĝigi.
Dishonest,
malhonesta.
Dishonesty,
malhonesteco.
Dishonour,
malhonori.
Dishonourable,
malhonora.
Disillusion, elreviĝo.
Disinfect, dezinfekti.
Disinterested,
malprofitema.
Disjoin, disligi.
Disjoint, elartikigi.
Disjunction, disigo.
Dislike, malŝati,
malameti.
Dislike, antipatio.
Dislocate, elartikigi.

Dislocate (to take to
pieces), dispecigi.
Dislocation,
elartikigo.
Dislodge, transloki.
Disloyal, malfidela.
Disloyalty, malfidelo.
Dismal, funebra.
Dismay, konsterni.
Dismember,
senmembrigi.
Dismiss, forsendi,
eksigi.
Dismount, elseligi.
Disobey, malobei.
Disobliging,
neservema.
Disorder, malordo,
senordeco.
Disorderly,
malordema.
Disorganise,
malorganizi.
Disown, forlasi, nei.
Disparity, neegaleco.
Dispatch, depeŝo.
Dispel, peli, forpeli.
Dispensary,
kuracilejo.
Dispense (to give
out), disdoni.
Disperse, dispeli.
Display, vidaĵo,
montraĵo.
Display (show,
pomp), lukso.
Displace, transloki.
Displease, malplaĉi.
Displeasure,
malplaĉo.
Disport, ludi.
Dispose, disponi.
Disposable,

disponebla.
Disposition, inklino.
Dispraise, mallaŭdi.
Disproof, refuto.
Disprove, refuti.
Dispute, disputo.
Dispute (quarrel),
malpaci.
Disputatious,
disputa.
Disqualify,
malkapabligi.
Disquiet,
maltrankviligi.
Disrespectful,
nerespekta.
Disappointment,
kontraŭaĵo.
Dissatisfied,
malkontenta.
Dissect, dissekcii.
Dissection, dissekcio.
Dissemble, hipokriti,
kaŝi.
Disseminate, dissemi.
Dissent, malkonsenti.
Dissenter,
alireligiulo.
Dissertation,
disertacio.
Dissimilar, malsama.
Dissimulate, kaŝi.
Dissimulation,
kaŝemo.
Dissipate, malŝpari.
Dissipation,
malŝparo.
Dissolute, diboĉa.
Dissolution, solvo.
Dissolve, solvi.
Disrespect,
malrespekti.
Disrespect,

malrespekto.
Dissuade, malkonsili.
Distaff, ŝpinilo.
Distance, interspaco.
Distant,
malproksima.
Distaste, tedo, naŭzo.
Distend, plilarĝigi,
ŝveli.
Distil, distili.
Distinct (clear),
klara.
Distinct, neta, klara.
Distinctive,
distingiga.
Distinguish, distingi.
Distort, tordigi.
Distortion (grimace),
grimaco.
Distract, distri.
Distraction, distreco.
Distress, ĉagrenigi.
Distress, mizerigo.
Distribute (scatter),
disŝuti.
Distribute (to share),
disdoni.
District, kvartalo.
Distrust, malfidi.
Distrust, malfido.
Distrustful,
malfidema.
Disturb, interrompi.
Disturbance,
tumulto.
Disunite, disigi.
Disunion, disiĝo.
Ditch, defluilo.
Ditto, sama, idemo.
Ditty, kanteto.
Dive, subakviĝi.
Diver (bird),
kolimbo.

Diverge,
malkonvergi.
Divers (various),
diversa.
Diverse, diversa.
Diversity, diverseco.
Divert, amuzi.
Divest, senvestigi.
Divide, dividi.
Dividend (finance),
rento.
Dividend (arith.),
dividato.
Divider, dividanto.
Divine, dia.
Divinity, dieco.
Divine service,
Diservo.
Division, divido.
Division (arith.),
dividado.
Divisor, dividonto.
Divorce (judicial),
eksedziĝo.
Divorce (judicial),
eksedziĝi.
Divorced, to be,
eksedziĝi.
Divulge, konigi.
Dizziness, kapturno.
Do, fari.
Do away with, to,
forigi.
Docile, obea.
Docility, obeemo.
Dock, ŝipejo.
Docket, karteto,
bileto.
Doctor, Doktoro.
Doctor (med.),
kuracisto.
Doctrine, dogmaro.
Document,

dokumento.
Doff, demeti.
Dog, hundo.
Dogged, obstina.
Doghouse,
hundodometo.
Dog kennel, hundejo.
Dogma, dogmo.
Dole, disdoni.
Doleful, funebra.
Doll, pupo.
Dollar, dolaro.
Dolphin, delfeno.
Dolt, malsaĝulo.
Domain, bieno.
Dome, kupolo.
Domestic, hejma.
Domestic, servisto—
ino.
Domicile, loĝejo.
Dominant, potenca.
Domination, potenco.
Dominion, regeco.
Dominion, regno.
Domino, domeno.
Donation, donaco,
oferdono.
Donkey, azeno.
Donor, donanto.
Doom, kondamno,
sorto.
Door, pordo.
Door curtain, pordo
kurteno.
Doorkeeper,
pordisto.
Dormant, ekdorma.
Dormer-window,
fenestreto.
Dormitory, dormejo.
Dorsal, dorsa.
Dose, dozo.
Dot, punkto.

Dote, amegi.
Double, duobligi.
Doubt, dubi.
Doubter, dubanto.
Doubtful, duba.
Doubtlessly, sendube.
Douche, duŝo.
Dough, knedaĵo.
Dove, kolombo.
Dovecot, kolombejo.
Down, lanugo.
Downs, sablaj montetoj.
Downfall, falego.
Dowry, doto.
Downwards, malsupre.
Doze, dormeti.
Dozen, dekduo.
Draft (bill of exchange), kambio.
Drag, treni, tiri.
Dragon, drako.
Dragon fly, libelo.
Dragoon, dragono.
Drake, anaso.
Drama, dramo.
Dramatical, drama.
Dramatist, dramaŭtoro.
Drape, drapiri.
Draper, drapvendisto.
Drastic, drastika.
Draught-board, dama tabulo.
Draughts (pieces), damoj.
Draughtsman, desegnisto.
Draw (water from well), ĉerpi.
Draw (pull), tiri.

Draw after (load, etc.), posttiri.
Draw (near), proksimiĝi.
Draw (lots), loti.
Draw (together), kuntiri.
Drawer, tirkesto.
Drawers (garment), kalsono.
Drawing (lots), lotado.
Dray, ŝarĝveturilo.
Dread, timi, timegi.
Dread, teruro, timo.
Dreadful, terurega.
Dream, sonĝi.
Dreary, malgaja.
Dredge, skrapi.
Dredger, skrapilego.
Dregs, feĉo.
Drench, akvumi.
Dress (clothe), vesti.
Dress (wound), bandaĝi.
Dressing case, necesujo.
Dress coat, frako.
Dressing gown, negliĝa vesto.
Dressmaker, kudristino.
Dressing room, tualetejo, vestejo.
Drill, bori.
Drill (tool), borilo.
Drill (military), ekzerco.
Drink, trinki.
Drink (to excess), drinki.
Drink, trinkaĵo.
Drinkable, trinkebla.

Drip, guteti.
Drive away (expel), forpeli.
Drive (in carriage), veturi.
Drive back (repel), repeli, repuŝi.
Drivel (to slaver), kraĉeti.
Driver (car, etc.), veturisto.
Droll, ridinda, ŝerca.
Drollery, ŝerco—ado.
Dromedary, unuĝiba kamelo.
Drone, burdo.
Droop (pine), malfortiĝi.
Drop, guto.
Dropsy, akvoŝvelo.
Dross, metala ŝaŭmo.
Drought, senpluveco.
Drove (cattle), bestaro, brutaro.
Drown, droni.
Drown (trans.), dronigi.
Drowsy, dorma.
Drub (beat), bati.
Drudge, laboregi.
Drug, drogo.
Druggist, drogisto.
Drum, tamburo.
Drum, of ear, oreltamburo.
Drunkard, drinkulo.
Drunkenness, ebrieco.
Dry, seka.
Dry up, sekiĝi.
Dry, one's self, sin sekigi.
Dry land, firmaĵo.

Dryness, sekeco.
Dual, duobla, dualo.
Dualism, dualismo.
Dubious, duba.
Ducat, dukato.
Duchess, dukino.
Duchy, duklando.
Duck, anasino.
Ducking, trempado.
Duct, tubo.
Ductile, etendebla.
Dude, dando.
Duel, duelo.
Duet, dueto.
Duke, duko.
Dukedom (duchy), duklando.
Dull (unpolished), malbrila.
Dull (sombre), malhela, nebula.
Dull (stupid), malklera.
Dull (blunt), malakra.
Dumb, muta.
Dumbness, muteco.
Dumb show, pantomimo.
Dunce, malklerulo.
Dung, sterko.
Dungheap, sterkaĵo.
Dungeon, malliberejo.
Dupe, trompi.
Duplicate, duobligi.
Duplicity, trompemo.
Durable, fortika.
Duration, daŭro.
During, dum.
Dusky, malhela.
Dust, polvo.
Dust, grain of, polvero.

Duster, viŝilo.
Dustman, kotisto.
Dutchman,
Holandano.
Duty, devo.
Duty (import),
imposto.
Dutiful, respektema.
Dwarf,
malgrandegulo.
Dwell, loĝi, restadi.
Dwelling, loĝejo.
Dwindle,
malgrandiĝi.
Dye, kolorigi.
Dye, kolorigilo.
Dyer, kolorigisto.
Dying, to be,
ekmorti.
Dying (person),
mortanto.
Dyke, digo.
Dynamics, dinamiko.
Dynamism,
dinamismo.
Dynamite, dinamito.
Dynasty, dinastio.
Dysentery, disenterio.
Dyspepsia, dispepsio.

E
Each (adj.), ĉia.
Each (pronoun), ĉiu.
Eager, avida.
Eagle, aglo.
Ear, orelo.
Ear (of corn), spiko.
Earl, grafo.
Earldom, graflando.
Early (adv.), frue.
Early (adj.), frua.
Earn, perlabori.

Earnest, diligenta.
Earnestly, forte,
fervore.
Earnestness, seriozeco.
Earring, orelringo.
Earth, tero.
Earthenware, fajenco.
Earthly, monda, tera.
Earthquake, tertremo.
Ease, komforto.
Ease, at, senĝene.
East, oriento.
Easter, Pasko.
Easterly, orienta.
Easy, facila.
Eat, manĝi.
Eatable, manĝebla.
Eaves, defluilo.
Ebb (and flow), forfluo
(kaj alfluo).
Ebony, ebono.
Ebriety, ebrieco.
Ebullition, bolado.
Eccentric, stranga.
Ecclesiastic, ekleziulo.
Ecclesiastical, eklezia.
Echo, eĥo.
Eclipse, mallumiĝo.
Ecliptic, ekliptiko.
Eclogue, eklogo.
Economical, ŝparema.
Economics, ekonomio.
Economise, ŝpari.
Economist,
ekonomiisto.
Economy, ŝparemo.
Ecstacy, ravo.
Eczema, ekzemo.
Eddy, turniĝadi.
Eddy, akvoturniĝo.
Eden, Edeno.
Edge, rando.
Edge (of tools),

tranĉrando.
Edible, manĝebla.
Edict, ordono.
Edifice, konstruaĵo.
Edify, edifi.
Edit, eldoni, redakti.
Edition, eldono.
Editor, eldonisto.
Educate, eduki.
Educated, klera.
Education (given), edukado.
Education (received), edukiteco.
Educator, edukisto.
Eel, angilo.
Efface, surstreki.
Effect (result), efiko.
Effect (impression), efekto.
Effect, efektivigi.
Effective, efektiva.
Effectively, efektive.
Effectual, efektiva.
Effervesce, ŝaŭmadi.
Efficacious, efika.
Efficacy, efikeco.
Effigy, figuro.
Efflorescence, florado.
Effluvium, malbonodoro.
Efflux, defluado.
Effort, peno.
Effrontery, senhonteco.
Effulgent, radiluma.
Egg, ovo.
Egg-shaped, ovoforma.
Egoism, egoismo.
Egoist, egoisto.
Egress, eliro.
Egyptian, Egipto.
Eh! he!

Eider-down, lanugo.
Eider-duck, molanaso.
Eight, ok.
Either, aŭ.
Ejaculation, ekkrio.
Eject, elĵeti.
Elaborate, prilabori.
Elastic, elasta.
Elastic, elastaĵo.
Elasticity, elasteco.
Elbow, kubuto.
Elder (tree), sambuko.
Elder, pliaĝa.
Eldest (first born), unuanaskito.
Elect (choose), elekti.
Elect (by ballot), baloti.
Election, elekto.
Elector, elektanto.
Electric, elektra.
Electricity, elektro.
Electrify, elektrigi.
Elegance, eleganteco.
Elegant, eleganta.
Elegy, elegio.
Element, elemento.
Elementary, elementa.
Elephant, elefanto.
Elevate, altigi.
Elevation (height), altaĵo.
Elf, koboldo, feino.
Elicit, eltiri.
Elide, elizii.
Eligible, elektebla.
Eligibility, elektebleco.
Eliminate, elmeti.
Elision, elizio.
Elite, eminentularo.
Ell, ulno.
Ellipse, elipso.
Elm, ulmo.

Elocution,
parolscienco.
Eloquence,
elokventeco.
Eloquent, elokventa.
Elope, forkuri.
Else, alie.
Elsewhere, aliloke.
Elude, lerte eviti.
Emaciated,
malgrasega.
Emanate, deveni.
Emancipate, liberigi.
Embalm, balzamumi.
Embankment, surbordo
bordmarŝejo.
Embark, enŝipiĝi.
Embarrass, embarasi.
Embarrassment,
embaraso.
Embellish, beligi,
ornami.
Embers, brulaĵo.
Emblem, emblemo.
Embolden, kuraĝigi.
Embossment, reliefo.
Embrace, ĉirkaŭpreni.
Embroider, brodi.
Embryo, embrio.
Embryology,
embriologio.
Emerald, smeraldo.
Emergency, ekokazo.
Emetic, vomilo.
Emigrant, elmigranto.
Emigrate, elmigri.
Emigration, elmigrado,
emigracio.
Eminence, altaĵo.
Eminence (title),
Moŝto.
Eminent, eminenta.
Emissary, emisario,

reprezentanto.
Emit, ellasi.
Emmet, formiko.
Emolument, salajro.
Emotion, kortuŝeco.
Emperor, imperiestro.
Emphatic, patosa,
akcentega.
Emphasis, patoso,
akcentego.
Emphasise, akcentegi.
Empire, imperio.
Employ (use), uzi.
Employ (hire), dungi.
Employment, ofico.
Empower, rajtigi.
Empress,
imperiestrino.
Empty, malplenigi.
Empty, malplena.
Empty (unoccupied),
neokupata.
Emulate, superemi.
Emulation, superemo.
Enable, ebligi.
Enact, reguli.
Enactment, regulo.
Enamel, emajlo.
Enamel, emajli.
Enamoured,
enamiĝinta.
Encase, enkasigi.
Enchant, ravi.
Enchantment, ensorĉo.
Enclose, enfermi.
Enclosed (herewith),
tie ĉi enfermita.
Encompass, ĉirkaŭi.
Encore, bis.
Encounter, renkonti.
Encourage, kuraĝigi.
Encyclopedia,
enciklopedio.

Encroach, trudi.
End, fini.
End, fino.
Endearment, kareso.
Endeavour, peni.
Endeavour, peno.
Endless, eterna.
Endow, doti.
Endure (continue),
daŭri.
Endure (tolerate),
toleri.
Endure (suffer), suferi.
Enema, klisterilo.
Enemy, malamiko.
Energetic, energia.
Energy, energio.
Enervate, malfortigi.
Enfranchise, afranki,
liberigi.
Engage, servigi, dungi.
Engage (to occupy),
okupi.
Engagement (promise)
, promeso.
Engagement (milit.),
ekbatalo.
Engine, maŝino.
Engineer, inĝeniero.
England, Anglujo,
Anglolando.
English, Angla.
Englishman, Anglo.
Engrave, gravuri.
Engraver, gravuristo.
Engraving, gravuraĵo.
Engross (fully
occupy), priokupi.
Enhale, enspiri.
Enigma, enigmo.
Enjoin, ordoni.
Enjoy, ĝui.
Enlarge, pligrandigi.

Enlighten, klerigi.
Enlist, varbi.
Enlistment, varbo.
Enliven, gajigi.
Enmity, malamikeco.
Ennoble, nobeligi.
Enormous, grandega.
Enough, sufiĉe.
Enquire, informiĝi.
Enquiry, informiĝo.
Enrage, furiozigi.
Enrapture, ravi.
Enrich, riĉigi.
Enrichment, riĉigo.
Enrol, varbi.
Ensign-bearer,
standardisto.
Enslave, sklavigi.
Ensue, sekvi.
Entangle, impliki.
Enter, eniri, enveni.
Enterprise, entrepreno.
Entertain, regali.
Entertain (amuse),
amuzi.
Entertain (consider),
konsideri.
Enthusiasm,
entuziasmo.
Enthusiast,
entuziasmulo.
Enthusiastic,
entuziasma.
Entice, allogi.
Entire, tuta.
Entirely, tute.
Entitle (to name),
titoli.
Entomb, entombigi.
Entomology,
entomologio.
Entr'acte, interakto.
Entrails, internaĵo.

Entrance, eniro.
Entrance, ĉarmi.
Entreat, petegi.
Entreaty, petego.
Entry, eniro.
Entwine, kunplekti.
Enumerate, denombri.
Enunciate, eldiri.
Envelop, envolvi.
Envelope, koverto.
Envenom, veneni.
Enviable, enviinda.
Envious, enviema.
Environs, ĉirkaŭaĵo.
Envoy, sendito.
Envy, envii.
Epaulet, epoleto.
Ephemeral, mallonga,
efemera.
Epic, epopea.
Epic, epopeo.
Epicure, epikuristo.
Epidemic, epidemio.
Epidermis, epidermo.
Epigram, epigramo.
Epilepsy, epilepsio.
Epileptic, epilepsia.
Epileptic (person),
epilepsiulo.
Epilogue, epilogo.
Epiphany, Epifanio.
Episcopacy,
episkopeco.
Episode, epizodo.
Epistle, letero.
Epistolary, letera.
Epitaph, epitafo.
Epithet, epiteto.
Epitome, resumo.
Epitomise, mallongigi.
Epoch, epoko.
Equable, egala.
Equal, egala.

Equality, egaleco.
Equalise, egaligi.
Equally, egale.
Equation, ekvacio.
Equator, ekvatoro.
Equilibrium, ekvilibro.
Equinox,
tagnoktegaleco.
Equipment (milit.),
armilaro.
Equitable, justa.
Equity, justeco.
Equivalent,
ekvivalenta.
Equivocal, dusenca.
Era, tempokalkulo.
Eradicate, elradikigi.
Erase, surstreki.
Eraser, skrapileto.
Erasure, surstrekaĵo.
Ere, antaŭ (ol).
Erect, starigi.
Erect, vertikala.
Erection, konstruo.
Ermine (animal),
ermeno.
Ermine (fur),
ermenfelo.
Erotic, erotika.
Err, erari.
Errand, komisio.
Erratic, erara.
Erratum, eraro.
Erroneous, erara.
Error, eraro.
Eructation, rukto.
Erudite (person),
instruitulo, klerulo.
Eruption, ekzantemo.
Eruption, volcanic,
elsputo, vulkana.
Erysipelas, erisipelo.
Escape, forkuri.

Escarpment, krutegaĵo.
Eschew, eviti.
Escort, gardistaro.
Escort, gardi.
Escutcheon, blazono.
Especial, speciala.
Especially, precipe.
Espouse, edziĝi.
Espouse (adopt),
alpreni.
Espy, vidi, ekvidi.
Essay (trial), provo.
Essay, provi.
Essence, esenco.
Essence (oil), oleo.
Essential, esenca.
Establish, fondi.
Estate, bieno.
Esteem, estimi.
Estimable, estiminda.
Estimate (appraise),
taksi.
Estimate, estimi.
*Estimate,
appraisement*, taksado.
Estimation, estimado.
Estrange, forigi.
Estuary, estuario.
Eternal, eterna.
Eternity, eterneco.
Ether, etero.
Ethereal, etera.
Ethical, etika.
Ethnography,
etnografio.
Ethology, etologio.
Etiology, etiologio.
Etiquette, etiketo.
Etymology,
vortodeveno.
Eucharist, Eŭkaristo.
Eulogize, laŭdegi.
Eulogy, laŭdego.

Euphonic, bonsona.
Euphonious, belsona.
Europe, Eŭropo.
European, Eŭropano.
Evacuate, malplenigi.
Evade, eviti.
Evangelical, evangelia.
Evaporate, vaporiĝi.
Evaporation, vaporiĝo.
Evasion, forkuro.
Evasion, artifiko.
Eve, antaŭtago.
Eve, evening, vespero.
Even (number),
parnombro.
Even, eĉ.
Even (level), ebena.
Even, to make, ebenigi.
Evening, vespero.
Evening party,
vesperkunveno.
Event, okazo.
Eventful, okazplena.
Ever, ĉiam.
Ever (whoever, etc.),
ajn (kiu ajn).
Everlasting, eterna.
Evermore, for, je
eterne.
Every, ĉiu.
Every kind of, ĉia.
Every manner, ĉiel.
Everyone, ĉiu.
Everyone's, ĉies.
Every reason, for, ĉial.
Everything, ĉio.
Everyway, ĉiel.
Everywhere, ĉie.
Evidence, evidenteco.
Evident, evidenta.
Evidently, evidente.
Evil, malbono, peko.
Evil, malbona, peka.

Evil doing, malbonfarado.
Evoke, elvoki.
Evolution, evolucio.
Ewe, ŝafino.
Ewer, kruĉego.
Exact, postuli.
Exact (precise), preciza.
Exact, ĝusta.
Exact, accurate, akurata.
Exactness, akurateco.
Exaggerate, trograndigi.
Exaggeration, trograndigo.
Exalt, laŭdegi.
Examination, ekzameno.
Examine, ekzameni.
Example, ekzemplo.
Exasperate, koleregigi.
Excavate, kavigi.
Excavate, kavigi, fosi.
Excavator, terfosisto.
Exceed, superi.
Excel, superi.
Excellence, boneco.
Excellency, Ekscelenco, Moŝto.
Excellent, bonega.
Except, krom.
Except, escepti.
Exception, escepto.
Excess, malmodereco.
Excessive, troa.
Excessively, troe.
Exchange, interŝanĝi.
Exchange, The, borso.
Excise officer, oficisto.
Excite, eksciti.
Excitement, ekscitego.

Exclaim, ekkrii.
Exclamation, point of, signo ekkria.
Exclude, eksigi.
Exclusion, eksigeco.
Exclusive, ekskluziva.
Excommunicate, ekskomuniki.
Excoriation, defrotaĵo.
Excrement, ekskremento.
Excrescence, elkreskaĵo.
Excruciate, turmentegi.
Exculpate, senkulpigi.
Excursion, ekskurso.
Excusable, pardonebla.
Excuse, pardoni, senkulpigi.
Execrable, abomena.
Execrate, malbenegi.
Execute (to do), fari.
Execute, ekzekuti.
Executioner, ekzekutisto.
Executive, regantaro.
Exemplar, ekzemplero.
Exemplary, ekzempla.
Exemplify, ekzempligi.
Exempt, liberigi.
Exempt, libera.
Exercise, ekzerci.
Exercise, ekzerco.
Exercise-book, kajero.
Exhale, odori.
Exhaust, konsumi.
Exhaustion, konsumiteco.
Exhibit, elmontri.
Exhibition, ekspozicio.
Exhort, admoni.
Exhume, elterigi.

Exigence, postulo—
eco.
Exigent, postula.
Exile, ekzili.
Exist, ekzisti.
Existence, ekzistaĵo.
Exit, eliro.
Exonerate, pravigi.
Exorbitant,
supermezura.
Exotic, alilanda.
Expanse, etendeco.
Expand, etendi.
Expect, atendi.
Expectation, atendo.
Expectorate, kraĉi.
Expedite, ekspedi.
Expedition (milit.),
militiro.
Expeditious, rapidega.
Expeditiously, rapide.
Expel, elpeli.
Expend, elspezi.
Expenditure,
elspezado.
Expense, elspezo.
Expensive, multekosta.
Experience, sperto.
Experience, senti.
Experienced, sperta.
Experiment,
eksperimenti.
Experiment,
eksperimento.
Expert, lerta.
Expert, an,
kompetentulo.
Expiate, elpagi.
Expiation, elpago.
Expiration (of time),
templimo.
Expire (to die), morti.
Expire (breathe out),

elspiri.
Explain, klarigi.
Explanation, klarigo.
Explication, klarigo.
Explicit, klara.
Explode, eksplodi.
Exploit, heroaĵo.
Exploit, ekspluati.
Explore, esplori.
Explorer, esploristo.
Explosion, eksplodo.
Export, eksteren sendi.
Expose, montri.
Exposition, ekspozicio.
Expostulate, rezonegi.
Expound, klarigi.
Express, esprimi.
Express-train, rapida
vagonaro.
Expression, esprimo.
Expressly, speciale.
Expulsion, elpelo.
Expunge, elstreki.
Exquisite, rava.
Extant, ekzistanta.
Extempore,
senprepara.
Extend, etendi.
Extension, etendo.
Extensive, vasta.
Exterior, eksteraĵo.
Exterminate, ekstermi.
External, ekstera.
Extinct, estingita.
Extinguish, estingi.
Extirpate, elradikigi.
Extol, laŭdegi.
Extort, eltiregi.
Extra, ekstra.
Extract, ekstrakti,
eltiri.
Extract, ekstrakto,
eltiro—aĵo.

Extraction (lineage), deveno.
Extraordinary, eksterorda.
Extravagance, malŝparo.
Extravagant, malŝparema.
Extreme, ekstrema.
Extremely, treege.
Extremity, ekstremaĵo.
Extricate, liberigi.
Exuberant, plenega.
Exude, guteti, malsorbiĝi, elsorbiĝi.
Exult, ĝojegi.
Exultation, ĝojego.
Eye, okulo.
Eyebrow, brovo.
Eyeglasses, lorno.
Eyelash, okulharo.
Eyelid, palpebro.

F

Fable, fablo.
Fabric (stuff), teksaĵo.
Fabric, fabriko.
Fabricate, fabriki.
Fabrication, fabrikado.
Fabulist, fablisto.
Fabulous, fabla.
Façade, antaŭa flanko.
Face, vizaĝo.
Facet, faceto.
Facetious, ŝerca.
Facilitate, faciligi.
Facility, facileco.
Facsimile, faksimilo.
Fact, fakto.
Fact, in (adv.), ja.
Faction, sekto.
Factious, malpaca.

Factor (agent), faktoro.
Factory, fabrikejo.
Faculty, fakultato.
Faculty, kapablo.
Fade, velki.
Fading, velkanto.
Fag, laboregi.
Fagot, brancaro.
Fail, manki.
Fail, malprosperi.
Fail (bankruptcy), bankroti.
Failure, malprospero.
Failing (fault), kulpo.
Faint, sveni.
Faint (swoon), sveno.
Faint hearted, timema.
Fair (market), foiro.
Fair (complexion), blonda.
Fair, justa.
Fair copy, neto.
Fairly, juste.
Fairy, feino.
Faith, fido.
Faithful, fidela.
Falcon, falko.
Fall, fali.
Fall, falo.
Fall (in price), malplikariĝo.
Fall off, away, defali.
Fall out (disagree), malpaci.
Fall (in ruins), ruiniĝi.
Fallacy, sofismo.
Fallow, senkulturega.
False, falsa.
Falsehood, mensogo.
Falsify, falsi.
Falsification, falsado.
Falsifier, falsinto.

Fame, famo.
Familiar, kutima.
Familiarize, kutimigi.
Familiarity, kutimeto.
Family, familio.
Famine, malsatego.
Famishing, to be, malsategi.
Famished, malsatega.
Famous, fama.
Fan, ventumi.
Fan, ventumilo.
Fanatic, fanatikulo.
Fanatical, fanatika.
Fanaticism, fanatikeco.
Fanciful, imaga.
Fancy, imagi.
Fanfaronade, fanfaronado.
Fang, kojna dento.
Fantastical, strangega.
Fantasy, fantazio.
Far, malproksima.
Far off (adv.), malproksime.
Farce, ŝerco.
Fare, bill of, manĝokarto.
Farewell, adiaŭ.
Farm, farmi.
Farm, farmo.
Farmhouse, farmodomo.
Farmer, farma mastro.
Farrier, forĝisto.
Fascinate, ensorĉi.
Fascination, ensorĉo.
Fashion (to form), formi.
Fashion (manner), maniero.
Fashion (dress), fasono.
Fashion, in such a, tiel.
Fast, fasti.
Fast, fasto.
Fast, to make, alligi.
Fast, rapida.
Fast-day, fasta tago.
Fasten, alligi.
Fastidious, malŝatema.
Fasting, fastinte.
Fat, grasa.
Fatal, fatala.
Fatalism, fatalismo.
Fatality, fatalo.
Fatally, fatale.
Fate, sorto.
Father, patro.
Fatherland, patrolando.
Father-in-law, bopatro.
Fatherhood, patreco.
Fatherly, patra.
Fathom, sondi.
Fathom-line, sondilo.
Fatigue, lacigi.
Fatigue, laceco.
Fatigued, laca.
Fatiguing, laciga.
Fatten, grasigi.
Faucet, krano.
Fault (error), eraro.
Fault, kulpo.
Faulty, mankhava.
Favour, favori.
Favour, favoro.
Favourable, favora.
Fawn, cervido.
Fawn-coloured, brunruĝa.
Fay, feo (m.), feino (f.).

Fealty, fideleco.
Fear, timi.
Fear, timo.
Feasible, farebla.
Feast, regali.
Feast (meal), regalo.
Feast (holiday), festeno.
Feast, festeni.
Feat, heroaĵo.
Feather, plumo.
Feather-duster, plumbalailo.
Feature (trait), trajto.
Febrile, febra.
February, Februaro.
Fecundate, fruktigi.
Federal, federa.
Federation (act), federo.
Federation (state), federacio.
Federative, federa.
Fee, pagi.
Feeble, malforta.
Feebleness, malforteco.
Feed, nutri.
Feel (touch), palpi.
Feel, senti.
Feeling, sento.
Feeling, palpo.
Feel one's way, palpeti.
Feign, ŝajnigi.
Feint, ŝaĵnigo.
Felicity, feliĉeco.
Fell, faligi.
Fellow, a good, karulo.
Fellow-citizen, samurbano.
Felly (felloe), radrondo.

Felon, krimulo.
Felt, felto.
Female, virino, ino.
Feminine, virinseksa, ina.
Feminism, feminismo, inismo.
Fen, marĉejo.
Fence, skermi.
Fencing, skermo.
Fence, palisaro.
Fend, defendi.
Fender, fajrgardo.
Fennel, fenkolo.
Ferment, fermenti.
Ferment (disturbance), tumulto.
Fern, filiko.
Ferocious, kruelega.
Ferocity, kruelego, kruelegeco.
Ferret, ĉasputoro.
Ferry, prami.
Ferry-boat, pramo.
Fertile, fruktodona.
Fertilize, fruktigi.
Fervency, fervoreco.
Fervent, fervora.
Fervour, fervoro.
Festal, festa.
Fester, ulceriĝi.
Festival, festo.
Festoon, festono.
Fetch, alporti.
Fetich, fetiĉo.
Fetichism, fetiĉismo.
Fetid, malbonodora.
Fetter, kateno.
Feud, malpacego.
Feudal, feŭdala.
Feudality, feŭdaleco.
Fever, febro.
Feverish, febra.

Few, kelkaj, malmultaj.
Fiance, fianĉo.
Fiancée, fianĉino.
Fiasco, fiasko.
Fibre, fibro.
Fickle, ŝanĝebla.
Fictitious, fiktiva.
Fiddle, violono.
Fiddler, violonisto.
Fidelity, fideleco.
Fidget, movadiĝi.
Fie! fi!
Field, kampo.
Fierce, kruelega.
Fiery, fervorega.
Fife, fifro.
Fig, figo.
Fight, batali.
Figure (represent), figuri.
Figure (cipher), cifero.
Figure (image), figuro.
Filament, fibro.
Filch, ŝteli.
File, fajli.
File (tool), fajlilo.
File (newspapers), legaĵo.
Filial, filia.
Filiation, genealogio.
Filigree, filigrano.
Fill, plenigi.
Fillet, lumbaĵo.
Filly, ĉevalidino.
Film, membrano, ŝeleto.
Filter, filtrilo.
Filth, malpuraĵo.
Filthy, malpurega.
Fin, naĝilo.
Final, fina.
Finally, fine.

Finance, financo.
Financial, financa.
Financier, financisto.
Find, trovi.
Fine, delikata.
Fine (penalty), mona puno.
Fine arts, belartoj.
Finery, ornamaĵo.
Finger, fingro.
Finish, fini.
Fir, abio.
Fire, fajro.
Fire, to set on, ekflamigi.
Fire-dog, kamenstableto.
Fire-engine, brulpumpilo.
Firing (guns, etc.), pafado.
Fireman (stoker), hejtisto.
Fireplace, kameno.
Fireside, hejmo.
Firework, fajraĵo, artfajraĵo.
Firm (fast), firma.
Firm (strong), fortika.
Firm (comm.), firmo.
Firmness, fortikeco.
Firmament, ĉielo.
First, unua.
Firstly, unue.
Firtree, pinarbo.
Fisc, fisko.
Fiscal, fiska.
Fish, fiŝo.
Fish, fiŝkapti.
Fisher, fiŝkaptisto.
Fishery, fiŝkaptado, fiŝkaptejo.
Fish-hook, fiŝhoko.

Fishing, fiŝkaptado.
Fishing-line,
hokfadeno.
Fish-market,
fiŝvendejo.
Fishmonger,
fiŝvendisto.
Fissure, fendeto.
Fist, pugno.
Fit (illness), atako.
Fit for, to be, taŭgi.
Fitly, alkonvena.
Five, kvin.
Fix, fiksi.
Fixed, fiksa.
Fixity, fikseco.
Flabby, mola.
Flag, standardo.
Flag (navy), flago.
Flagon, botelego.
Flagstone, ŝtonplato.
Flagrant, flagranta.
Flail, draŝilo.
Flake, neĝero, floko.
Flambeau, torĉo.
Flame, flami.
Flame, flamo.
Flank, flanko.
Flannel, flanelo.
Flap, klapo.
Flare, brilego.
Flash (lightning),
fulmo.
Flash (of wit), spritaĵo.
Flask, boteleto.
Flat, plata.
Flat (music), duontono
sube.
Flatten, platigi.
Flatter, flati.
Flatterer, flatulo.
Flattering, flatema.
Flavour, gusto.

Flaw, difekto.
Flax, lino.
Flay, senhaŭtigi.
Flea, pulo.
Flee, flugi.
Fleece, ŝaflano.
Fleecy, laneca.
Fleet (quick), rapida.
Fleet, ŝiparo.
Flesh (meat), viando.
Flesh, karno.
Flexibility,
fleksebleco.
Flexible, fleksebla.
Flexion, flekso.
Flicker, lumŝanceli.
Flight, forkuro.
Flight (birds), flugado.
Fling, ĵeti.
Flint (mineral), siliko.
Flippant, babila.
Flirt, amindumeti,
koketi.
Flirt, koketulino.
Flirtation, koketeco.
Flit, flirti.
Float (intrans.), naĝi.
Float (trans.), flosi.
Flock (congregation),
zorgitaro.
Flock, aro.
Flog, skurĝi.
Flood, superakvego.
Floor, planko.
Floor (storey), etaĝo.
Florid, ruĝega.
Florin, floreno.
Florist, floristo.
Flotilla, ŝipareto.
Flour, faruno.
Flourish (brandish),
svingi.
Flow, flui.

Flow (of blood),
sangverŝo.
Flow away, deflui.
Flower, flori.
Flower-bed, florbedo.
Flower-garden,
florejo.
Fluctuate, ŝanceliĝi.
Flue, kamentubo.
Fluent, elokventa,
fluanta.
Fluid, fluaĵo.
Fluid, flua.
Flute, fluto.
Flutter, flugeti, flirti.
Flux, alfluo.
Fly, flugi.
Fly, muŝo.
Fly away, forflugi.
Foal, ĉevalido—ino.
Foam, ŝaŭmi.
Foam, ŝaŭmo—aĵo.
Foam (sea),
marŝaŭmo.
Focus, fokuso.
Fodder, furaĝo.
Fœtid, malbonodora.
Foe, kontraŭulo,
malamiko.
Fog, nebulo.
Foil (weapon), rapiro,
skermilo.
Fold, faldi.
Fold (sheep), ŝafejo.
Folding-screen,
ventoŝirmilo.
Foliage, foliaro.
Follow, sekvi.
Following, the,
sekvanta.
Follows, that which,
jena.
Folly, malspriteco.

Fond, ama.
Foment, vivigi.
Fondle, dorloti.
Fondness, ameco.
Font, baptakvujo.
Food, nutraĵo.
Fool, simplanimulo.
Foolish, malsaĝa.
Foolishness,
malsaĝeco.
Foot, piedo.
Foot (measure), futo.
Foot, on, piedire.
Foot-bridge,
piedponto.
Footman, lakeo.
Footpath, trotuaro.
Footprint, piedsigno.
Foot-soldier,
infanteriano.
Footway, piedvojo.
Fop, dando.
For, ĉar.
For (on account of),
pro.
For, por.
Forage, furaĝo.
Forbear, toleri.
Forbearance, tolero.
Forbearing, tolerema.
Forbid, malpermesi.
Force, devigi.
Forcible, devigebla.
Ford, transirejo.
Fore, antaŭa.
Forearm, antaŭbrako.
Foreboding,
antaŭsento.
Forehead, frunto.
Foreign, alilando.
Foreigner, alilandulo.
Foreman, submajstro.
Foremost, unua.

Forenoon,
antaŭtagmezo.
Forepart (ship),
antaŭparto.
Forerunner, antaŭulo.
Foresee, antaŭvidi.
Foresight, antaŭzorgo.
Forest, arbaro.
Foretell, antaŭdiri.
Forethought,
antaŭzorgo.
Forewarn, averti.
Forge, forĝi.
Forge, forĝejo.
Forget, forgesi.
Forgetful, forgesa.
Forgetfulness,
forgeseco.
Forget-me-not,
miozoto.
Forgive, pardoni.
Forgiveness, pardono.
Fork, forko.
Form (to fashion),
alformi.
Form (shape), formo.
Formal, ceremonia.
Formation, formo.
Former (the), tiu.
Formerly, iam, antaŭe.
Formidable,
timeginda.
Formulate, formuli.
Formulary, protokolo.
Formula, formulo.
Forsake, forlasi.
Fort, fortikaĵeto.
Fortify (milit.),
fortikigi.
Fortify, fortigi.
Fortitude, kuraĝeco.
Fortnight, du
semajnoj.

Fortress, fortikaĵo.
Fortune, riĉeco.
Forward! antaŭen!
Forward (in advance),
antaŭe.
Forward, ekspedi,
sendi.
Fossil, elfosataĵo.
Foster, nutri.
Foster child,
suĉinfano.
Foul, malpura.
Foulard, silktuko.
Found, fondi.
Foundation, fondo,
fondaĵo.
Founder (ship),
ŝipperei.
Foundry, fandejo.
Fountain, fontano.
Four, kvar.
Fowl (domestic),
kortbirdo.
Fox, vulpo.
Fraction, partumo.
Fracture, rompo.
Fragile, facilrompa.
Fragment, fragmento.
Fragrance,
bonodoreco.
Frail, kaduka.
Frame, enkadrigi.
Frame, kadro.
Framework, trabaĵo.
Franc, franko.
France, Francujo,
Franclando.
Frank, sincera.
Frank (letters),
afranki.
Frankly, sincere.
Frankness, sincereco.
Frantic, furioza.

Fraternal, frata.
Fraternity, frateco.
Fraternize, fratiĝi.
Fraud, trompo.
Fraudulent, trompa.
Fray, batalo.
Freckle, lentugo.
Free, libera.
Free (gratis), senpage.
Freedom, libereco.
Freemason,
framasono.
Freeze, glaciiĝi.
Freight (load), ŝarĝi.
Frenchman, Franco.
Frenzy, frenezeco.
Frequent, ofta.
Frequent, vizitadi.
Frequency, ofteco.
Fresco, fresko.
Fresh, freŝa.
Fret, malkvietiĝi.
Friar, monaĥo.
Friction, frotado.
Friend, amiko.
Friendly, amika.
Friendship, amikeco.
Frigate, fregato.
Fright, timo.
Frighten, timigi.
Frightful, terura.
Frigid, glaciiga.
Fringe, franĝo.
Frisk, salteti.
Fritter, fritaĵo.
Frivolity, vaneteco.
Frivolous, malserioza.
Friz (curl), frizi.
Frock-coat, frako.
Frog, rano.
Frolic, petoleco.
Frolicsome, petolema.
Front, antaŭa flanko.

Frontier, landlimo.
Frost, frosto.
Froth, ŝaŭmo.
Froward, malvirta.
Frown, sulkigi.
Fructify, fruktodoni.
Frugal, ŝparema.
Fruit, frukto.
Fruitery, fruktejo.
Fruitful, fruktoporta.
Fruit-garden, fruktejo.
Fruitless, vana.
Fruitlessly, vane.
Frustrate, malhelpi.
Fry, friti.
Fry (spawn), frajo.
Frying-pan, pato,
fritilo.
Fuel, brulaĵo.
Fugitive, forkuranto.
Fugue (mus.), fugo.
Fulfil, plenumi.
Full, plena.
Full-aged, plenaĝa.
Fume, fumo.
Fun, ŝercado.
Function, funkcio.
Functionary, oficisto.
Fundamental,
fundamenta.
Fundholder, rentulo.
Funeral, enterigiro.
Funereal, funebra.
Funnel, funelo.
Funny, ridinda.
Fur, felo.
Furious, furioza.
Furnace, forno,
fornego.
Furnish (provide),
provizi.
Furnish (a house),
mebli.

Furniture, meblaro.
Furniture (piece of), meblo.
Furrier, felisto.
Furrow (wrinkle), sulko.
Furrow, tersulko.
Further, plie.
Further, plimalproksima.
Fury, furiozo.
Fury (mythol.), furio.
Fuse, fandi.
Fusilade, pafado.
Fusion, fandiĝo.
Fustian, fusteno.
Futile, vana.
Future, estonta.
Futurity, estonteco.

G

Gadfly, tabano.
Gaff, hokstango.
Gag, silentigi, buŝumi.
Gaiety, gajeco.
Gain, gajni.
Gain (of a watch), trorapidi.
Gainsay, kontraŭdiri.
Gait, irado.
Gaiter, gamaŝo.
Gale, ventego, blovado.
Gall, galo.
Gall-nut, gajlo.
Gallant, amisto.
Gallant, ĝentila.
Gallant, brava.
Gallery, galerio.
Galley, remŝipego.
Gallicism, galicismo.

Gallop, galopi.
Gallows, pendigilo.
Galvanism, galvanismo.
Gambol, salteti.
Game (play), ludo.
Game, ĉasaĵo.
Game-bag, ĉasaĵujo.
Gamekeeper, ĉasgardisto.
Gamut, gamo.
Gander, anserviro.
Gang, bando.
Ganglion, ganglio.
Gangrene, gangreno.
Gaol, malliberejo.
Gaoler, gardisto.
Gap, breĉo.
Gap, manko.
Gape, oscedegi.
Garb, vesto.
Garden, ĝardeno.
Gardener, ĝardenisto.
Gardenia, gardenio.
Gardening, ĝardenlaborado.
Gargle, gargari.
Gargle, gargaraĵo.
Garland, girlando.
Garlic, ajlo.
Garment, vesto.
Garner, provizi.
Garnish, ornami.
Garniture, garnituro.
Garret, subtegmento.
Garrison, garnizono.
Garrote, ĉirkaŭligi.
Garter, ŝtrumpligilo.
Gas, gaso.
Gaseous, gasa.
Gash, tranĉadi.
Gasometer, gasometro.

Gasp, spiregi.
Gastric, stomaka.
Gate, pordego.
Gather, kolekti.
Gather together, kolekti.
Gathering, kolekto.
Gaudy, luksema.
Gauge, mezuri.
Gaunt, malgrasa.
Gauntlet, ferganto.
Gauze, gazo.
Gawky, mallerta.
Gay, to be, gaji.
Gay, gaja.
Gaze, rigardegi.
Gazelle, gazelo.
Gazette, gazeto.
Gear (machinery), ilaro.
Gehenna, Geheno.
Gelatine, gelateno.
Gem, brilianto, ĝemo.
Gendarme, ĝendarmo.
Gender, sekso.
Genealogy, genealogio.
General, ĝenerala.
General (milit.), generalo.
Generate, produkti, naski.
Generation, generacio.
Generosity, malavareco.
Generous, malavara.
Genial, bonvola.
Genitive, genitivo.
Genius, genio.
Genteel, ĝentila.
Gentle, dolĉa.
Gentleman, sinjoro.

Gently, dolĉe.
Genuflect, genufleksi.
Genuine, vera.
Genus, gento.
Geography, geografio.
Geology, geologio.
Geometry, geometrio.
Geranium, geranio.
Germ, ĝermo.
German, Germano.
German (adj.), Germana.
Germinate, ĝermi.
Gerund, gerundio.
Gesture, gesto.
Get (receive), ricevi.
Get (procure), havigi.
Get (with infinitive), igi, iĝi.
Get dirty, malpuriĝi.
Get ready, pretigi, pretiĝi.
Ghastly, palega.
Gherkin, kukumeto.
Ghost, fantomo.
Giant, grandegulo.
Gibbet, pendigilo.
Gibbous, ĝiba.
Gibe, moki.
Giddiness, kapturno.
Giddy, to make, kapturnigi.
Gift, donaco.
Gift, to make a, donaci.
Gifted, talenta.
Gild, orumi.
Gill (fish), branko.
Gilliflower, levkojo.
Gimlet, borileto.
Gin, ĝino.
Ginger, zingibro.
Gingerbread,

mielkuko.
Gipsy, nomadulo.
Giraffe, ĝirafo.
Gird, zoni.
Girdle, zono.
Girl, knabino.
Give, doni.
Give back, redoni.
Give up, forlasi.
Give evidence, atesti.
Give notice, sciigi.
Glacier, glaciejo.
Glad, ĝoja.
Gladden, ĝojigi.
Glade, maldensejo.
Gladiator, gladiatoro.
Glance, ekrigardi.
Gland, glando.
Glare, brilego.
Glass (substance),
vitro.
Glass (vessel), glaso.
Glass, pane of,
vitraĵo.
Glass-case,
vitromeblo.
Glass, looking,
spegulo.
Glass-works,
vitrofarejo.
Glassy, vitreca.
Glaucous (colour),
marverda.
Glaze, vitrumi.
Glaze (pottery),
glazuri.
Glaze (ice cakes, etc.),
glaciumi.
Glaze (polish), poluri.
Glazier, vitraĵisto.
Gleam, lumeti.
Gleam, lumeto.
Glean, postrikolti.

Glee, ĝojo.
Glen, valeto.
Glide, gliti.
Glimmer, lumeto.
Glimpse, videto,
ekvido.
Glisten, brili.
Glitter, brilegi.
Globe, globo.
Globe (earth),
terglobo.
Globular, globa.
Globule, globeto.
Gloom, mallumo.
Gloom (sadness),
malgajo.
Gloomy (sad),
malgaja.
Gloomy, malluma.
Glorify, glori.
Glorious, glora.
Glory, gloro.
Gloss, poluri.
Glove, ganto.
Glow, brili.
Glow-worm, lampiro.
Glucose, glikozo.
Glue, gluo.
Glue, glui.
Glut, sato.
Glut, satigi.
Glutinous, gluanta.
Glutted, satega.
Glutton, manĝegulo.
Gluttonous,
manĝegema.
Gluttony,
manĝegemo.
Glycerine, glicerino.
Gnash, grinci.
Gnat, kulo.
Gnaw, mordeti.
Gnome, gnomo.

Go, iri.
Go along, vojiri.
Go astray, erari, vagadi.
Go away, foriri.
Go back, reiri.
Go before, antaŭiri.
Go beyond, trapasi, preterpasi.
Go in, eniri.
Go out, eliri.
Go out (of a light), estingiĝi, elbruli.
Go over, transiri.
Go through, trairi.
Go down (ship), ŝipperei.
Go on foot, piediri.
Go on a pilgrimage, pilgrimi.
Goad, instigilo.
Goal (aim), celo.
Goat, kapro.
Goatherd, kapristo.
Goblet, pokalo.
Goblin, koboldo.
God, Dio.
Godfather, baptopatro.
Godhead, Diaĵo.
Godless, malpia.
Godliness, sankteco.
Godly, sankta.
Gold, oro.
Golden, ora.
Goldfinch, kardelo.
Goldsmith, oraĵisto.
Goloche, galoŝo.
Gondola, gondolo.
Good, bona.
Good, to do, bonfari.
Good (welfare), bonstato.

Good-for-nothing, sentaŭgulo.
Good-bye, adiaŭ.
Goodness, boneco.
Goods (effects), posedaĵo.
Goods (merchandise), komercaĵo.
Goods train, by, malrapidire.
Goose, ansero.
Goose, anserino.
Gooseberry, groso.
Gorge, valego.
Gorge, supersatigi.
Gorgeous, belega.
Goshawk, akcipitro.
Gosling, anserido.
Gospel, Evangelio.
Gossip, babilaĵo.
Gourd, kukurbo.
Gourmand, manĝegulo.
Gout, podagro.
Govern, regi.
Government, registaro.
Governess, guvernistino.
Governor, reganto.
Gown, robo.
Grace, gracio.
Graceful, gracia.
Gracious, gracia.
Gradation, gradeco.
Grade (rank), rango.
Gradual, grada.
Gradually, grade.
Graduate, gradigi.
Graduation, gradigo.
Graft, inokuli.
Grain of corn, grenero.

Grain of dust, polvero.
Grammar, gramatiko.
Gramme, gramo.
Granary, grenejo.
Grand, belega.
Grandfather, avo.
Grandson, nepo.
Granite, granito.
Grant, permesi.
Grape, vinbero.
Grapeshot, kugletaĵo.
Graphite, grafito.
Grapnel, ankreto.
Grapple, ekkapti.
Grasp, premi.
Grass, herbo.
Grass-plot, herbejo.
Grasshopper, akrido.
Grate, fajrujo.
Grate, raspi, froti.
Grateful, dankema.
Grater, raspilo.
Gratification, kontentigo.
Grating, krado.
Grating noise, akra sono.
Gratis, senpage.
Gratitude, dankeco.
Gratuitous, senpaga.
Gratuitously, senpage.
Gratuity (tip), trinkmono.
Grave, tombo.
Grave, grava.
Gravel, ŝtonetaĵo.
Graver, gravurilo.
Gravity, graveco.
Gravy, suko.
Gray, griza.
Graze (rub slightly), tuŝeti.

Graze cattle, paŝti.
Grazing ground, paŝtejo.
Grease, graso.
Grease, ŝmiri.
Great, granda.
Greatcoat, palto.
Great-grandfather, praavo.
Greatness, grandeco.
Greedy (eager), avida.
Greedy, manĝegema.
Green, verda.
Green (village), komunejo.
Greenhouse, varmejo.
Greenish, dubeverda.
Greek, Greko.
Greet, saluti.
Grenade, grenado.
Grenadier, grenadisto.
Grey, griza.
Greyhound, leporhundo.
Gridiron, kradrostilo.
Grief, malĝojo.
Grievance, plendkaŭzo.
Grieve, malĝoji.
Grieve (trans.), malĝojigi.
Grimace, grimaco.
Grime, malpureco.
Grin, grimaci.
Grind, pisti.
Grind the teeth, grinci.
Grind (corn), mueli.
Grip, premego.
Grit, sablego.
Groan, ĝemi.
Groats, grio.
Grocer, spicisto.

Groin, ingveno.
Groom, ĉevalisto.
Groove, kavo,
radsigno.
Grope, palpeti.
Gross (in manner),
maldelikata.
Grotesque, groteska.
Grotto, groto.
Ground, tero.
Ground-floor,
teretaĝo.
Group, grupo.
Group, grupigi.
Grouse, tetro.
Grove, arbetaro.
Grow, kreski.
Grow (become), —
iĝi.
Grow young, juniĝi.
Growl, bleki, blekadi.
Growth, kresko.
Grub (insect),
tervermeto.
Grudge, malameco.
Gruff, malĝentila.
Grumble, riproĉegi.
Grunt, bleki.
Guarantee, garantio.
Guarantee, garantii.
Guard, gardi.
Guard (milit.),
gvardio.
Guardian, gardanto,
zorganto.
Gudgeon, gobio.
Guess, diveni.
Guest, gasto.
Guide, gvidi.
Guide, gvidisto.
Guile, artifiko.
Guileless, senartifika.
Guillotine, gilotino.

Guilt, kulpo.
Guilty, to be, kulpiĝi.
Guinea, gineo.
Guitar, gitaro.
Gulf, golfo.
Gull, trompi.
Gullet, faringo,
ezofago.
Gully, valeto.
Gulp, engluti.
Gum, gumo.
Gum, gumi.
Gun, pafilo.
Gun (cannon),
pafilego.
Gun-carriage,
subpafilego.
Gunpowder, pulvo.
Gunsmith,
armilfaristo.
Gunnery, pafilado.
Gush, ŝpruci.
Gust, ekventego.
Gut, intestotubo.
Gutter, defluilo.
Gutter-spout, defluilo.
Gymnast,
gimnastikisto.
Gymnasium,
gimnastikejo.
Gypsum, gipso.
Gyrate, turniĝi.

H

Ha! ha!
Haberdasher,
fadenisto.
Habit, kutimo.
Habit, vesto.
Habit of, to be in the,
kutimi.
Habitation, loĝejo.

Habitual, kutima.
Habituate, kutimigi.
Hack, haki.
Hack (horse),
ĉevaleto.
Hackney-coach,
fiakro.
Hag, malbelulino.
Haggard, sovaĝa.
Haggle, marĉandi.
Hail, hajli.
Hail, hajlo.
Hailstone, hajlero.
Hair, haro.
Hair, head of, hararo.
Hairdresser, frizisto.
Hairy, haraĵa.
Halberd, halebardo.
Halcyon, alciono.
Hale, sana.
Half, duono.
Hall, vestiblo.
Hallow, sanktigi.
Hall-porter, pordisto.
Hallucination,
halucinacio.
Halt, halti.
Halting-place,
haltejo.
Halter, kolbrido.
Halves, by, duone.
Ham, ŝinko.
Hamlet, vilaĝeto.
Hammer, martelo.
Hammer, martelumi.
Hammock, pendlito.
Hamper, korbo.
Hamper, malhelpi.
Hamstring,
subgenuo.
Hand, mano.
Hand-barrow,
puŝveturilo.

Handcuff, mankateno.
Handful, plenmano.
Handicraft,
manfarado.
Handkerchief,
naztuko.
Handle, manpreni.
Handle, tenilo.
Handmade,
manfarita.
Handshake,
manpremo.
Handsome, bela.
Handy, lerta,
oportuna (of things).
Hang (intrans.),
pendi.
Hang up, pendigi.
Hanker, deziregi.
Hansom, kabrioleto.
Hap, okazi.
Hapless, malfeliĉa.
Haply, eble.
Happen, okazi.
Happiness, feliĉo.
Happy, feliĉa.
Harangue, parolado.
Harass, enuigi, lacigi.
Harass (milit.),
atakadi.
Harbinger, antaŭulo.
Harbour, haveno.
Hard, malmola.
Hard (difficult),
malfacila.
Hard (severe),
severega.
Harden (to make
hard), malmoligi,
hardi.
Harden (to become
hardy), hardiĝi.
Hardly, apenaŭ.

Hardness, malmoleco.
Hardwareman, kuirilvendisto.
Hardy, hardita.
Hark! aŭskultu.
Hare, leporo.
Hairbrained, sencerba.
Harem, haremo.
Haricot-bean, fazeolo.
Harlequin, arlekeno.
Harm, malutili.
Harm, malutilo.
Harmonica, harmoniko.
Harmonious, harmonia.
Harmonize, harmoniigi.
Harmony, harmonio.
Harness, jungi.
Harness, jungaĵo.
Harp, harpo.
Harpoon, harpuno.
Harpy, harpio.
Harrier, leporhundo.
Harrow (to rake), erpi.
Harrow, erpilo.
Harsh (rough), maldolĉa.
Harsh (severe), severega.
Harsh (of voice), raŭka.
Hart, cervo.
Harvest (crop), rikolto.
Harvest-time, rikolto.
Hash, viandmiksaĵo.
Hasp, alkroĉi.

Hassock, kuseno.
Haste, rapideco.
Hasten, rapidi.
Hasten (trans.), rapidigi.
Hasty, rapida.
Hat, ĉapelo.
Hatch, elŝeligi.
Hatchet, hakilo.
Hate, malami.
Hateful, malaminda.
Hatred, malamo.
Haughty, aroganta.
Haunch, kokso.
Haunt, vizitadi.
Hautboy, hobojo.
Have, havi.
Haven, haveno.
Havoc, ruinigo.
Hawk, akcipitro.
Hawk (for sale), kolporti.
Hawthorn, kratago.
Hay, fojno.
Hay-loft, fojnejo.
Hazard, hazardi.
Hazard, hazardo.
Hazardous, hazarda.
Haze, nebuleto.
Hazel-nut, avelo.
He, li.
Head, kapo.
Headache, kapdoloro.
Head-dress (coiffure), kapvesto.
Headland, promontoro.
Headlong, senpripensa, e.
Headstrong, obstina.
Heal, kuraci.
Health, sano.

Health, toast a,
toasti.
Healthy, sana.
Heap, amaso.
Heap up, amasigi.
Hear, aŭdi.
Hearken, aŭskulti.
Hearse, ĉerkveturilo.
Heart, koro.
Heart (cards), kero.
Heart, by, parkere.
Heart, to learn by,
parkeri.
Hearth, fajrujo,
hejmo.
Heartrending,
korŝiranta.
Heartsease, violo.
Hearty, korega.
Heat, hejti.
Heat, varmeco.
Heath, stepo, erikejo.
Heather (plant),
eriko.
Heathen, idolano.
Heathenism,
idolservo.
Heaven, ĉielo.
Heaviness,
multepezeco.
Heavy, peza.
Hebdomadary,
ĉiusemajna.
Hebraism,
Hebreismo.
Hebrew, Hebreo.
Hectare, hektaro.
Hectogramme,
hektogramo.
Hectolitre, hektolitro.
Hedge, plektobarilo.
Hedgehog, erinaco.
Heed, atenti.

Heedful, atenta.
Heedless, senatenta.
Heel, kalkano.
Heel (of shoe, etc.),
kalkanumo.
Heifer, bovidino.
Height, alteco, altaĵo.
Heinous, kruelega.
Heir, heredanto.
Heliotrope,
heliotropo.
Helix, ŝraŭbego.
Hell, infero.
Hellenism,
Helenismo.
Hellish, infera.
Helm, direktilo.
Helmet, kasko.
Helmsman,
direktilisto.
Help, helpi.
Helpful, helpema.
Helpmate,
kunhelpanto.
Hem, borderi.
Hem, bordero.
Hemisphere,
duonsfero.
Hemorrhage,
sangado.
Hemorrhoids,
hemorojdo.
Hemp, kanabo.
Hen (fowl), kokino.
Henbane, hiskiamo.
Hence, de nun.
Henceforth, de nun.
Hepatic, hepata.
Heptagon, sepangulo.
Her, ŝin.
Her (possessive), ŝia.
Hers, ŝia.
Herald, heroldo.

Heraldic, heraldika.
Heraldry (science), heraldiko.
Heraldry, blazono.
Herb, herbo.
Herbalist, herbovendisto.
Herbivorous, herbomanĝanta.
Herd, brutaro.
Herdsman, paŝtisto.
Here, tie ĉi, ĉi tie.
Here are, jen estas.
Here is, jen estas.
Hereafter, de nun.
Hereat, ĉi tie.
Hereditary, hereda.
Heretic, herezulo.
Heretical, hereza.
Herewith, tie ĉi aldonita.
Heritage, heredo.
Hermit, ermito.
Hernia, hernio.
Hero, heroo.
Heroic, heroa.
Heroine, heroino.
Heroism, heroeco.
Heron, ardeo.
Herring, haringo.
Hesitate, ŝanceliĝi.
Hesitation, ŝanceliĝo.
Hew, dehaki.
Hexagon, sesangulo.
Hexameter, heksametro.
Hiatus, manko.
Hiccough, singulto.
Hidden, kaŝita.
Hide, kaŝi.
Hide (skin), haŭto.
Hideous, malbelega.
Hiding-place, kaŝejo.

Hierarchy, hierarĥio.
Hieroglyphic, hieroglifo.
High, alta.
Highlander, montano.
Highness (title), moŝto.
High-tide, alfluo.
Highway, vojo.
Highwayman, rabisto.
Hill, monteto.
Hillock, altaĵeto.
Hilt, tenilo.
Him, lin.
Himself, sin mem.
Hind, cervino.
Hinder, posta.
Hinder, malhelpi.
Hinderance, malhelpo.
Hindermost, lasta.
Hindoo, Hindo.
Hindrance, malhelpo.
Hindu, Hindo.
Hinge, ĉarniro.
Hint, proponeti.
Hip, kokso.
Hippodrome, hipodromo.
Hippopotamus, hipopotamo.
Hire, dungi.
Hire, cost of, salajro.
Hireling, salajrulo.
His, lia, sia.
Hiss, sibli.
Historian, historiskribanto.
History, historio.
History, natural, naturscienco.
Hit, frapi.
Hit against, ektuŝegi.

Hitch, malhelpaĵo.
Hive, abelujo.
Ho! ho!
Hoard, amaso.
Hoarfrost, prujno.
Hoarse, raŭka.
Hoarseness, raŭkiĝo.
Hoax, mistifiki.
Hobble, lamiri.
Hobby, amuzaĵo.
Hoe, sarki.
Hoe, sarkilo.
Hog, porkviro.
Hoist, suprenlevi.
Hold, teni.
Hold one's tongue,
silentiĝi.
Hole, truo.
Hole, to make a,
truigi.
Holiday (feast), festo.
Holiday, libertempo.
Holiness, sankteco.
Holla, ho! he!
Hollow, kava.
Hollow, kavigi.
Holly, ilekso.
Holy, sankta.
Homage, riverenco.
Home, hejmo.
Home, at, hejme.
Homœopathy,
homeopatio.
Homicide,
hommortigo.
Homonym, samnoma.
Honest, honesta.
Honesty, honesteco.
Honey, mielo.
Honeycomb,
mieltavolo.
Honeysuckle,
lonicero.

Honour, honori.
Honour, honoro.
Honourableness,
honorindeco.
Hood, kapuĉo.
Hoof, hufo.
Hook, hoko.
Hoop, ringego.
Hoot (of owl),
pepegi, pepegadi.
Hope, espero.
Hope, esperi.
Hops, plant, lupolo.
Horizon, horizonto.
Horizontal,
horizontala.
Horn, korno.
Horn (hunting),
ĉaskorno.
Horoscope,
horoskopo.
Horrible, teruriga.
Horrid, terura.
Horror, teruro.
Hors d'oeuvres,
almanĝaĵoj.
Horse, ĉevalo.
Horsemanship,
rajdarto.
Horse-radish, kreno.
Horseshoe, hufferaĵo.
Horticulture,
ĝardenkulturo.
Hose, ŝtrumpaĵo.
Hose, ledtubo.
Hosier,
ŝtrumpvendisto.
Hospitable, gastama.
Hospital,
malsanulejo,
hospitalo.
Hospitality, gastamo.
Host, mastro.

Host, Hostio.
Hostage, garantiulo.
Hostile, kontraŭa,
malamika.
Hot, varmega.
Hot air stove,
hejtaparato.
Hothouse, varmejo.
Hotel, hotelo.
Hound, hundo.
Hour, horo.
House, domo.
House, to keep,
mastrumi.
Housekeeping,
mastraĵo.
Housewife, mastrino.
Hovel, kajuto,
terdometo.
Hover, flirtegi.
How, kiel.
How (what manner),
kiamaniere.
How many, kiom da.
How much, kiom da.
However, tamen.
Howsoever, tamen.
Howl, hundblekegi.
Howitzer,
bombardilo.
Hub (of wheel),
radcentro.
Hubbub, bruado.
Huddle,
kunproksimiĝi.
Hue (colour), nuanco.
Hug, ĉirkaŭprenegi.
Huge, grandega.
Hum, kanteti.
Hum, zumi.
Human, homa.
Humane, humana.
Humanity, humaneco.

Humanity (mankind),
homaro.
Humble, humila.
Humble, humiligi.
Humble, to be,
humiliĝi.
Humerus, humero.
Humid, malseka.
Humidity, malsekeco.
Humiliate, humiligi.
Humility, humileco.
Humming-bird,
kolibro.
Humorous, humora.
Humour, humoro.
Hump, ĝibo.
Hunchback, ĝibulo.
Hunger, malsato.
Hungry, malsata.
Hungry, to be,
malsati.
Hundred, 100, cent.
Hundredweight,
centfunto.
Hunt, ĉasi.
Hunting-lodge,
ĉasdometo.
Hurdle, brancbarileto.
Hurl, alĵeti.
Hurrah, hura.
Hurricane, uragano.
Hurry, rapidi.
Hurry (trans.),
rapidigi.
Hurt (to wound),
vundi.
Hurt, malutili.
Hurtful, malutila.
Husband, edzo.
Husbandman,
terkulturisto.
Hush, silentigi.
Husk, ŝelo.

Hussar, husaro.
Hustle, puŝegi.
Hut, budo.
Hutch, kesto.
Hyacinth, hiacinto.
Hydra, hidro.
Hydrogen, hidrogeno.
Hydropathy,
akvokuraco.
Hydrophobia,
hidrofobio.
Hydrostatic,
hidrostatika.
Hyena, hieno.
Hygrometer,
higrometro.
Hygrometry,
higrometrio.
Hymn, himno.
Hyperbole, hiperbolo.
Hyphen, streketo.
Hypnotic, hipnota.
Hypnotism,
hipnotismo.
Hypnotize, hipnotigi.
Hypochondria,
hipoĥondrio.
Hypocrisy,
hipokriteco.
Hypocrite,
hipokritulo.
Hypocritical,
hipokrita.
Hypothesis, hipotezo.
Hypotenuse,
hipotenuzo.
Hyssop, hisopo.
Hysterical, histeria.
Hysterics, histerio.

I

I, mi.

Ibis, ibiso.
Ice, glacio.
Ice, an, glaciaĵo.
Iceberg, glacierego,
glacimonto.
Icicle, pendglacio.
Icelander, Islandano.
Idea, ideo.
Ideal, idealo.
Identical, identa.
Identify, identigi.
Idiocy, idioteco.
Idiom (a peculiar
expression), idiotismo.
Idiom (general sense),
idiomo.
Idiot, idiotulo.
Idle, senokupa.
Idleness, senokupeco.
Idol, idolo.
Idolatry, idolservado.
Idolize, amegi, adori.
If, se.
Ignis fatuus, erarlumo.
Ignite, ekbruligi.
Ignoble, malnobla.
Ignominy, malnobleco.
Ignorance, nescio.
Ignorant of, to be,
nescii.
Ignorant, malklera.
Ignore, neobservi.
Ill, malbono.
Ill, malbone.
Ill, to be, malsani.
Ill-bred, maledukita.
Illegal, malleĝa.
Illegible, nelegebla.
Illegitimate, nelaŭleĝa.
Illegitimate, malrajta.
Illiberal, avara.
Illicit, malpermesita.
Illiterate, malklera.

Illness, malsano.
Illogical, mallogika.
Illude, iluzii.
Illuminate, ilumini.
Illumination, iluminado.
Illusion, iluzio.
Illustrate, ilustri.
Illustrated, ilustrita.
Illustration, ilustrajô.
Illustrious, fama.
Image, figuro.
Imaginary, fantazia.
Imagination, fantazio.
Imagine, imagi.
Imbecile, malspritulo.
Imbibe, sorbigi.
Imbue, penetri, inspiri.
Imitate, imiti.
Imitation, imito.
Immaculate, senmakula.
Immaterial, negrava.
Immature, nematura.
Immediate, tuja.
Immediately, tuj.
Immense, vasta.
Immense (size), grandega.
Immerge, trempi.
Immerse, subakvigi.
Immigrate, enmigri.
Immigrant, enmigranto.
Imminent, minaca.
Immobility, senmoveco.
Immoderate, malmodera.
Immodest, nemodesta.
Immolate, oferbuĉi.
Immoral, malbonmora.
Immorality, malbonmoreco.
Immortal, senmorta.
Immortality, senmorteco.
Immovable, senmova, nemovebla.
Immutable, neŝanĝebla.
Imp, diableto.
Impair, difekti.
Impart, komuniki, sciigi.
Impartial, senpartia.
Impartiality, senpartieco.
Impatience, malpacienco.
Impatient, malpacienca.
Impassive, kvieta, stoika.
Impeach, kulpigi, denunci.
Impediment, baro.
Impel, antaŭen puŝi.
Impend, minaci.
Impenetrable, nepenetrebla.
Imperative, ordona.
Imperfect, neperfekta.
Imperfection, difektajô.
Imperial, imperia.
Imperishable, nepereema.
Impermeable, nepenetrebla.
Impersonal, nepersona.
Impertinent, malrespekta.
Imperturbable, stoika.
Impetuous, vivega.
Impetus, antaŭenpuŝo.

Impiety, malpieco.
Impious, malpia.
Implacable, venĝema.
Implant, enradiki.
Implement, ilo.
Implicate, impliki.
Implied, neesprimita.
Implore, petegi.
Impolite, malĝentila.
Impolitic, nesaĝema.
Import, enporti.
Importance, graveco.
Important, grava.
Importunate, trudema.
Importune, trudi,
trudiĝi.
Impose (put on), trudi.
Impose on, trompi.
Impossible, neebla.
Impost, imposto.
Impostor, trompanto.
Impotence, neebleco.
Impoverish, malriĉigi.
Impracticable,
nefarebla.
Impregnable, fortika.
Impress, impresi.
Impress (print), presi.
Impression (printing),
presaĵo.
Impression, impreso.
Impressionable,
impresebla.
Impressive, impresa.
Imprison, malliberigi.
Improbable,
neverŝajna.
Improper, nedeca.
Impropriety, nedececo.
Impromptu,
senprepara.
Improve, plibonigi.
Improvement,

plibonigo.
Improvident,
malspxarema.
Improvise, improvizi.
Imprudent,
nesingardema.
Impudent, senhonta.
Impulse, puŝo.
Impure, malpura.
Impurity, malpureco.
Impute, alkalkuli.
In, en.
In front, antaŭe.
In place of, to put,
anstataŭi.
In that manner,
tiamaniere.
Inability, neebleco.
Inaccessible,
neatingebla.
Inaccurate, neakurata.
Inaction, senokupo.
Inactive, senokupa.
Inadvertence,
malatenteco.
Inane, malplena.
Inanimate, senviva.
Inappreciable,
netaksebla.
Inappropriate, nedeca.
In as much as, tial ke.
Inattention,
neatenteco.
Inaudible, neaŭdebla.
Inauspicious, nefavora.
Incalculable,
nekalkulebla.
Incapable, nekapabla.
Incapacity,
nekapableco.
Incarnate, korpigi.
Incarnation, korpiĝo.
Incendiary,

brulkrimulo.
Incense, bonodorfumo.
Incense, furiozigi.
Incest, sangadulto.
Incentive, kaŭzo.
Inch, colo.
Incident, okazaĵo.
Incision, tranĉo.
Incite, instigi, inciti.
Inclination, inklino.
Incline, inklini.
Incline (slope), deklivo.
Include, enhavi.
Incoherent, sensenca.
Income, rento.
Incommode, ĝeni.
Incomparable, nekomparebla.
Incompatible, nekunigebla.
Incompetent, nekompetenta.
Incomplete, neplena.
Incomprehensible, nekomprenebla.
Inconceivable, neimagebla.
Inconsistent, nekonsekvenca.
Inconsolable, nekonsolebla.
Inconstant, ŝanĝema.
Incontestable, nedisputebla.
Inconvenient, maloportuna.
Incorporeal, spirita.
Incorrect, malkorekta.
Incorrigible, plimalobea, nerebonigebla.
Incorrupt, honesta.

Incorruptible, neputrebla.
Incorruption, senputreco.
Increase (grow), kreskiĝi.
Increase, plimultigi.
Incredible, nekredebla.
Incredulous, nekredema.
Incriminate, kulpigi.
Inculcate, enradiki.
Incurable, neresanigebla.
Indebtedness, ŝuldeco.
Indecent, maldeca.
Indecision, nedecideco.
Indeed, do, efektive, ja.
Indefatigable, senlaca.
Indefinite, nedifinita.
Indemnify, kompensi.
Indemnity, kompenso.
Independence, sendependeco.
Independent, sendependa.
Indeterminate, nedifinita.
Index (names), nomaro.
Index, tabelo.
India-rubber, kaŭĉuko.
Indicate, montri.
Indicative (gram.), indikativo.
Indict, kulpigi.
Indifferent, indiferenta.
Indigenous, enlanda.
Indigent, malriĉa.
Indigestible, nedigestebla.

Indigestion, malbona digestado.

Indignant, to be, indigni.

Indirect (through an intermediary), pera.

Indirectly (through an intermediary), pere.

Indirect (devious), malrekta.

Indiscreet, maldiskreta.

Indispensable, necesega.

Indisposed (ill), malsaneta.

Indisposition, malsaneto.

Indisputable, nedisputebla.

Indissoluble, nesolvebla.

Indistinct, malklara.

Individual, individuo.

Individual, individua.

Indivisible, nedividebla.

Indolent, senenergia.

Indomitable, nedresebla.

Indorse, dorseskribi.

Indubitable, neduba.

Induce, decidigi, alkonduki.

Indulge, indulgi.

Indulge (one's self), indulgiĝi.

Indulgence, indulgo.

Industrious, diligenta.

Industry (business), industrio.

Inebriate, ebrii.

Ineffectual, vana.

Ineligible, neelektebla.

Inert, senmova.

Inertia, inercio.

Inestimable, netaksebla.

Inevitable, neevitebla.

Inexact, malĝusta.

Inexhaustible, nekonsumebla.

Inexpedient, nenecesa, nekonvena.

Inexperience, malsperteco.

Inexplicable, neklarigebla.

Inexpressible, neesprimebla.

Inextricable, nemalplektebla.

Infallible, neerarebla.

Infallibility, neerarebleco.

Infallibly, neerareble.

Infamous, malglora, malfama.

Infamy, malgloro, malfamo.

Infancy, infaneco.

Infant, infaneto.

Infantile, infana.

Infantry, infanterio.

Infatuation, delogiteco.

Infect, infekti.

Infelicity, malfeliĉeco.

Infer, impliki.

Inferior, an, subulo.

Inferior, malsupera.

Inferiority, malsupereco.

Infernal, infera.

Infidelity, malfideleco.

Infinite, senlima.

Infinitive (gram.),

infinitivo.
Infinity, multego.
Infirm, malforta.
Infirmary, malsanulejo.
Infirmity, malforteco.
Inflame, flamigi.
Inflammable, bruliĝema.
Inflammation, brulumo.
Inflate, ŝveligi.
Inflect, fleksi.
Inflexible, nefleksebla, rigida.
Inflict, punon doni.
Influence, influi.
Influence, influo.
Influenza, gripo.
Inform, informi.
Inform, sciigi.
Informed, to be, sciiĝi.
Infrequent, malofta.
Infuze, infuzi.
Ingenious, sagaca.
Ingenuity, lerteco.
Ingenuous, naiva.
Ingot, fandaĵo.
Ingratitude, sendankeco.
Ingredient, elementaĵo.
Ingress, enigo.
Inhabit, loĝi.
Inhale, enspiri.
Inherit, heredi.
Inheritance, heredaĵo.
Inhuman, nehumana.
Iniquity, malboneco, maljusteco.
Initial (letter), ĉeflitero.
Initiate, iniciati.
Initiator, iniciatoro.

Inject, enŝprucigi.
Injection (medical), klistero.
Injurious, difektiga.
Injury, difektaĵo.
Injury (wound), vundo.
Injustice, maljusteco.
Ink, inko.
Inkstand, etc., inkujo.
Inmate, loĝanto.
Inn, gastejo.
Innocence, senkulpeco.
Innocent, senkulpa.
Innumerable, nekalkulebla.
In order to, por.
In order that, por ke.
Inoculate, inokuli.
Inodorous, senodora.
Inoffensive, neofendema.
Inopportune, neĝustatempa.
Inquest, enketo.
Inquietude, maltrankvileco.
Inquire, demandi.
Inquiry, demando.
Inquisition, inkvizicio.
Inquisitive, sciama.
Inquisitor, inkvizitoro.
Inroad, ekokupo.
Insalubrious, malsaniga.
Insane, freneza.
Insanity, frenezeco.
Insatiable, nesatigebla.
Inscribe, enskribi.
Inscription, surskribo.
Inscrutable, neserĉebla.
Insect, insekto.
Insecure, danĝera.

Insensible, sensenta.
Insert, enmeti.
Insert (print), enpresi.
Insertion, enpresaĵo.
Inseparable, sendisiĝa.
Inside, interne.
Inside out, returnite.
Insidious, insida.
Insight, elsciado.
Insignificant,
sensignifa.
Insincere, nesincera.
Insinuate, proponeti.
Insipid, sengusta.
Insist, insisti.
Insnare, allogi, kapti.
Insobriety,
malsobreco.
Insolent, insultema.
Insoluble, nesolvebla.
Insolvent,
nepagokapabla.
Insomnia, sendormo.
Insomuch, tial ke.
Inspect, ekzameni.
Inspector, inspektoro.
Inspiration, inspiro.
Inspiration (breath),
enspiro.
Inspire, enspiri.
Inspire, inspiri.
Instalment, partpago.
Install, loĝigi.
Instance,
ekzemplodoni.
Instance, ekzemplo.
Instant, momento.
Instant, in an,
momente.
Instantaneous, subita.
Instead of, anstataŭ.
Instead of, to put,
anstataŭi.

Instep, piedartiko.
Instigate, instigi.
Instill, infuzi.
Instinct, instinkto.
Institute, fondi.
Institute, instituto.
Institution, institucio.
Instruct, instrui.
Instruction, instrukcio.
Instruction (teaching),
instruado.
Instructive, instrua.
Instructor, instruisto.
Instrument (mus.),
muzikilo.
Instrument (wind),
blovinstrumento.
Instrument (string),
kordinstrumento.
Instrument (tool), ilo.
Insubordination,
ribeleto—ado.
Insufferable,
nesuferebla.
Insufficient, nesufiĉa.
Insular, insula.
Insulate, soligi, izoli.
Insult, insulti.
Insurance, asekuro.
Insure, asekuri.
Insurgent, ribelanto.
Insurrection, ribelo.
Insusceptible,
sensentema.
Intact, sendifekta.
Integer, tutcifero.
Integral (math.),
integrala.
Integrity, rekteco.
Intellect, inteligenteco.
Intelligence,
inteligenteco.
Intelligence (news),

sciigo.
Intelligent, inteligenta.
Intemperance,
malsobreco.
Intemperate, malsobra.
Intend, intenci.
Intense, ega.
Intensity, egeco.
Intent, celo.
Intention, intenco.
Intentional, intenca.
Inter, enterigi.
Intercalate, intermeti.
Intercede, propeti.
Intercept, interkapti.
Intercession, propeto.
Intercessor, propetulo.
Intercourse, interrilato.
Interdict, malpermesi.
Interest, procento.
Interest, interesi.
Interest one's self in,
interesiĝi je.
Interesting, interesa.
Interfere, sin intermeti.
Interior, interno.
Interjection,
interjekcio.
Interline, interlinii.
Interlocutor,
interparolanto.
Interloper, trudulo.
Interlude, interakto.
Intermeddle,
enmiksiĝi.
Intermediate, intera,
intermeza.
Interment, interigo.
Interminable, senfina.
Intermission,
intermito.
Intermit, intermiti.
Intermittent, intermita.

Internal, interna.
Internally, interne.
International,
internacia.
Internationalist,
Internaciisto.
Internationality,
internacieco.
Interpose, intermeti.
Interprete, traduki.
Interpreter, tradukisto.
Interrogate, demandi.
Interrogation, denotes,
ĉu.
Interrogation, note of,
signo demanda.
Interrogatory,
demanda.
Interregnum,
interregno.
Interrupt, interrompi.
Intersect, intersekcii.
Interval (space),
interspaco.
Interval (time),
intertempo.
Intervene, sin
intermeti.
Intervention,
intermeto.
Interview, intervidiĝo.
Interweave, kunplekti.
Intestate,
sentestamenta.
Intestine, internaĵo.
Intimacy, intimeco.
Intimate, intima,
intimulo.
Intimate, sciigi.
Intimation, sciigo.
Intimidate, timigi.
Into, en (with
accusative).

Intolerable,
netolerebla.
Intolerant, netolerema.
Intoxicate, ebriigi.
Intoxicated, ebria.
Intoxication, ebrieco.
Intractable,
nedresebla.
Intransitive,
netransitiva.
Intrepid, kuraĝega.
Intricate, malsimpla.
Intrigue, intrigi.
Intrinsic, vera.
Introduce, prezenti,
enkonduki.
Introduction,
enkonduko.
Introduction (preface),
antaŭparolo.
Intruder, trudulo.
Intrusion, trudo.
Intrust, komisii.
Inundate, superakvi.
Inure, kutimigi.
Inutility, senutilo.
Invade, enpenetri.
Invalid, nula.
Invalid, malsanetulo.
Invalidate, nuligi.
Invaluable, netaksebla.
Invariable, neŝanĝebla.
Invasion, ekokupado.
Invent, elpensi.
Invention, elpenso.
Inventory, katalogo.
Invert, interŝanĝi.
Invest (money),
procentdoni.
Investigate, esplori.
Inveterate, enradikita.
Invigorate, vivigi.
Invincible, nevenkebla.

Invisible, nevidebla.
Invitation, invito.
Invite, inviti.
Invoice, fakturo.
Invoke, alvoki.
Involuntary, senvola.
Iodine, jodo.
Irascible, ekkolerema.
Ire, kolero.
Iris (anat.), iriso.
Iris (bot.), irido.
Irishman, Irlandano.
Irksome, peniga,
enuiga.
Iron, fero.
Iron (linen, etc.), gladi.
Iron, an, gladilo.
Ironer (fem.),
gladistino.
Ironmonger,
patvendisto.
Irony, ironio.
Irradiate, radii.
Irregular, neregula.
Irreligious, malpia.
Irreparable,
neriparebla.
Irrepressible,
nehaltigebla.
Irreproachable,
neriproĉinda.
Irresolute, ŝanceliĝa,
nedecida.
Irreverence,
malriverenco.
Irritable, incitebla.
Irritate, inciti.
Is, estas.
Island, insulo.
Islander, insulano.
Isle, insulo.
Isolate, izoli.
Israelite, Izraelido.

Issue, eldoni.
Issue (offspring),
idaro.
Issue, elflui.
Isthmus, terkolo.
It, ĝi, ĝin.
Italian, Italo.
Italic (writing),
kursiva.
Itch, juki.
Itching, juko.
Item, ero.
Iteration, ripetado.
Itinerant, vojaĝanta.
Ivory, elefantosto.
Ivy, hedero.

J

Jabber, babili.
Jack, roasting,
turnrostilo.
Jackass, azenviro.
Jackal, ŝakalo.
Jacket, jako, ĵaketo.
Jade (tire), lacigadi.
Jaded, laca.
Jagged, denta.
Jaguar, jaguaro.
Jail, malliberejo.
Jailer, gardisto.
Jam, fruktaĵo.
January, Januaro.
Japan (polish), laki.
Japan, Japanujo.
Japanese, Japano.
Jar, botelego.
Jasmine, jasmeno.
Jaundice,
flavmalsano.
Javelin, ĵetponardo.
Jaw, makzelo.
Jawbone,

makzelosto.
Jay, garolo.
Jealousy, ĵaluzo.
Jeer, mokadi.
Jelly, ĝelateno.
Jeopardy, danĝero.
Jerk, ekskuo.
Jersey (garment),
trikoto.
Jessamine, jasmeno.
Jest, ŝerci.
Jest, ŝerco.
Jesuit, Jezuito.
Jesus, Jesuo.
Jetsam, fuko.
Jetty, digo.
Jew, Hebreo.
Jewel, juvelo.
Jewel-box, juvelujo.
Jeweller, juvelisto.
Jewess, Hebreino.
Jilt, koketulino.
Jingle, tinti.
Job, tasketo.
Jockey, rajdisto.
Jocose, ŝercema.
Jocular, ŝercema.
Join, kunigi.
Join hands,
manplekti.
Join together, kuniĝi.
Join with, kunigi.
Joiner, lignaĵisto.
Jointly, kune.
Joint (anatomy),
artiko.
Joint (carpentering),
kuniĝo.
Joist, trabo.
Joke, ŝerci.
Jolly, gajega.
Jolt, ekskui.
Jostle, puŝegi.

Jot, joto.
Journal (book keeping), taglibro.
Journal (a paper), ĵurnalo.
Journey (by car, etc.), veturi.
Journey (travel), vojaĝi.
Journey, vojaĝo.
Journeyman, taglaboristo.
Jovial, ĝojega.
Jowl, buŝego.
Joy, ĝojo.
Joyous, ĝoja.
Jubilant, ĝojega.
Jubilee, jubileo.
Judge, juĝi.
Judge (legal), juĝisto.
Judge, juĝanto.
Judgment (legal), juĝo.
Judicial, juĝa.
Judicious, prudenta.
Jug, kruĉo.
Juggle, ĵongli.
Juggler, ĵonglisto.
Jugglery, ĵonglado.
Juice, suko.
Juicy, suka.
July, Julio.
Jumble, miksi.
Jump, salti.
Junction, kuniĝo.
June, Junio.
Junior, neplenaĝa.
Juror, ĵurinto.
Jury, juĝantaro.
Juryman, ĵurinto.
Just (time), ĵus.
Just (fair), justa.

Justice, justeco.
Justice (correctness), praveco.
Justify, pravigi.
Justly, juste.
Juvenile, juna.
Juxtaposition, apudmeto.

K

Kaleidoscope, kalejdoskopo.
Kangaroo, didelfo.
Keel, kilo.
Keen (sharp), akra.
Keep, teni, gardi.
Keep silence, silentiĝi.
Keeper, gardanto.
Keepsake, memoraĵo.
Keg, bareleto.
Kennel, hundejo.
Kernel, kerno.
Kettle, bolilo.
Key, ŝlosilo.
Key (of piano, etc.), klavo.
Keyboard, klavaro.
Keystone, ĉefŝtono.
Kick, piedfrapo.
Kid, kaprido.
Kidnap, forŝteli.
Kidney, reno.
Kill, mortigi.
Kill (animals), buĉi.
Kilogramme, kilogramo.

Kilolitre,
kilolitro.
Kilometre,
kilometro.
Kin, parenceco.
Kind (species),
speco.
Kind, bona.
Kindle, ekbruligi.
Kindness,
boneco.
Kindred,
parencaro.
King, reĝo.
Kingdom,
reĝolando,
reĝlando.
Kingfisher,
alciono.
Kingly (adj.),
reĝa.
Kingly (adv.),
reĝe.
King's evil,
skrofolo.
Kinsfolk,
parencaro.
Kinsman,
parenco.
Kiss, kisi.
Kitchen, kuirejo.
Kitchen-garden,
legoma ĝardeno.
*Kitchen-
gardener,*
legomĝardenisto.
Kitchen-jack,
turnrostilo.
Kitchen utensils,
kuirilaro.
Kite (bird),
milvo.
Kite (toy),

flugludilo.
Knack, lerteco.
Knacker,
defelisto.
Knapsack,
tornistro.
Knave, fripono.
Knave (cards),
lakeo.
Knavery,
friponeco.
Knead, knedi.
Kneading-trough,
knedujo.
Knee, genuo.
Kneecap,
genuosto.
Kneel,
genufleksi.
Knell,
mortsonorado,
funebra
sonorado.
Knife, tranĉilo.
Knife-blade,
tranĉanto.
Knight, kavaliro.
Knit, triki, trikoti.
Knitting-needle,
trikilo.
Knob, butono.
Knock, frapi.
Knock down,
disĵeti, deĵeti.
Knot, ligtubero.
Knot (bow),
banto.
Knot (in wood),
lignotubero.
Knout, skurĝo.
Know, scii.
Know (to be
acquainted with),

koni.
Knuckle, artiko.
Kopeck, kopeko.
Koran, Korano.

L

Label, surskribeto.
Laborious, laborema.
Laboratory, laborejo.
Labour, laboro.
Labour, labori.
Labour, manual,
manlaboro.
Labourer, laboristo.
Labyrinth, labirinto.
Lac (lacquer), lako.
Lace, laĉi.
Lace, pasamento.
Lace (of shoe, etc.),
laĉo.
Lacerate, disŝiri.
Lack, bezono.
Lacker, lacquer, laki.
Lackey, lacquey,
lakeo.
Laconic, lakona.
Laconism,
lakonismo.
Lad, knabo, junulo.
Ladder, ŝtupetaro.
Lade, ŝarĝi.
Lading, bill of,
garantiita letero.
Lading, ŝarĝo—ado.
Lady, sinjorino,
nobelino.
Lag, malakceli.
Laical, nereligia.
Lair, nestego.
Laity, nereligiuloj.
Lake, lago.
Lamb, ŝafido.

Lame, to be, lami.
Lament, bedaŭri.
Lamentable,
bedaŭrinda.
Lamp, lampo.
Lampoon, satiro.
Lamprey, petromizo.
Lance, lanco.
Lancet, lanceto.
Land (goods),
elŝipigi.
Land (a country),
lando.
Land (of persons),
elŝipiĝi.
Land (soil), tero.
Landgrave,
landgrafo.
Landing (place),
plataĵo.
Landlord, bienulo,
landsinjoro.
Landmark,
terlimŝtono.
Landscape, pejzaĝo.
Landslip, terdisfalo.
Lane, strateto.
Language, lingvo.
Language (speech),
lingvaĵo.
Languid, malfortika.
Languish, malfortiĝi.
Lank, maldika.
Lantern, lanterno.
Lap, leki, lekumi.
Lapis lazuli, lapis
lazuro.
Lapse (of time),
manko, daŭro.
Larceny, ŝtelo.
Larch, lariko.
Lard, porkograso.
Larder, manĝaĵejo.

114

Large, granda.
Largely, grandege.
Lark, alaŭdo.
Larva, larvo.
Larynx, laringo.
Lascivious,
voluptema.
Lash (to tie), alligi.
Lash (to whip),
skurĝi.
Lass, junulino.
Lassitude, laciĝo.
Lasso, kaptoŝnuro.
Last (continue),
daŭri.
Last, lasta.
Last but one,
antaŭlasta.
Latch, pordrisorto,
fermilo.
Late, malfrua.
Late, to be, malfrui.
Late (deceased),
mortinto.
Lately, antaŭ ne
longe.
Lateness, malfrueco.
Latent, kaŝita.
Lateral, flanka.
Lath, paliseto.
Lathe, tornilo.
Lather, sapumi.
Lather, sapumaĵo,
ŝaŭmaĵo.
Latin, Latina.
Latter, lasta, tiu ĉi.
Lattice, palisplektaĵo.
Laud, laŭdi.
Laudable, laŭdebla.
Laudation, laŭdego.
Laugh, ridi.
Laughable, ridinda.
Laughter, ridado.

Laundress, lavistino.
Laundry, lavejo.
Laurel, laŭro.
Lava, lafo.
Lavish, malŝpara.
Law, a, regulo, leĝo.
Law, the,
leĝoscienco.
Lawful, rajta.
Lawn, herbejo.
Lawsuit, proceso.
Lawyer, legisto.
Lax, laksa.
Laxative, laksilo.
Lay (song), kanto.
Lay (trans. v.), meti.
Lay (eggs), demeti
(ovojn).
Lay bare, senigi.
Lay hold of, ekkapti.
Lay open, malkovri.
Lay waste, ruinigi.
Layer (stratum),
tavolo.
Layman, nereligiulo.
Laziness,
mallaboreco.
Lazy, mallaborema.
Lead, konduki.
Lead (metal),
plumbo.
Lead astray, deturni.
Lead away,
dekonduki.
Leaf (tree), folio.
Leaf, folio.
League (union), ligo.
Leaguer, ligano.
Leak, guteti.
Lean, klini.
Lean, malgrasa.
Lean, to grow,
malgrasiĝi.

Leap, salti.
Leap forward, antaŭensalti.
Leap year, superjaro.
Learn, lerni.
Learn (news, etc.), sciiĝi.
Learn (thoroughly), ellerni.
Learned (man), klerulo, scienculo.
Lease, lukontrakto.
Leash, ligilo.
Least, malplej.
Least, at, almenaŭ.
Leather, ledo.
Leave, lasi.
Leave (bequeath), testamenti.
Leave (depart), deiri.
Leave off, ĉesi.
Leaven, fermentilo.
Leavings (food), manĝrestaĵo.
Lecture, parolado.
Leech, hirudo.
Leer, flanken rigardi.
Lees, feĉo.
Left, on the, maldekstre.
Leg (limb), kruro.
Leg (of a fowl, etc.), femuro.
Leg of mutton, ŝaffemuro.
Legacy, heredaĵo.
Legal, leĝa.
Legation (place), senditejo.
Legation, senditaro.
Legend, legendo.
Legible, legebla.
Legion, legio.

Legislate, leĝdoni.
Legislative, leĝiganta.
Legislator, leĝfaranto.
Legitimate, rajta.
Legitimate, laŭleĝa.
Leisure, libertempo.
Lemon, citrono.
Lemonade, limonado.
Lemon tree, citronarbo.
Lend, prunti, pruntedoni.
Lender, pruntanto.
Length, longeco.
Length, in, laŭlonge.
Lengthen, plilongigi.
Leniency, malsevereco.
Lenient, malsevera.
Lent (40 days before Easter), granda fasto.
Lentil, lento.
Leopard, leopardo.
Leper, leprulo.
Leprosy, lepro.
Leprous, lepra.
Less, malpli.
Lessee, luanto.
Lessen, plimalgrandigi.
Lesson, leciono.
Lessor, luiganto.
Let (house, etc.), luigi.
Let (before an infinitive), lasi.
Let down, mallevi.
Lethargy, letargio.
Letter, capital, granda litero.
Letter (alphabet),

litero.
Letter (epistle),
letero.
Letter (registered),
rekomendita letero.
Letter of advice,
ricevavizo.
Letter of exchange,
kambio.
Letter-box, poŝta
kesto, leterkesto.
Letter-carrier (postman),
leteristo.
Letter-case, leterujo.
Lettuce, laktuko.
Level (instrument),
nivelilo.
Level, nivela.
Level (flat), ebena.
Lever, levilo.
Levity, malseriozo.
Lewd, malĉasta.
Lexicon, leksikono.
Liable, responda.
Liability, respondeco.
Liar, mensogulo.
Libation, oferverŝo.
Libel, kalumnii.
Liberal (generous),
malavara.
Liberate, liberigi.
Libertine,
malĉastulo.
Liberty, libereco.
Librarian,
bibliotekisto.
Library, biblioteko.
Libretto, libreto.
License, permeso.
Licentiate, licencato.
Licentious,
malbonmora.

Lichen, likeno.
Lick (lap), leki.
Lie (rest on), kuŝi.
Lie down, kuŝiĝi.
Lie, mensogo.
Lien, garantiaĵo.
Lieu (in lieu of),
anstataŭ.
Lieutenant,
leŭtenanto.
Life, vivo.
Lifeguard,
korpogardisto.
Lifelong, dumviva.
Lifetime, dumvivo.
Lift, levi.
Lift up, altlevi.
Lift, homlevilo.
Ligament, tendeno.
Ligature, bandaĝilo.
Light, lumi.
Light, lumo, lumeco.
Light (weight),
malpeza.
Lighten, malpezigi.
Lightning, fulmo.
Lightning-conductor,
fulmoŝirmilo.
Lighthouse, lumturo.
Like, ameti.
Like, simila.
Like (adv.), tiel.
Likelihood, verŝajno.
Likeness (similarity),
simileco.
Likeness (portrait),
portreto.
Likely (adj.), ebla,
verŝajna.
Likely (adv.), eble,
verŝajne.
Likewise, simile.
Lilac, siringo.

Lilac (colour),
siringkolora.
Lily, lilio.
Limb, membro.
Lime, kalko.
Lime tree, tilio.
Limestone,
kalkŝtono.
Limit, limigi.
Limit, limo.
Limp, lami, lameti.
Limpid, klarega.
Linden, tilio.
Line, linio.
Line, subŝtofi.
Linen, tolo.
Linen (the washing),
tolaĵo.
Linen, baby,
vestaĵeto.
Linen-room, tolaĵejo.
Linger, prokrastiĝi.
Lining, subŝtofo.
Link (of chain),
ĉenero.
Link, torĉo.
Lint, ĉarpio.
Lion, leono.
Lip, lipo.
Liquefy, fluidigi.
Liquid, fluida.
Liquid, fluidaĵo.
Liquidate, likvidi.
Liquidation, likvido.
Liquidator,
likvidanto.
Liquor, likvoro.
Liquorice, glicirizo.
Lisp, lispi.
List, registro.
List of names,
nomaro.
List (index), tabelo.

Listen, aŭskulti.
Listless, senvigla.
Litany, litanio.
Literal, laŭlitera.
Literally, laŭlitere.
Literary, literatura.
Literateur,
literaturisto.
Literature, literaturo.
Lithe, aktiva.
Lithograph, litografi.
Lithographer,
litografisto.
Lithography,
litografarto.
Litigation,
procesado.
Litigious, procesema.
Litre, litro.
Litter (animals),
kuŝejo.
Litter, pajlaĵo.
Little, a, iom.
Little (not much, not
many), malmulte.
Little (small),
malgranda.
Littleness,
malgrandeco.
Littoral, marbordo.
Liturgy, liturgio.
Live, vivi.
Live (dwell), loĝi.
Live long! vivu!
Lively, vigla.
Liver, hepato.
Livery, livreo,
uniformo.
Living, viva.
Lizard, lacerto.
Lo! jen.
Load, ŝarĝi.
Load (weapon),

ŝargi.
Load, ŝarĝo.
Loadstone, magneto.
Loaf, bulkego.
Loan, prunto.
Loathe, malamegi.
Loathsome, naŭziza.
Lobby, vestiblo.
Lobster, omaro.
Local, loka.
Locality, loko.
Loch, lago.
Lock, ŝlosi.
Lock, seruro.
Lock (hair), buklo.
Lock (of canal, etc.),
kluzo.
Lockjaw, tetano.
Locomotive,
lokomotivo.
Locksmith, seruristo.
Lodge (small house),
dometo.
Lodge (dwell), loĝi.
Lodger, luanto.
Lodgings, loĝejo.
Loft (corn), grenejo.
Loftiness (character),
nobleco.
Lofty, altega.
Log, ŝtipo.
Logarithm,
logaritmo.
Logic, logiko.
Logogriph,
logogrifo.
Loins, lumboj.
Loiter, vagi.
Lone, lonely, sola.
Loneliness, soleco.
Long, longa.
Long for, sopiri pri.
Longitude, longo.

Long time,
longatempe.
Long while,
longatempe.
Look, mieno, vizaĝo.
Look at, rigardi.
Look for, serĉi.
Looking-glass,
spegulo.
Look out (man),
observisto.
Loom, teksilo.
Loop (of ribbons),
banto.
Loose, ellasa.
Loosen, ellasi.
Lop, ĉirkaŭhaki.
Lord, the, la Sinjoro.
Lord's Supper,
Sankta vespermanĝo.
Lordly, nobla.
Lose, perdi.
Lose, at play,
malgajni.
Lose time (of a
watch, etc.),
malrapidi.
Lose one's self,
perdiĝi.
Lose one's way,
vojperdi.
Loss, perdo.
Lot (destiny), sorto.
Lot, lotaĵo.
Lots, to cast, loti.
Lottery, loterio.
Loud, laŭta.
Loudly, laŭte.
Loudness, laŭteco.
Lough, lago.
Lounger, vagulo.
Louse, pediko.
Love, ami.

Love, to make, amindumi.

Lover, amanto, amisto.

Low (cry of a cow), bleki.

Low (sound), basa.

Low (not loud), mallaŭta.

Low (not high), malalta.

Lower, mallevi.

Lower price, rabati.

Lowly, humila.

Lowliness, humileco.

Loyal, fidela.

Loyalty, fideleco.

Lozenge (geom.), lozanĝo.

Lozenge, pastelo.

Lucid, klara.

Luck, ŝanco, bonŝanco.

Lucky, ŝanca, bonŝanca.

Lucrative, profita.

Ludicrous, ridinda.

Luggage, pakaĵo.

Lukewarm, varmeta.

Lull, kvietigi.

Lullaby, lulkanto.

Luminary, lumigilo.

Luminous, lumiga.

Lump, bulo.

Lunacy, lunatikeco.

Lunar, luna.

Lunatic, lunatikulo.

Lunch, tagmezomanĝo.

Lung, pulmo.

Lurch, ŝanceliĝi.

Lure, trompi, logi.

Lurid, malhela.

Lurk, sin kaŝi (insideme).

Luscious, bongusta.

Lust, avideco.

Lustre (lamp), lustro.

Lustre, brilo.

Lusty, fortega.

Lute, liuto.

Lutheran, luterano.

Luxury, lukso.

Luxurious, luksa.

Lyceum, liceo.

Lye, lesivo.

Lymph, limfo.

Lynx, linko.

Lyre, liro.

M

Macadam, makadamo.

Macaroni, makaronio.

Machine, maŝino.

Machine, sewing, stebilo.

Machinery, radaro, maŝinaro.

Machinist, maŝinisto.

Mad, freneza.

Madam, sinjorino.

Madden, frenezigi.

Madly, freneze.

Madness, frenezeco.

Madrigal, madrigalo.

Magazine, revuo, gazeto.

Magazine (store-house), magazeno.

Maggot, akaro.

Magic, magio.

Magician, magiisto.

Magisterial, majstrata.

Magistrate, magistrato.

Magnanimous, grandanima.

Magnet, magneto.
Magnetise, magnetizi.
Magnetism,
magnetismo.
Magnificent, belega.
Magnify, pligrandigi.
Magnitude, grandeco.
Magpie, pigo.
Mahogany, mahagono.
Mahomet, Mahometo.
Mahometan,
Mahometano.
Maid, fraŭlino.
Maiden, virgulino.
Maidenly, virga.
Maid-servant,
servistino.
Mail, poŝto.
Mail (armour), maŝo.
Maim, vundegi.
Mainly, ĉefe.
Maintain, subteni.
Maintain (assert),
pretendi.
Maintenance,
subtenado.
Maize, maizo.
Majestic, majesta.
Majesty, majesto.
Major (milit.), majoro.
Major (mus.), dura.
Majority (age),
plenaĝo.
Majority, plimulto.
Make, fari.
Make glad, ĝojigi.
Make good, rebonigi.
Make haste, rapidiĝi.
Make holy, sanktigi.
Make known, sciigi.
Make longer,
plilongigi.
Make an obeisance,

riverenci.
Make public, publikigi.
Make stronger,
plifortigi.
Make younger,
plijunigi.
Malachite, malakito.
Malady, malsano.
Malcontent,
malkontentulo.
Male, viro.
Malediction, malbeno.
Malefactor, krimulo.
Malevolence,
malbonvolo.
Malicious, malica.
Malign, kalumnii.
Malignant, malicema.
Malleable, etendebla.
Mallet, martelego.
Mallow, malvo.
Malt, bierhordeo,
hordeo trempita.
Maltreat, bati.
Mama, patrinoto.
Mammal,
mamsuĉbesto.
Man, homo.
Man (male), viro.
Manage, administri.
Management,
administrado.
Manager,
administranto.
Mandate, skribordono,
komando.
Mandarin, Mandarino.
Mane, kolhararo.
Manganese, mangano.
Mange, bestjuko—
skabio.
Manger, manĝujo.
Mangle (to maim),

121

senmembrigi.
Manhood, vireco.
Mania, manio.
Maniac, frenezulo.
Manifest, elmontri.
Manifest, evidenta.
Manifest, klara.
Manifesto, manifesto.
Manifold,
multenombra.
Manikin, kvazaŭhomo.
Mankind, homaro.
Manly, vira.
Manliness, vireco.
Manna, manao.
Manner, maniero.
Manner, in this,
tiamaniere.
Manner, in that, tiel.
Mannered, bonmora.
Manners, moroj.
Manœuvre (milit.),
manovro.
Manometer,
manometro.
Mansion, domego.
Manslaughter,
mortbato.
Mantle, mantelo.
Manual, mana.
Manual, lernolibro.
Manufactory,
fabrikejo.
Manufacture, fabriki.
Manufacture, fabriko.
Manure, sterko.
Manuscript,
manuskripto.
Many, multo.
Many, multaj.
Many of, multe da.
Many, how, kiom.
Many, so, tiom.

Map, karto,
geografikarto.
Mar, difekti,
malbonformigi.
Maraud, rabeti.
Marble, marmoro.
Marble (plaything),
globeto.
March (month), Marto.
March, marŝi.
March, marŝado.
Marchioness,
markizino.
Mare, ĉevalino.
Margin, marĝeno.
Marguerite (daisy),
lekanto.
Marigold, kalendulo.
Marine, mara.
Marine, marsoldato.
Mariner, maristo.
Marionette, marioneto.
Maritime, mara.
Mark (sign), signo.
Mark, marko.
Market, vendejo.
Marl, kalkargilo.
Marmalade, fruktaĵo.
Marmot, marmoto.
Marquis, Markizo.
Marriage (state),
edzeco.
Marriage (ceremony),
edziĝo, edziniĝo.
Marriageable,
edzigebla.
Married, to get,
edz(in)iĝi.
Marry a man, edzigi.
Marry a woman,
edzinigi.
Marry (unite),
geedzigi.

Marry, geedziĝi.
Marsh, marĉo.
Marshal, marŝalo.
Marsh mallow, alteo.
Mart, vendejo.
Martial, militama—ema.
Marten, mustelo.
Martingale, kapdetenilo.
Martyr, turmentito.
Martyr, suferanto.
Martyrdom, turmento.
Martyrdom, sufero.
Marvel, miri.
Marvel, mirindaĵo.
Marvellous, mirinda.
Masculine, vira.
Masculine, virseksa.
Mash, miksaĵo.
Masher, dando.
Mask, masko.
Mask, maski.
Mason, masonisto.
Masquerade, maskitaro.
Mass, meso.
Mass, amaso.
Massacre, elmortigi.
Massacre, buĉado.
Massive, masiva.
Mast, masto.
Master (of house), mastro.
Master (teacher), instruisto.
Master (of profession), majstro.
Mr., sinjoro.
Masterpiece, ĉefverko.
Mastic, mastiko.
Masticate, maĉi.
Mastication, maĉado.

Mastiff, korthundo.
Mat, mato.
Match, alumeto, egaligi.
Match-box, alumetujo.
Match, kompari, egaligi.
Matchless, nekomparebla.
Matchmaker, alumetisto.
Match (marriage), svatisto.
Mate, ŝipoficiro.
Mate, kunulo.
Material (cloth), ŝtofo.
Material, materialo.
Materialism, materialismo.
Materialist, materialisto.
Maternal, patrina.
Maternity, patrineco.
Mathematician, matematikisto.
Matrimony, geedzeco.
Matrix, utero.
Matron, patrino.
Matron, patronino, estrino.
Matter, ŝtofo.
Matter, materialo.
Matter (pus), puso.
Mattock, pikfosilo.
Mattress, matraco.
Mature, matura.
Mature, maturigi—iĝi.
Maturity, matureco.
Maul, bategi.
Maxillary, makzela.
Maxim, proverbo.
Maximum, maksimumo.

123

May (month), Majo.
May-bug, majskarabo.
Mayhap, eble.
Mayor, urbestro.
Maze, labirinto.
Mazurka, mazurko.
Me, (al) mi, min.
Meadow, herbejo.
Meagre (poor),
malriĉa.
Meal (flour), faruno.
Meal, manĝo.
Mean (math.),
mezakvanto.
Mean (paltry),
malgrandanima.
Mean (stingy),
troŝpara.
Mean, signifi.
Meaning, signifo.
Meaning (of a word),
senco.
Means of, by, per.
Means, by no, neniel.
Measles, morbilo.
Measure, mezuri.
Measure (quantity),
mezuro.
Measure, mezurilo.
Measure (time, mus.),
takto.
Measurement,
mezuraĵo—eco.
Meat, viando.
Mechanic, metiisto.
Mechanic (engineer),
meĥanikisto.
Mechanism,
meĥanismo.
Mechanics, meĥaniko.
Mechanical, meĥanika.
Medal, medalo.
Medallion, medaliono.

Meddle, enmiksiĝi.
Mediæval, mezepoka.
Mediate, peri.
Mediate, pera.
Mediator, perulo.
Medical, medicina.
Medicament, kuracilo.
Medicinal, medicina.
Medicine, kuracilo.
Medicine (art),
medicino.
Mediocre, malboneta.
Meditate, mediti.
Meditation, medito.
Mediterranean,
Mezomaro.
Medium (spiritualism),
mediumo.
Medium, meza.
Meek, humilega.
Meet, renkonti.
Meeting, renkonto.
Meeting (of club, etc.),
kunveno.
Meeting-place,
kunvenejo.
Melancholy,
melankolio.
Melancholy,
melankolia.
Mellow, matura.
Melodious, melodia.
Melody, melodio.
Melodrama,
melodramo.
Melon, melono.
Melt, fluidiĝi.
Member (limb),
membro.
Member (of club),
klubano.
Membrane, membrano.
Memento, memoraĵo.

Memorable,
memorinda.
Memorandum, noto.
Memorial, memoraĵo.
Memory, memoro.
Menace, minaci.
Menacing, minaca.
Menagery, bestejo.
Mend, fliki.
Mendacity,
mensogeco.
Mendicant, almozulo.
Menial, servulo.
Menses, monataĵo.
Mental, spirita.
Mention, citi, nomi.
Menu, manĝokarto.
Mercantile, komerca.
Mercenary, dungato.
Mercenary,
subaĉetebla.
Merchandise,
komercaĵo.
Merchant, negocisto.
Merciful, kompata—
ema.
Mercury, hidrargo.
Mercy, kompato—eco.
Mere, nura.
Merely, nure.
Meridian, meridiano.
Merino, merinolano.
Merit, merito.
Merit, meriti.
Mermaid, sireno.
Merriment, gajeco.
Merry, gaja.
Mesh, maŝo.
Mess, kunmanĝi.
Message, depeŝo.
Messenger, sendito.
Messiah, Savonto,
Mesio.

Messmate,
kunmanĝanto.
Metal, metalo.
Metallic, metala.
Metallurgy,
metalurgio.
Metaphor, metaforo.
Mete, dividi, disdoni.
Meteor, meteoro.
Meteorology,
meteorologio.
Meter, mezurilo.
Method, metodo.
Metre, metro.
Metric, metra.
Metropolis, ĉefurbo.
Mettle, fervoro,
kuraĝo.
Mew, katbleki.
Miasma, miasmo.
Mica, glimo.
Microbe, mikrobo.
Microscope,
mikroskopo.
Midday, tagmezo.
Middle, centro.
Middle, meza.
Midnight, noktomezo.
Midsummer, duonjaro,
somermezo.
Midwife, akuŝistino.
Mien, mieno.
Might, potenco.
Mighty, potenca.
Mignonette, resedo.
Migrate, migri.
Milch, laktodona.
Mild, dolĉa.
Mildew, ŝimo.
Mildness, dolĉeco.
Mile, mejlo.
Militant, milita.
Military, milita.

Military man, militisto.
Militia, militantaro.
Milk, melki.
Milk, lakto.
Mill, muelilo.
Mill-house, muelejo.
Miller, muelisto.
Millenium, miljaro.
Millet, milio.
Milligram, miligramo.
Millimeter, milimetro.
Milliner, ĉapelistino.
Millinery, galanterio.
Million, miliono.
Milt, laktumo.
Mimic, imiti.
Mince, haketi.
Mind (heed), atenti.
Mind (a patient), flegi.
Mind, spirito.
Mind (see after), zorgi.
Mindful, zorga.
Mine, mia, mian.
Mine (pit), mino.
Mine, subfosi.
Miner, ministo.
Mineral, mineralo.
Mineralogy,
mineralogio.
Mingle, miksi.
Miniature, miniaturo.
Minimum, minimumo.
Minister (religious),
pastro.
Minister (polit.),
ministro.
Ministry, ministraro.
Minor (age),
neplenaĝa.
Minor (mus.), molo,
mola.
Minority (age),
neplenaĝo.

Minority, malplimulto.
Minstrel, bardo,
kantisto.
Mint, mento.
Minute, menueto.
Minuet (time), minuto.
Minute (note), noto.
Minute, malgrandega.
Minutiæ, detaleto.
Miracle, miraklo.
Miraculous, mirakla.
Mire, ŝlimo, koto.
Mirror, spegulo.
Mirth, gajeco, kun—.
Miry, ŝlimhava.
Misapply, eraralmeti.
Misapprehend,
malkompreni.
Misapprehension,
malkompreno.
Misanthrope,
homevitulo.
Misbehave,
malbonkonduti.
Miscalculation,
kalkuleraro.
Miscarry, malsukcesi.
Miscellaneous,
miksita, diversa.
Mischance, malfeliĉo.
Mischief, malboneco,
malpraveco.
Mischievous,
malbonema.
Misconception,
malkompreno—eco.
Misconduct,
malbonkonduti.
Miscreant, malbonulo.
Misdeed, malbonfaro.
Misdemeanour,
krimeto.
Miser, avarulo.

Miserable, malgaja.
Miserly, avara.
Misery, mizero.
Misfortune, malfeliĉo.
Misinterpretation,
kontraŭsenco.
Misgiving, dubo.
Mishap, malfeliĉo.
Misinform, malsciigi.
Mislay, erarigi,
neĝustmeti, trompi.
Mislead, erarigi.
Mislead (deceive),
trompi.
Misplaced, neĝustloka.
Misprint, preseraro.
Misrepresent,
falsreprezenti.
Miss, manki.
Miss, Fraŭlino.
Missile, ĵetarmilo.
Missing, manka.
Mission, misio.
Missionary, misiisto.
Mist, nebuleto.
Mistake, eraro.
Mistaken, to be,
trompiĝi.
Mistletoe, visko.
Mistress (house),
mastrino.
Mistress (lover),
amantino.
Mistress (school),
instruistino.
Mistrust, malfido.
Mistrust, suspekti.
Misty, nebuleta.
Misunderstand,
malkompreni.
Misuse, maluzi,
malbonuzi.
Mite, akaro.

Mite (coin), monereto.
Mitre, mitro.
Mitigate, moderigi.
Mix, miksi.
Mixture, miksaĵo.
Moan, ĝemi.
Moat, fosaĵo.
Mob, amaso.
Mobile, movebla.
Mobilise, mobilizi.
Mock, moki.
Mockery, moko—eco.
Mode, modo.
Model, modelo.
Model, modeli.
Moderate, modera.
Moderate, moderigi.
Moderation,
modereco.
Modern, moderna.
Modest, modesta.
Modesty, modesteco.
Modify, ŝanĝi.
Modulate, moduli.
Modulation,
modulado.
Moiety, duono.
Moist, malseketa.
Moisten, malseketigi.
Moisture, malseketaĵo.
Molasses, mielsiropo.
Molar, vanga dento.
Mole (animal), talpo.
Molest, turmenti,
lacigi.
Mollify, moderigi.
Mollusk, molusko.
Moment (time),
momento.
Momentous, gravega.
Monarch, monarĥo.
Monarchy, monarĥejo.
Monastery, monaĥejo.

127

Monday, Lundo.
Monetary, mona.
Money, mono.
Money-order,
poŝtmandato.
Mongrel, hibrida.
Monitor, avertulo,
avertanto.
Monk, monaĥo.
Monkey, simio.
Monograph,
monografo.
Monogram,
monogramo.
Monologue, monologo.
Monomania,
monomanio.
Monopolise,
monopoligi.
Monopoly, monopolo.
Monosyllable,
unusilabo.
Monotonous (of form),
unuforma.
Monotonous (of tone),
unutona.
Monster, monstro.
Monstrous, monstra.
Month, monato.
Monthly (adj.),
ĉiumonata.
Monument,
monumento.
Mood, modo.
Moody, silentema.
Moon, luno.
Moonlight, lunbrilo.
Moor, stepo.
Moor (a ship, etc.),
alligi per ŝnurego.
Moot, disputebla.
Mope, malĝojiĝi.
Moral, morala.

Morality, moraleco.
Morals, etiko, moro.
Morass, marĉejo—aĵo.
Morbid, malsana.
Mordant, morda.
More (than), pli (ol).
More, plu.
More, the—the more,
ju pli—des pli.
Moreover, plie.
Morgue, mortulejo.
Moribund, mortanto.
Morning, mateno.
Morocco (leather),
marokeno.
Morose, malgaja.
Moroseness,
malgajeco.
Morrow, morgaŭtago.
Morsel, peceto.
Mortal (subject to
death), mortema.
Mortal (deadly),
mortiga.
Mortal, a, mortonta—
o.
Mortality (effect),
mortado.
Mortality (state),
morteco.
Mortar, a, pistujo.
Mortar (milit.),
bombardilo.
Mortar (building),
mortero.
Mortgage, hipoteko.
Mortification,
humiligo.
Mortification,
gangreno.
Mortify, gangreni.
Mortify, humiligi.
Mosaic, mozaiko.

Mosquito, kulo.
Moss, musko.
Most, plej.
Mostly, pleje.
Moth, tineo.
Mother, patrino.
Motion, movo.
Motionless, senmova.
Motive, kaŭzo.
Motive, moviga.
Motor, movilo, motoro.
Motto, devizo.
Mould, modelilo.
Mould (soil), tero.
Mouldy, ŝima.
Mouldy, to get, ŝimiĝi.
Moult, ŝanĝi plumojn.
Moult (birds), ŝanĝi plumojn.
Mound, remparo, digo.
Mount, supreniri.
Mount, monteto.
Mountain, monto.
Mountaineer, montano.
Mountainous, monta.
Mountain-range, montaro.
Mountebank, ĵonglisto.
Mourn, malĝoji, ploregi.
Mournful, funebra.
Mourning (dress), funebra vesto.
Mouse, muso.
Mouse, shrew, soriko.
Mouse-trap, muskaptilo.
Moustache, lipharoj.
Mouth, buŝo.
Mouth (of river), enfluo.

Movable, movebla.
Move, movi.
Move (furniture), transloĝiĝi.
Move in (dwelling), enloĝi.
Move out (dwelling), elloĝiĝi.
Move (feelings), kortuŝi.
Moved (to be), kortuŝiĝi.
Movement, movado.
Mow, falĉi.
Much, multe da.
Much, multa.
Much, so, tiom.
Much, how, kiom da.
Much, too, tro multe.
Mucus, muko.
Mud, ŝlimo, koto.
Muddle (of liquors), malklarigi.
Muddle (bungle), fuŝi, konfuzi.
Muddle (bungle), konfuzo.
Mudguard, kotŝirmilo.
Muff, mufo.
Muffle, envolvi.
Mug, pokaleto, poteto.
Mulberry, moruso.
Mulct (fine), mona puno, monpuno.
Mule, mulo.
Muleteer, mulisto.
Mulish, obstina.
Multiple, multoblo.
Multiplicand, multigato.
Multiplication, multigado.
Multiplied, multigita.

Multiplier, multiganto.
Multiply (trans.),
multigi.
Multiply (intrans.),
multiĝi.
Mumble, murmuri.
Mummy, mumo.
Munch, maĉi.
Mundane, monda.
Municipal, urba.
Munificence,
malavareco.
Munificent, malavara.
Murder, mortigi.
Murder, mortigo.
Murderer, mortiganto.
Murky, malhela,
malluma.
Murmur, murmuri.
Muscat wine,
muskatvino.
Muscle, muskolo.
Muscular, muskola.
Muse, muzo.
Muse, revi.
Museum, muzeo.
Mushroom, fungo.
Music, muziko.
Musical, muzika.
Musician, muzikisto.
Music (to play),
muziki.
Muskrat, miogalo.
Musket, pafilo.
Muslin, muslino.
Mussel, mitulo.
Must (verb), devas.
Must, mosto.
Mustard, mustardo.
Mustard plant, sinapo.
Mustard-plaster,
sinapa kataplasmo.
Muster, kunvenigi.

Musty, malfreŝa.
Mutation, ŝanĝado.
Mute, muta.
Mute, mutulo.
Mutilate, vundegi.
Mutinous, ribela.
Mutiny, ribelo.
Mutter, murmuri.
Mutton, ŝafaĵo.
Mutton, leg of,
ŝaffemuro.
Mutual, reciproka.
Mutually, reciproke.
Muzzle (for a dog),
buŝumo.
Muzzle, buŝumi.
My, mia, mian.
Myoptic, miopa,
miopema.
Myopy, miopeco.
Myosotis, miozoto.
Myriad, miriado.
Myriametre,
miriametro.
Myrrh, mirho.
Myrtle, mirto.
Mysterious, mistera.
Mystery, mistero.
Mystify, mistifiki.
Mystification,
mistifiko.
Myth, mito.
Mythology, mitologio.

N

Nadir, nadiro.
Nail (of finger, etc.),
ungo.
Nail, najli.
Naive, naiva.
Naked, nuda.
Name, nomi.

Name, Christian, baptonomo.
Namely, nome.
Namesake, samnomulo.
Nankeen, nankeno.
Nap (doze), dormeti.
Nape, nuko.
Napkin, buŝtuko.
Narcissus, narciso.
Narcotic, narkotiko.
Narrate, rakonti.
Narrative, rakonto.
Narrow, mallarĝa.
Narrowly, mallarĝe.
Narrowness, mallarĝeco.
Nasal, naza.
Nasty, malagrabla.
Natation, naĝarto.
Nation, nacio.
National, nacia.
Nationality, nacieco.
Native, landano, enlandulo.
Native, enlanda.
Native-land, patrujo.
Nativity, naskiĝo.
Natural (music), naturo.
Natural, natura.
Naturalism, naturalismo.
Naturalist, naturalisto.
Naturally, nature.
Naturally (of course), kompreneble.
Naturalness, naturaleco.
Nature, naturo.
Naught, nulo.
Naughty, malbona.
Nausea, naŭzo.

Nauseate, naŭzi.
Nauseous, naŭza.
Nautical, ŝipa.
Naval, ŝipa.
Nave (church), navo.
Nave (wheel), aksingo.
Navigable, ŝipirebla.
Navigate, marveturi.
Navigation, marveturado.
Navy, ŝiparo.
Navvy, terfosisto.
Nay, ne.
Near, proksima.
Near by, apud.
Nearly, preskaŭ.
Nearness, proksimeco.
Neat, pura, deca.
Neatness, pureco, dececo.
Nebulous, nebula.
Necessary, necesa.
Necessity, neceseco.
Neck, kolo.
Neck (of vase), nazeto.
Neck (of land), terkolo.
Neckcloth, koltuko.
Necklace, ĉirkaŭkolo.
Necktie, kravato.
Necrology, nekrologio.
Necromancer, nekromancisto, sorĉisto.
Nectar, nektaro.
Need, bezoni.
Need, malriĉeco.
Needful, bezona, necesa.
Needle, kudrilo.
Needy, malriĉa.
Negation, neado.
Negative, nea.
Neglect, ne zorgi pri.

Neglected, nezorgita.
Neglectful, senzorga.
Negligent, malatenta.
Negligence, malatento.
Negotiate, negoci.
Negotiation, negocado.
Negro, nigrulo.
Neigh, ĉevalbleki.
Neighbour, najbaro.
Neighbourhood,
ĉirkaŭaĵo.
Neighbouring,
samlima.
Neither, nek.
Neo-Latin, novlatina.
Neologism,
neologismo.
Nephew, nevo.
Nepotism, nepotismo.
Nerve, nervo.
Nervous, nerva.
Nervousness, nerveco.
Nest, nesto.
Nestle, kuŝiĝeti.
Nestling, birdido.
Net, reto.
Netting, retaĵo.
Nettle, urtiko.
Network, retaĵo.
Neuralgia, neŭralgio.
Neuter, neŭtra.
Neutral, neŭtrala.
Neutrality, neŭtraleco.
Never, neniam.
Nevertheless, tamen.
New, nova.
News, sciigo, novaĵo.
Newspaper, ĵurnalo.
New Year's Day,
novjartago.
Next, sekvanta.
Next (near),
plejproksima.

Nibble, mordeti.
Nice, agrabla.
Niche, niĉo.
Nick (notch), tranĉeti.
Nickel, nikelo.
Nickname, moknomo.
Nicotine, nikotino.
Niece, nevino.
Niggard, avarulo.
Nigh, proksima.
Nigh (time), baldaŭa.
Night, nokto.
Nightly, nokta.
Night, by, nokte.
Nightingale,
najtingalo.
Night-watch, nokta
patrolo.
Nightmare, terursonĝo.
Nimble, vigla.
Nimbus, glorkrono.
Nine, naŭ.
Ninny, simplanimulo.
Nip, pinĉi.
Nippers, prenileto.
Nitre, salpetro.
Nobility, nobelaro.
Noble, nobla.
Nobleman, nobelo.
Nobleness, nobleco.
Nobody, neniu.
Nocturnal, nokta.
Nocuous, pereiga.
Nod (beckon),
signodoni.
No, ne.
No one, neniu.
Noise, bruo.
Noisome, naŭza,
malbonodora.
Noisy (of children),
petola.
Nomad, migranto.

Nomadic, migranta.
Nom-de-plume, pseŭdonomo.
Nomenclature, nomaro.
Nominal, nominala.
Nominative, nominativo.
Nonchalance, apatio.
Nonconformist, nekonformisto.
Nondescript, nepriskriba.
None, neniom.
Nonentity, neestaĵo.
Nonsense, sensencaĵo, malsaĝeco.
Non-success, malprospero.
Nook, anguleto.
Noon, tagmezo.
Noose, ligotubero.
Nor, nek.
Normal, normala.
North, nordo.
Northerly, norda.
Northern, norda.
Nose, nazo.
Nosebag, manĝujo.
Nosegay, bukedo.
Nostril, naztruo.
Not, ne.
Notable, fama, grava.
Notary, notario.
Note, noti, rimarki.
Note (music), noto.
Note (letter), letereto.
Notebook, notlibreto.
Note of exclamation, signo ekkria.
Note of interrogation, signo demanda.
Nothing, nenio.

Notice, rimarki.
Notice (public), surskribo.
Notice, avizo.
Notification, sciigo.
Notify, sciigi.
Notion, ekkono.
Notoriety, konateco.
Notorious, malglora.
Notwithstanding, tamen.
Nought, nulo.
Nought, nenio.
Noun, substantivo.
Nourish, nutri.
Nourishing, nutra.
Nourishment, nutraĵo.
Novel (romance), romano.
Novelty, novaĵo.
November, Novembro.
Novice, novulo.
Noviceship, noviceco.
Novitiate, provtempo.
Novitiate (place), novicejo.
Now, nun.
Nowadays, nuntempe.
Nowhere, nenie.
Noxious, malutila, venena.
Nozzle, nazeto.
Nude, nuda.
Nudity, nudeco.
Null, nuliga.
Nullify, nuligi.
Numb, rigidigi.
Numbness, rigideco.
Number (quantity), nombro.
Number, numero.
Numeral, numero.
Numerical, nombra.

Numerous, multa.
Numerously, multege.
Nun, monaĥino.
Nuncio, nuncio.
Nunnery, monaĥinejo.
Nuptial, edziĝa.
Nurse (a child), varti.
Nurse, nutristino.
Nurse, flegistino.
Nurse (hospital), malsanulistino.
Nurse (wet), suĉigistino.
Nurseling, suĉinfano.
Nursemaid, vartistino, infanistino.
Nursery (horticulture), plantejo, florkulturejo.
Nursery, infanĉambro.
Nurture, elnutri.
Nut, nukso.
Nut (of a screw), ŝraŭbingo.
Nutmeg, muskato.
Nutriment, nutraĵo.
Nutritious, nutra.
Nymph, nimfo.

O

Oaf, idiotulo.
Oak, kverko.
Oakum, stupo.
Oar, remilo.
Oasis, oazo.
Oath (legal), ĵuro.
Oath (curse), blasfemo.
Oatmeal, grio.
Obduracy, obstineco.
Obdurate, obstina.
Obedience, obeo.
Obedient, obea.

Obeisance, riverenco.
Obelisk, obelisko.
Obese, grasega.
Obesity, vastkorpeco.
Obey, obei.
Obituary, nekrologio.
Object (end, aim), celo.
Object, kontraŭparoli.
Object, objekto.
Objection, kontraŭparolo.
Objectionable, riproĉeblinda.
Objective (purpose), celo.
Oblation, ofero.
Obligation, devo.
Obligatory, deviga.
Oblige (compel), devigi.
Oblige (render service), fari komplezon.
Obliged, to be, devi.
Obliging, servema.
Oblique, oblikva.
Obliquity, oblikveco.
Obliterate, surstreki.
Oblivion, forgeso.
Oblivious, forgesa.
Oblong, longforma.
Obnoxious, ofendega.
Obscene, malbonmora, malĉasta.
Obscure, mallumigi.
Obscure, malhela.
Obscurity, senlumeco, mallumeco.
Obsequies, enterigiro.
Observance (rite), ceremonio—ado.
Observant, observema.

Observation,
observo—ado.
Observatory,
observatorio.
Observe (make a
remark), rimarki.
Observe (see), vidi.
Obsolete, troantikva.
Obstacle, baro,
kontraŭaĵo.
Obstinacy, obstineco.
Obstinate, to be,
obstini.
Obstinate, obstina.
Obstruct, obstrukci.
Obstruction, baro,
obstrukco.
Obtain, ricevi, atingi.
Obtrude, trudi.
Obtrusion, trudo—
eco.
Obtrusive, trudema.
Obtuse, malakra,
malinteligenta.
Obverse, antaŭa
flanko.
Obviate, malhelpi.
Obvious, videbla,
evidenta.
Occasion, okazo.
Occasional, okaza.
Occult, kaŝata.
Occupant, okupanto,
loĝanto.
Occupation, okupo.
Occupy, okupi.
Occupied with, to be,
okupiĝi pri.
Occur, okazi.
Occurrence, okazo.
Ocean, oceano.
Oceania, Oceanio.
Ochre, okro.

Octave, oktavo.
October, Oktobro.
Ocular, okula.
Ocularly, okule.
Oculist, okulisto.
Odd (peculiar),
stranga.
Odd (number), nepara.
Oddly, strange.
Ode, odo.
Odious, malaminda.
Odium, malamo.
Odour, odoro.
Odorous, odora.
Of, de.
Of (after noun of
measure, etc.), da.
Off, be! foriru!
Offence, peketo,
ofendo.
Offend, ofendi.
Offender, ofendanto.
Offensive, ofenda.
Offer (propose),
propono.
Offer (present),
prezenti.
Offer (sacrifice), oferi.
Offering, oferdono,
oferaĵo.
Offertory, mona
kolektado.
Office (divine),
Diservo.
Office (function),
ofico.
Office, printing,
presejo.
Office, oficejo.
Office, post, poŝta
oficejo.
Officer (military),
oficiro.

Officer, non-
commissioned,
suboficiro.
Official, oficisto.
Official, oficiala.
Officiate, agi.
Officious, agama.
Offspring, ido, idaro.
Often, ofte.
Oh! ho!
Oil, oleo.
Oilcloth, vakstolo.
Ointment, ŝmiraĵo.
Old (not new),
malnova.
Old (aged), maljuna.
Old, to grow,
maljuniĝi.
Old, to make,
maljunigi.
Old age, maljuneco.
Olden (time), antikva.
Oldness, malnoveco.
Oligarchy, oligarkio.
Olive, olivo.
Olive-shaped,
olivforma.
Olive tree, olivarbo.
Omelet, ovaĵo.
Omen, antaŭsigno.
Ominous, gravega.
Omission, formetado.
Omit, formeti, forigi.
Omnibus, omnibuso.
Omnipotent, ĉiopova.
Omnipresence,
ĉieesto.
Omniscient, ĉioscia.
On, sur.
Once, foje, unu fojon.
Once upon a time,
iam.
One, unu.

One day (sometime),
iam.
One-eyed, unuokula.
Oneness, unueco.
Onion, bulbo.
Only, nur.
Onset, atako.
Ontology, ontologio.
Onward, antaŭe, n.
Onyx, onikso.
Ooze, traguteti.
Opal, opalo.
Opaque, maldiafana.
Open, malfermi.
Open, to throw,
malfermegi.
Open (candid),
nekaŝema.
Open (uncork, etc.),
malŝtopi.
Open (of flowers),
ekflori.
Open-hearted,
malkovranima.
Openly, nekaŝeme,
tutkora.
Opera, opero.
Opera-glass, lorneto.
Opera-house, operejo.
Operate (surgery),
operacii.
Operate, funkcii.
Operatic, opera.
Operation, operacio.
Operative, metiisto.
Operative, agebla.
Operetta, opereto.
Opinion, to be of an,
opinii.
Opium, opio.
Opponent, kontraŭulo.
Opportune,
ĝustatempa.

136

Opportunity, okazo.
Oppose, kontraŭmeti,
kontraŭbatali.
Opposed to, to be,
kontraŭstari.
Opposite (in
opposition), kontraŭa.
Opposite facing),
kontraŭe.
Opposition,
kontraŭmeto—ado.
Oppress, subpremi.
Oppressor, tirano,
subpremanto.
Opprobrium,
malnobleco, malgloro.
Optics, optiko.
Optical, optika.
Optician, optikisto.
Optimism, optimismo.
Optimist, optimisto.
Option, elekto—aĵo.
Opulence, riĉeco.
Opulent, riĉa.
Opusculum, libreto,
broŝuro.
Or, aŭ.
Oracle, orakolo.
Oral, voĉa, parola.
Orange, oranĝo.
Orange (colour),
oranĝkolora.
Orangery, oranĝerio.
Oration, parolado.
Orator, oratoro,
parolisto.
Oratory (chapel),
preĝejeto.
Oratory, elokventeco.
Orchard, fruktarbejo.
Orchestra, orkestro.
Ordain, ordeni.
Ordeal, provo,

ekzameno.
Order, to put in,
ordigi.
Order (goods), mendi.
Order (command),
ordoni.
Orders (instructions),
instrukcio.
Order (for goods),
mendo.
Order (postal),
mandato.
Order (a decoration),
ordeno.
Order (arrangement),
ordo.
Orderly, orda.
Orderly (military),
servosoldato.
Ordinance, ordono.
Ordinary, kutima,
ordinara.
Ordnance, artilerio.
Ore, minaĵo.
Organ (music),
orgeno.
Organ, organo.
Organic, organa.
Organism, organismo.
Organize, organizi.
Organization,
organizo.
Orient, oriento.
Oriental, orienta.
Orifice, truo, buŝo.
Origin, deveno.
Original, originala.
Originate, devenigi—
iĝi.
Ornament, ornamo.
Ornament, ornami.
Ornaments (jewellery,
etc.), juvelaro.

Ornamentation, ornamaĵo.
Ornithology, ornitologio.
Orphan, orfo—ino.
Orphanage, orfejo.
Orthodox, ortodoksa.
Orthography, ortografio.
Ortolan, hortulano.
Oscillate, vibri, balanciĝi.
Osier, saliko.
Ossify, ostiĝi.
Ostensible, videbla.
Ostentation, fanfaronado, trudpompo.
Ostentatious, trudpompa.
Ostracism, ostracismo.
Ostrich, struto.
Other, alia.
Otherwise, alie, cetere.
Otter, lutro.
Ought (should), devus (devi).
Ounce, unco.
Our, ours, nia.
Oust, forpeli.
Out (prep.), ekster.
Out (prefix), el.
Outbid, plioferi, superoferi.
Outcast, ekzilo, elpelito.
Outcome, elveno.
Outer, ekstera.
Outermost, plejekstera.
Outfit, vestaro.
Outlaw, forpeli.
Outlaw, elpelito.

Outlay, elspezo.
Outlet, eliro.
Outline, skizo, konturo.
Outlive, postvivi.
Outpost, antaŭposteno.
Outrage, insultegi, perforti.
Outrage, perforto.
Outright, tute.
Outset, komenco.
Outskirts, ĉirkaŭaĵo.
Outside, ekstere.
Outstanding (unpaid), nepagita.
Oval, ovala.
Ovary, ovujo.
Ovation, laŭdado.
Oven, forno.
Over (above), super.
Overall, surtuto.
Overbearing, aŭtokrata, fierega.
Overcast, malklara, nuba.
Overcharge, supertakso.
Overcoat, supervesto.
Overcome, venki.
Overflow, superflui.
Overhaul (examine), ekzameni.
Overhead, supre.
Overlook (inspect), viziti, ekzameni, esplori.
Overlook (excuse), senkulpigi, pardoni.
Overlook, malatenti, malintenci.
Overplus, preteraĵo, plimultaĵo.
Overpower, venki,

submeti.
Overrun, enpenetri.
Overseer, observisto,
oficisto.
Overstep, transpaŝi.
Overtake, atingi.
Overthrow, renversi.
Overture (music),
uverturo.
Overture (proposal),
propono.
Overturn, renversi.
Overweening,
tromemfida.
Overwhelm, premegi.
Owe, ŝuldi.
Owl, strigo, gufo.
Own, propra.
Own (possess), posedi,
havi.
Owner (of property,
etc.), bienulo.
Ox, bovo.
Oxide, oksido.
Oxygen, oksigeno.
Oyster, ostro.

P

Pa, patreto, paĉjo.
Pace, paŝi.
Pace (step), paŝo.
Pacific, pacema.
Pacifically, pace,
paceme.
Pacification, pacigo.
Pacify, trankviligi,
pacigi.
Pachydermatous,
dikhaŭta.
Pack, paki.
Pack up, enpaki.
Pack (hounds),

hundaro.
Package, pakado,
pakaĵo.
Packer, pakisto.
Packet, pako—aĵo.
Packet-boat,
kurierŝipo.
Pack-saddle, ŝarĝselo.
Pad, vati.
Padding, vato—aĵo.
Paddle (to row),
remeti.
Paddock, kampeto.
Padlock, penda seruro.
Pagan, idolano.
Page-boy, paĝio,
lakeeto.
Page, paĝo.
Pageant, vidaĵo,
parado.
Pagoda, pagodo.
Pail, sitelo.
Pain, dolori.
Painful, dolora.
Painless, sendolora.
Paint, pentri, kolori.
Paint, kolorilo,
kolorigilo.
Paint (rouge), ruĝilo.
Painter (artist),
pentristo.
Painter (workman),
kolorigisto.
Painting (art),
pentrarto.
Painting, pentrado.
Painting (picture),
pentraĵo.
Pair, kunigi.
Pair, paro.
Palace, palaco.
Palanquin, palankeno.
Palate, palato.

Palatable, bongusta.
Pale, to become,
paliĝi.
Pale, pala.
Paleness, paleco.
Paleography,
paleografio.
Paleontology,
paleontologio.
Paletot, palto.
Paling, palisaro—aĵo.
Palisade, palisaro—
aĵo.
Pall, supersati.
Pall, ĉerkokovrilo.
Palliasse, pajla
matraco.
Pallid, palega.
Pallet, paletro.
Palm (of hand),
manplato.
Palm, palmobranĉo.
Palm-tree, palmarbo.
Palpable, palpebla.
Palpitate, korbati,
palpiti.
Palpitation, korbato—
ado.
Palsy, paralizeto.
Paltry, triviala.
Pamper, dorloti.
Pamphlet, pamfleto.
Pan, tervazo.
Pane, vitraĵo.
Panegyric, laŭdado.
Panegyrist, laŭdegisto.
Panel, enkadraĵo.
Pang, doloro.
Panic, teruro.
Pannier, korbego.
Pansy, violo.
Pant, spiregi.
Pantaloons, pantalono.

Pantheism, panteismo.
Pantheist, panteisto.
Panther, pantero.
Pantomime,
pantomimo.
Pantry, manĝaĵejo.
Pap, kaĉo.
Papa, patreto, paĉjo.
Papal, papa.
Paper, papero.
Paper-hanger,
paperkovristo,
tapetisto.
Paper-maker,
paperisto.
Paper-manufactory,
paperfarejo.
Paper-mill,
paperfarejo.
Paper-shop,
ĵurnalvendejo.
Papyrus, papiruso.
Parable, komparaĵo.
Parabola, parabolo.
Parade, paradi.
Parade (place),
promenejo.
Parade, vidaĵo,
luksaĵo.
Paradise, paradizo.
Paradox, paradokso.
Paragon,
perfektmodelo,
perfektaĵo.
Paragraph, paragrafo.
Parallel, paralela.
Paralyze, paralizi.
Paralysis, paralizo—
ado.
Paralytic, paralizito—
ulo.
Paramount, superega.
Paramour, kromviro—

ino.
Parapet, randmuro.
Paraphrase, parafrazo.
Parasite, parazito.
Parasitic, parazita.
Parasol, sunombrelo.
Parboil, duonboli.
Parcel, pako, pakaĵo.
Parcel out, dispecigi,
dividi.
Parcels-office,
pakaĵejo.
Parcel-post, poŝta
paketo.
Parch, sekigi.
Parchment,
pergameno.
Pardon, pardoni,
senkulpigi.
Pardon, pardono.
Pardonable,
pardonebla.
Pare, ŝeli.
Parenthesis, parentezo.
Parents, gepatroj.
Parentage, naskiĝo,
deveno.
Parental, gepatra.
Paring, ŝelo—aĵo.
Parish, paroĥo.
Parishioner, paroĥano.
Parish-priest,
paroĥestro.
Parity, egaleco.
Park, parko.
Parley, paroladi.
Parliament, house of,
parlamentejo.
Parliamentary,
parlamenta.
Parlour, parolejo.
Parochial, paroĥa.
Parody, parodio.

Parole, parolo je la
honoro.
Paroxysm, frenezo,
frenezado.
Parricide,
patromortiginto.
Parroquet, papageto.
Parrot, papago.
Parry, lerte eviti,
skermi.
Parsimony,
parcimonio.
Parsley, petroselo.
Parsnip, pastinako.
Parson, pastro.
Parsonage, pastra
domo.
Part, parto, porcio.
Part, on my part,
miaflanke.
Part, to depart, foriri.
Part, to separate,
disiĝi, malkuniĝi.
Partake, partopreni.
Parterre, florbedo.
Parterre (theatre),
partero.
Partial, partia.
Partiality, partieco.
Participant,
partoprenanto.
Participate, partopreni.
Participle, participo.
Particle, pecero,
pecereto.
Particular, speciala.
Partisan, partiano.
Partition, dividi.
Partition, divido,
partituro.
Partition-wall, maldika
muro.
Partly, parte.

141

Partner,
partoprenanto, kunulo.
Partridge, perdriko.
Party, partio.
Parvenu, elsaltulo.
Pass (intrans.), pasi.
Pass (trans.), pasigi.
Pass, to let, preterlasi.
Pass by, preteriri.
Pass on, preterpasi.
Pass over, across,
transpasi.
Pass through, trapasi.
Pass (passport),
pasporto.
Passable, nebona.
Passage (a way), aleo.
Passage, trairejo.
Passage (voyage),
vojiro, vojaĝo.
Passenger, vojaĝanto.
Passer-by, pasanto.
Passion, manio, pasio.
Passion, kolera,
kolerega, pasio.
Passionate, pasia,
kolerema.
Passive, pasiva.
Passport, pasporto.
Password, signaldiro.
Past, estinta.
Past, estinteco.
Paste, pasto.
Pasteboard, kartono.
Pastel, paŝtelo.
Pastille, pastelo.
Pastime, amuzaĵo.
Pastor, pastro.
Pastoral, kampa.
Pastry, pasteco.
Pastry-shop, kukejo.
Pasture, herbejo,
paŝtejo.

Pasturage, paŝtaĵo,
paŝtejo.
Pat, frapeti.
Patch, fliki.
Patchwork, flikaĵo.
Patella, genuosto.
Patent, patento.
Patentee, patentito.
Paternal, patra.
Paternity, patreco.
Path, vojo, vojeto.
Pathetic, kortuŝanta.
Pathology, patologio.
Pathos, patoso.
Patience, pacienco.
Patient, pacienca.
Patient, a,
malsanulo—ino.
Patois, provinca
lingvaĵo.
Patriarch, patriarko.
Patrimony, hereda
propraĵo.
Patriot, patrioto.
Patriotism,
patriotismo.
Patrol, patrolo.
Patrol (night), nokta
patrolo.
Patron, proktektanto,
patrono.
Patronage, protekto.
Patronize, favori,
protekti.
Patron saint, patrona
sanktulo.
Patrons (clients),
klientaro.
Patter, guteti.
Pattern, patrono,
modelo.
Paunch, ventro.
Pauper, malriĉulo,

almozulo.
Pause, paŭzo.
Pave, pavimi.
Pavement, pavimo.
Paving-stone,
pavimero.
Pavilion, tendo,
paviliono.
Paw, piedego.
Pawn (chess), soldato.
Pawn, garantiaĵo.
Pawnbroker, pruntisto.
Pawnbroker's,
pruntoficejo.
Pawn-office,
pruntoficejo.
Pay, pagi.
Pay (military), soldo.
Pay (in full), elpagi.
Payable, pagebla.
Payment (wages, etc.),
pago.
Pea, pizo.
Peace, paco.
Peace, to make, pacigi.
Peaceable, pacema.
Peaceably, pace.
Peaceful, pacema.
Peacefully, pace.
Peach, persiko.
Peacock, pavo.
Peak, pinto, pintaĵo.
Peak (of cap, etc.),
ŝirmileto.
Peal (of bells),
sonorilaro.
Pear, piro.
Pear-tree, pirarbo.
Pearl, perlo.
Pearl, mother of,
perlamoto.
Peasant, vilaĝano,
kamparano.

Peat, torfo.
Pebble, marŝtono,
ŝtoneto.
Peccadillo, peketo.
Peculiar, stranga.
Pecuniary, mona.
Pedagogue, pedagogo.
Pedagogy, pedagogio.
Pedal, pedalo.
Pedant, pedanto.
Peddler, kolportisto.
Peddle, kolporti.
Pedestal, piedestalo.
Pedestrian, piediranto.
Pedigree, deveno,
genealogio.
Pediment, fruntaĵo.
Peel (fruit, etc.), ŝelo.
Peel, senŝeligi.
Peep, rigardeti.
Peer, nobelo.
Peer, esplori, serĉi.
Peerage, nobelaro.
Peerless, senegala,
nekomparebla.
Peevish, malafabla,
ĉagrena.
Peevishness,
malafableco.
Peg (a hook), kroĉilo,
lignanajlo.
Peg, ŝtopileto.
Pelerine, manteleto.
Pelf, mono.
Pelican, pelikano.
Pelisse, pelto.
Pellet, kugleto, buleto.
Pellicle, membraneto.
Pell-mell, intermiksita,
e.
Pellucid, diafana.
Pelt, felo.
Pen, plumo.

143

Pen (to enclose),
barĉirkaŭi, enfermi.
Pen (sheep fold),
ŝafejo.
Pen-name,
pseŭdonomo.
Penal, puna.
Penal servitude,
punlaboro.
Penalty, puno,
monpuno.
Penance, to do,
pentofari.
Penance, puno.
Penchant, inklino—
emo.
Pencil (lead), krajono.
Pencil (slate), grifelo.
Pendant, pendaĵo.
Pendulum, pendolo.
Penetrate, penetri.
Penetrable, penetrebla.
Penetration, akra
sento.
Penholder, plumingo.
Peninsula, duoninsulo.
Penitence, pento.
Penitent, a,
konfesanto.
Penitent, penta.
Penitentiary,
pentfarejo.
Penknife, tranĉileto.
Pennant, flageto.
Penny, penco.
Penniless, senmona.
Pension, pensio.
Pensioner, pensiulo.
Pensive, pensa,
pensema.
Pentagon, kvinangulo.
Pentecost, pentekosto.
Penultimate,

antaŭlasta.
Penurious, avara.
Penury, malriĉeco.
Peony, peonio.
People, popolo, homoj.
Peopled, homhava.
Pepper, pipro.
Pepper-box, piprujo.
Pepper-caster, piprujo.
Peradventure, eble,
hazarde.
Perambulate, promeni,
trairi.
Perambulator,
infanveturilo.
Perceive (to see),
ekvidi.
Perceive, senti.
Percentage, procento.
Perceptible, palpebla,
sentebla.
Perception (by sight),
vido, videco.
Perception, sento.
Perch (for birds, etc.),
stango.
Perch (fish), perko.
Percolate, traguti.
Perdition, ruinego,
perdego.
Peremptory, absoluta.
Perennial, persista.
Perfect, perfektigi.
Perfect, perfekta.
Perfection, perfekteco.
Perfidious, perfida.
Perfidy, perfido,
perfideco.
Perforate, trabori,
trapiki.
Perform (to do),
efektivigi, fari.
Perform (fulfil),

plenumi.
Performer, faranto.
Perfume, parfumi.
Perfume, parfumo,
odoro.
Perfumer, parfumisto.
Perfumery (manufactor
y), parfumfarado.
Perhaps, eble.
Perigee, perigeo.
Peril, danĝero.
Perimeter, perimetro,
ĉirkaŭmetro.
Period, periodo.
Periodic—al, perioda.
Periodicity, periodeco.
Periphrase,
ĉirkaŭfrazo.
Periphery, ĉirkaŭo,
periferio.
Perish, perei.
Perishable, pereema.
Peristyle, peristilo.
Peritoneum, peritoneo.
Periwig, peruko.
Periwinkle (plant),
vinko.
Perjury, ĵurrompo.
Permanent, konstanta,
daŭra.
Permeable, penetrebla.
Permission, permeso.
Permissive, permesa.
Permit, permesi.
Permutation,
interŝanĝo.
Pernicious, pereiga.
Perpendicular,
perpendikulara.
Perpetrate, elfari.
Perpetual, eterna.
Perpetuate, daŭrigi.
Perplex, konfuzi,

ĉagrenegi.
Perplexity, konfuzeco,
ŝanceliĝo.
Perron, perono.
Perruquier, perukisto.
Persecute, persekuti.
Persecution,
persekutado.
Perseverance, persisto.
Persevere, persisti.
Persist, persisti.
Persistance, persisto—
ado.
Persistent, persista.
Persistency, persisteco.
Person, persono.
Personage, persono.
Personal, persona.
Personality,
personeco.
Personate, reprezenti.
Personate, personiĝi,
imiti.
Personification,
personiĝo.
Perspective,
perspektivo.
Perspicuous, sagaca.
Perspicacity, sagaceco.
Perspiration, ŝvito.
Perspire, ŝviti.
Persuade, konvinki.
Persuasive, konvinka.
Pert, malrespekta.
Pertinacious, trudpeta.
Pertinacity, obstineco,
persisteco.
Perturb, konfuzi,
turmenteti.
Perturbation,
turmentado.
Peruke, peruko.
Perusal, legado.

145

Peruse, legadi, ellegi.
Pervade, penetri.
Perverse, obstina, kontraŭa.
Pervert, malkonverti, malverigi.
Perversion, malkonverto, malverigo, malveriĝo.
Pervious, penetrebla.
Pest, pesto.
Pester, enui, turmenteti.
Pestiferous, pesta.
Pestilence, pesto.
Pestilential, pesta, pestiga.
Pestle, pistilo.
Pet, dorloti.
Petal, florfolieto.
Petard, petardo.
Petition, petegi.
Petition, petskribo.
Petrify, ŝtonigi.
Petroleum, petrolo.
Petticoat, subjupo.
Pettish, malĝentila.
Petty, malgranda.
Petulance, petoleco.
Petulant, petola.
Pew, preĝbenko.
Pewter, stano.
Phantom, apero, fantomo.
Pharmacist, farmaciisto.
Pharmacy (place), farmaciejo, apoteko.
Pharmacy (science), farmacio.
Pharos, lumturo.
Pharynx, faringo.
Phase, fazo.

Pheasant, fazano.
Pheasantry, fazanejo.
Phenomenon, fenomeno.
Phial, boteleto.
Philanthropist, filantropo.
Philanthropy, filantropeco.
Philatelic, filatela.
Philatelist, filatelisto.
Philately, filatelo.
Philologist, filologiisto.
Philology, filologio.
Philosopher, filozofo.
Philosophise, filozofii.
Philosophy, filozofio.
Phlegm, flegmo, muko.
Phlegmatic, flegma.
Phoenix, fenikso.
Phonetic, fonetika.
Phonograph, fonografo.
Phosphorus, fosforo.
Photograph, fotografaĵo.
Photographer, fotografisto.
Photography, fotografarto.
Phrase, frazero.
Phraseology, frazeologio.
Phthisis, ftizo.
Phthisical, ftiza.
Physic, kuracilo.
Physical, fizika.
Physician, fizikisto, kuracisto.
Physics, naturscienco, fiziko.

Physiognomy,
fizionomio.
Physiology, fiziologio.
Piano, fortepiano.
Piaster, piastro.
Pick (choose), elekti.
Pick (implement),
pikfosilo.
Pickaxe, pikfosilo.
Picket (military),
pikedo.
Pickle (to salt), pekli.
Pickle (liquid),
peklakvo.
Pickpocket, fripono.
Picnic, kampfesteno.
Picquet (cards),
pikedo.
Pictorial, ilustrita.
Picture, pentraĵo.
Picturesque, pentrinda.
Pie, pasteĉo.
Piebald, multkolora.
Piece (to patch), fliki.
Piece, peco.
Piecemeal, peco post
peco.
Pier (pillar),
pontkolono.
Pier (landing place),
enŝipigejo.
Pierce, trabori, penetri.
Piety, pieco.
Pig, porko.
Pigeon, kolombo.
Pigeon-hole (for
papers, etc.), faketaro.
Pigeon-house,
kolombejo.
Pigmy, pigmeo.
Pike (fish), ezoko.
Pike (tool), pikilego.
Pike (weapon),

ponardego.
Pile up, amasigi.
Pile (logs), ŝtiparo.
Pile (support), paliso,
subteno.
Pile (heap), amaso—
aĵo.
Pile (electric), elektra
pilo.
Piles, hemorojdo.
Pilfer, ŝteleti.
Pilferer, ŝtelisto.
Pilgrim, pilgrimanto.
Pilgrimage,
pilgrimo—ado.
Pill, pilolo.
Pillage, rabegi—ado.
Pillar, kolono.
Pillory, punejo.
Pillow, kapkuseno.
Pillow-case,
kusentego.
Pilot, piloto, gvido.
Pimple, akno.
Pin, pinglo.
Pince-nez, nazumo.
Pincers, prenilo.
Pinch, pinĉi.
Pinch (of snuff, etc.),
preneto.
Pine (languish),
konsumiĝi.
Pine away (plants,
etc.), sensukiĝi.
Pining, sopiranta.
Pineapple, ananaso.
Pine tree, pinarbo.
Pinion (feather),
plumaĵo, flugilo.
Pinion (to bind), ligi.
Pink (flower), dianto.
Pink (color), rozkolora.
Pinnacle, pinto, supro.

Pioneer, pioniro.
Pious, pia.
Pip (disease in birds),
pipso.
Pip (of fruit), grajno.
Pipe (tube), tubo,
tubeto.
Pipe (for tobacco),
pipo.
Piquancy, pikeco.
Piquant, pika.
Pique, ofendi.
Piracy, marrabo—ado.
Pirate, marrabisto.
Piscina, naĝejo.
Pistil (botany), pistilo.
Pistol, pafileto.
Piston, piŝto.
Pit (well, etc.), puto,
fosaĵo, kavo.
Pit (theatre), partero.
Pitch (to smear with),
kalfatri.
Pitch, peĉo.
Pitch (of ships),
subakviĝi.
Pitcher, kruĉo.
Pitchfork, forkego.
Piteous, kompatinda.
Pitfall, enfalujo.
Pith, suko.
Pitiable, kompatinda.
Pitiful, kompatinda.
Pitiless, senkompata.
Pity, kompati, bedaŭri.
Pity, it is a, estas
domaĝo.
Pivot, akso.
Placable, kvietebla,
kvietema.
Placard, afiŝo,
kartego.
Place (to put), meti.

Place, loko.
Place, a public, placo.
Place of abode,
restadejo.
Placid, kvieta.
Plagiarist,
verkoŝtelisto.
Plague, pesto—ego.
*Plague-
stricken* (person),
pestulo.
Plain, malbela.
Plain, senornama.
Plainly, simple, klare.
Plainness, simpleco.
Plaint, plendo.
Plaintive, plenda.
Plait (with straw),
pajloplekti.
Plait, plekti.
Plait, plektaĵo.
Plait (hair), harligo.
Plan, plano.
Plan (geometrical),
plato.
Plane, raboti.
Plane (tool), rabotilo.
Planet, planedo.
Plank, tabulo.
Plant, planti.
Plant, kreskaĵo.
Plantation, plantejo.
Plaster, plastro, gipso.
Plastron,
brustoŝirmilo.
Plate, stanumi.
Plate, telero.
Plate (stereotype),
kliŝaĵaro, kliŝaĵo.
Plateau, plataĵo.
Platform, plataĵo,
estrado.
Platinum, plateno.

Platitude, plateco.
Platter, pladego.
Plaudit, aplaŭdego.
Plausible, verŝajna, aprobebla.
Play (a game), ludi.
Play (piano, etc.), ludi.
Play about, ludeti, petoli.
Play (joke), ŝerci.
Play (theatrical), teatraĵo.
Player, ludanto.
Playful, petola.
Playhouse (theatre), teatro.
Plaything, ludilo.
Playtime, ludtempo.
Plead, procesi, proparoladi.
Pleasant, plaĉa.
Pleasant (manner), dolĉega.
Please, plaĉi.
Please, if you, se vi bonvolas, se plaĉos al vi.
Pleasure, to give, plaĉi.
Pleasure, with, plezure.
Plebeian, malnobelo.
Pledge, garantiaĵo.
Plenitude, pleneco.
Plenteous, sufiĉega.
Plenty, sufiĉa, sufiĉega.
Pleonasm, pleonasmo.
Pliable, fleksebla.
Pliant, fleksebla.
Pliantness, fleksebleco.
Pliers, prenilo—eto.

Plod on, diligentiĝi.
Plot, konspiri, intrigi.
Plot (league), intrigo, konspiro.
Plot (of land), terpeco.
Plough, plugi.
Plough, plugilo.
Ploughshare, plugfero.
Pluck (fowl), plumtiregi, senplumigi.
Pluck (courage), kuraĝo.
Plug, ŝtopilego.
Plum, pruno.
Plumage, plumaro, plumaĵo.
Plumbago, grafito.
Plumber, plumbisto.
Plume, plumfasko.
Plummet, sondilo.
Plump, dika.
Plumpness, dikeco.
Plunder, rabadi.
Plunge, subakviĝi.
Plural, multenombro
Plush, pluŝo.
Poach, ĉasoŝteli.
Poach (eggs, etc.), boleti.
Poacher, ĉasoŝtelisto.
Pocket, poŝo.
Pod, ŝelo.
Poem, poemo.
Poesy, poezio.
Poet, poeto.
Poetize, versi.
Poetry, poezio, poeziaĵo.
Poetry, a piece of, versaĵo.
Poignant, dolorega.
Point, punkto.
Point (cards), poento.

Point (tip of), pinto.
Point (to sharpen), pintigi.
Point out, montri, signali.
Points (railway), relforko.
Poise, balanci, ekvilibri.
Poison, veneno.
Poisonous, venena.
Poke the fire, inciti la fajron.
Poker, fajrincitilo.
Polar, polusa.
Pole (wooden), stango.
Pole (shaft of car), timono.
Pole (geography), poluso.
Polecat, putoro.
Polemic, disputo, polemiko.
Police, polico.
Policeman, policano.
Polish, poluri.
Polish (substance), polurajô.
Polished (manners), ĝentila.
Polite, ĝentila.
Politic, saĝa.
Political, politika.
Politician, politikisto.
Politics, politiko.
Poll (vote), voĉdoni, baloti.
Poll (of head), verto.
Pollen, florsemo.
Pollute, malpurigi.
Poltroon, timulo—egulo.
Poltroonery, timeco—egeco.
Polygon, multangulo.
Polyp, polipo.
Polypus, polipo.
Polytechnic, politekniko, a.
Pomade, pomado.
Pomatum, pomado.
Pomegranate, pomgranato.
Pompous, pompa.
Pond, lageto.
Ponder, pripensi, reveti.
Ponderous, multepeza.
Poniard, ponardo.
Pontiff, ĉefpastro.
Pontoon, boatoponto.
Pony, ĉevaleto.
Poodle, pudelo.
Pool, marĉlageto.
Poop, posta parto.
Poor, malriĉa.
Pope, papo.
Poplar, poplo—arbo.
Poppy, papavo.
Poppy-coloured, punca.
Populace, popolo—amaso.
Popular, populara.
Population, loĝantaro.
Populous, popola.
Porcelain, porcelano.
Porch, vestiblo.
Porcupine, histriko.
Pore, trueto.
Pork, porkajô.
Porous, trueta.
Porphyry, porfiro.
Porpoise, fokseno.
Port (harbour), haveno.

150

Portable, portebla.
Portend, antaŭsciigi.
Porter (doorkeeper),
pordisto.
Porter, portisto.
Portfolio, paperujo.
Portion (allot), dividi.
Portion, porcio, parto,
doto.
Portmanteau, valizo,
vestkesto.
Portrait, portreto.
Portraiture (art),
pentrarto.
Position (place), loko.
Position, situacio.
Positive, pozitiva.
Possess, posedi.
Possessive, poseda.
Possessor, posedanto.
Possible, to render,
ebligi.
Possible, ebla.
Possibility, ebleco.
Possibly, eble.
Post (military),
posteno.
Post (wooden pole),
stango, fosto.
Post (position), ofico.
Post (letters, etc.),
poŝto.
Postal, poŝta.
Postcard, poŝtkarto.
Postman, poŝtisto,
leteristo.
Post-office, poŝta
oficejo.
Poster (placard), afiŝo,
kartego.
Poste-restante,
poŝtrestante.
Posterior, posta,

malantaŭ.
Posterity, idaro,
posteularo.
Postillion, kondukisto.
Postscript,
postskribaĵo.
Postulate, petado.
Posture, teniĝo.
Pot, poto.
Potash, potaso.
Potato, terpomo.
Potency, potenco.
Potent, potenca.
Potential, potencebla,
poviga.
Potter, potisto.
Pottery (art),
potfarado.
Pottery, a, potfarejo.
Pouch, saketo.
Poultice, kataplasmo.
Poultry, kortbirdaro.
Poultry-yard,
kortbirdejo.
Pound (grind), pisti.
Pound (money), livro.
Pound (weight), funto.
Pour out (liquids),
verŝi.
Pour out, ŝuti.
Pout, kolereti.
Poverty, malriĉeco.
Powder (hair, etc.),
pudri.
Powder (gun), pulvo.
Powder, pulvro, pudro.
Power, povo, potenco.
Power (of attorney),
konfidatesto.
Powerful, multepova.
Powerless, senpotenca.
Practical, praktika.
Practice (custom),

151

kutimo.
Practice, praktiko, kutimo, uzado.
Practise, praktiki.
Prairie, herbejo.
Praise, laŭdi.
Prank, petoleco—aĵo.
Prate, babili.
Prattle, babili.
Pray (religious), preĝi.
Pray (to request), peti.
Prayer, preĝo.
Prayer-book, preĝlibro.
Preach, prediki.
Preacher, predikisto.
Preaching, predikado.
Preamble, antaŭparolo.
Prebendary, kanoniko.
Precarious, duba, necerta.
Precaution, antaŭzorgo, singardo.
Precede, antaŭiri.
Precedence, antaŭeco.
Precedent, antaŭaĵo.
Precentor, kantoro.
Precept, ordono.
Preceptor, guvernisto.
Precinct, limo.
Precious, multekosta.
Precipice, krutegaĵo.
Precipitancy, trorapideco.
Precipitate, trorapida.
Precipitation, trorapideco.
Precise, preciza.
Precisely, ĝuste.
Precision, precizeco, akurateco.
Preclude, eksigi, malhelpi.

Precocious, frumatura.
Precocity, frumaturo—eco.
Precursor, antaŭulo.
Predatory, rabadega.
Predecessor, antaŭulo.
Predestination, sortdifino.
Predetermination, antaŭdecido.
Predict, antaŭdiri, profetadi.
Prediction, antaŭdiro.
Predisposition, inklino.
Predominate, superregi.
Preface, antaŭparolo.
Prefect, prefekto.
Prefer, preferi.
Preferable, preferinda.
Preferably, prefere.
Preference, prefero.
Prefix, prefikso.
Pregnancy, gravedeco.
Pregnant, graveda.
Prehension, preno.
Prehistoric, pratempa.
Prejudice, antaŭjuĝo.
Prejudge, antaŭjuĝi.
Prejudicial, malutila.
Prelate, episkopo, ĉef—.
Preliminary, antaŭafero, antaŭpreparo.
Prelude, antaŭludaĵo.
Premature, antaŭtempa.
Premeditate, pripensi.
Premeditation, pripensado.
Premier, ĉefa, unua.

Premises, propreco—ajo.
Premium, at a, premie.
Premium (reward), premio.
Premonitory, antaŭsciiga.
Pre-occupation, priokupado.
Prepare, prepari, pretigi.
Preparation, preparo—ado.
Prepay, antaŭpagi, afranki.
Preponderance, superrego.
Preposition, prepozicio.
Presage, antaŭsigno.
Presbyter, pastro.
Presbytery, pastrejo.
Prescribe, ordoni.
Prescription (med.), recepto.
Presence, apudesto, ĉeesto.
Present, to be, ĉeesti, apudesti.
Present, to make a, donaci.
Present, prezenti.
Present (gift), donaco.
Present (time), nuntempa, estanteco.
Present, at, nune.
Presentative, donaco, prezento.
Presentiment, antaŭsento.
Presently, tuj.
Preserve (jam, etc.), konservi.

Preserve, antaŭgardi.
Preservation, antaŭzorgo.
Preservative, antaŭgardo—ado.
Preside, prezidi.
President, prezidanto.
Press (squeeze), premi.
Press (machine), premilo.
Press (newspapers), gazetaro.
Press forward, antaŭiri.
Press-gang, varbigistaro.
Pressure, premo—ado.
Pressing (urgent), neprokrastebla, urĝa.
Presumably, supozeble.
Presume, supozi.
Presumption, tromemfideco, tromemfido.
Presumptuous, tromemfida.
Pretence, preteksto.
Pretend (to claim), pretendi.
Pretend, preteksti.
Pretend (to feign), ŝajnigi.
Pretentious, afektema.
Preternatural, supernatura, preternatura.
Pretext, preteksto.
Pretty, beleta.
Prevail, superi.
Prevalent, ĝenerala, rega.
Prevaricate, malveriĝi.

153

Prevent, malhelpi, eksigi.
Previous, antaŭa.
Prey, kaptaĵo.
Price, prezo, kosto.
Price—current, prezaro.
Priceless (valuable), senpreza, netaksebla.
Price lists, prezaro.
Prick, piki.
Prick, pikilo.
Prickly, pika.
Pride, malhumileco, fiereco.
Priest, pastro.
Priesthood, pastreco.
Prim, afekta, preciza.
Primary, elementa, unua.
Primeval, primitiva.
Primitive, primitiva, originala.
Primrose, primolo.
Prince, reĝido, princo.
Principal, estro, ĉefo.
Principal, precipa.
Principality, princlando.
Principle, principo.
Print, presi.
Print (picture), gravuraĵo.
Printer, presisto, preslaboristo.
Printed matter, presaĵo.
Printing-press, presilo.
Prior (title), ĉefabato.
Prior, antaŭa.
Priority, antaŭeco.
Prism, prismo.
Prison, malliberejo.

Prisoner, malliberulo.
Prisoner of war, militkaptito.
Private, privata.
Privateer, marrabisto.
Privation, senigo.
Privilege, privilegio.
Privily, sekrete.
Prize, premio.
Prize, ŝati.
Probable, kredinda—ebla.
Probability, kredebleco, kredindeco, iĝebleco.
Probation, provtempo.
Probationer, novico.
Probe, sondi, esplori.
Probity, honesteco.
Problem, problemo.
Proboscis, rostro.
Proceed, procedi.
Proceedings (law), proceso—ado.
Proceeding, procedo.
Procession, procesio.
Process, procedo, rimedo.
Proclaim, proklami.
Procrastinate, prokrasti.
Procure, havigi.
Procuration, konfidatisto.
Prodigal, malŝpara.
Prodigality, malŝparemo.
Prodigious, mireginda.
Prodigy, miregindaĵo.
Produce, produkti.
Produce, produktaĵo.
Product, produktaĵo.
Production, produkto.

Productive,
fruktoporta.
Proem, antaŭdramo,
antaŭdiro.
Profanation,
malpiegaĵo.
Profane, malpia.
Profanity, malpieco.
Profess, anonci,
profesi.
Profession (occupation
), profesio.
Professor, profesoro.
Proffer, proponi,
prezenti.
Proficient,
kompetenta.
Profile, profilo.
Profit, profito, gajno.
Profitable, profita.
Profligate, diboĉulo.
Profound (deep),
profunda.
Profound (learned),
lernega, klerega.
Profundity,
profundeco.
Profuse, sufiĉega,
supermezura.
Progeny, ido, idaro.
Prognostic,
antaŭsigno.
Programme,
programo.
Progress, progreso.
Progression,
progresado.
Prohibit, malpermesi.
Prohibition,
malpermeso.
Project (protrude),
elstari.
Project, projekto.

Projectile, ĵetaĵo,
pafaĵo.
Proletarian, proletaria,
o.
Prolific, multinfana,
fruktoporta.
Prolix, trolonga.
Prologue,
antaŭskribaĵo,
antaŭverko.
Prolong, plilongigi.
Promenade, promeni.
Promenade (act),
promenado.
Promenade (place),
promenejo.
Prominent, eminenta,
rimarkinda.
Promiscuous, miksa,
konfuza.
Promise, promesi.
Promontory,
promontoro.
Promote (advance),
antaŭenigi.
Promoter, iniciatoro.
Prompt (quick), rapida.
Prompter,
memorigisto.
Promptitude, rapideco.
Promptly, rapide, tuj.
Promulgate, publikigi.
Promulgation,
publikigado, sciigado.
Prone (inclined to),
inklina, ema.
Prone (downward),
terenkuŝa.
Proneness, emo,
inklino.
Prong, forkego.
Pronominal, pronoma.
Pronoun, pronomo.

155

Pronounce, elparoli.
Pronunciation, elparolado.
Proof (for press), presprovaĵo.
Proof, pruvo, provo.
Prop, subtenaĵo, subteno.
Propaganda, propagando.
Propagandism, propagandismo.
Propagate, propagandi.
Propel, antaŭen puŝi, irigi.
Propensity, emo, inklino.
Proper (exact), ĝusta.
Proper, konvena.
Property, propreco, posedaĵo.
Prophecy, profetaĵo.
Prophesy, profetaĵi.
Prophet, profeto.
Propinquity, proksimeco.
Propitiate, favorigi, trankviligi.
Propitious, favora.
Proportional, proporcia.
Proposal, propono.
Propose, proponi.
Proposition, propono.
Proposition (gram.), propozicio.
Proprietor, posedanto.
Propriety, konveneco.
Pro rata, proporcie.
Prorogue, prokrasti.
Prosaic, proza.
Proscribe, ekzili.

Prose, prozo, prosaĵo.
Prosecute, persekuti.
Proselyte, prozelito.
Prospect, vidaĵo.
Prospective, antaŭvida, estonta.
Prospectus, prospekto.
Prosper, prosperi.
Prosperity, prospereco.
Prosperous, prospera.
Prostrate (one's self), terenkuŝiĝi.
Prosy, teda.
Protect, protekti.
Protection, protekto.
Protector, protektanto, zorganto.
Protectorate, protektorato.
Protégé, protektato.
Protest, protesti.
Protestation, protestado.
Protestant, protestanto.
Protocol, protokolo.
Protrude, elstari.
Protuberance, ŝvelaĵo.
Proud, to be, fieriĝi.
Proud, fiera, vanta.
Prove, pruvi, konstati.
Provender, bestnutraĵo.
Proverb, proverbo.
Provide, provizi.
Provided that, se nur.
Providence, antaŭzorgo, singardemo.
Provident, zorgema, ŝparema.
Province, provinco.
Provincial, provincano.

Provision, provizaĵo, manĝaĵo.
Provisional, provizora.
Provocation, incitego—ado.
Provoke, incitegi.
Prow, antaŭa parto.
Prowess, valoreco, kuraĝegeco.
Prowl, vagi.
Proximate, proksima, apuda.
Proximity, proksimeco, apudeco.
Proxy, anstataŭulo.
Prudence, singardemo.
Prudent, singardema, prudenta.
Prune, ĉirkaŭhaki.
Prune, seka pruno.
Pruning shears, branĉotondilo.
Prussian, a, Pruso.
Prussic acid, ciana acido.
Pry, serĉi, rigardeti.
Psalm, psalmo.
Psalmody, psalmokantado.
Psalter, psalmaro.
Pseudonym, pseŭdonomo.
Psychology, psikologio.
Puberty, viriĝo.
Public, publika.
Publican, drinkejmastro.
Public-house, drinkejo.
Publicity, publikigo, publikigeco.
Publish, publikigi, eldoni.

Puerile, infana.
Puff, blovi.
Puff up, plenblovi.
Pug-dog, mopseto.
Pull, tiri.
Pull out, eltiri.
Pull together, kuntiri.
Pullet, kokidino.
Pulley, rulbloko.
Pulmonary, pulma.
Pulmonic person, ftizulo.
Pulp, molaĵo.
Pulpit, tribuno, predikseĝo.
Pulsation, pulsbatado.
Pulse, pulso.
Pulverize, pulvorigi.
Pump, pumpi.
Pump, pumpilo.
Pumice-stone, pumiko.
Pumpkin, kukurbo.
Punch (drink), punĉo.
Punch and Judy, pulĉinelo.
Punctilious, precizema.
Punctual, ĝustatempa, akurata.
Punctuality, akurateco.
Punctuate, interpunkcii.
Punctuation, interpunkcio.
Puncture, trapiki.
Pungent, pika, morda.
Punish, puni.
Punishment, puno—ado.
Puny, malgranda, malfortika.
Pupil (scholar), lernanto.

Pupil (of eye), pupilo.
Puppet, pupo,
marioneto.
Puppy, hundido.
Purchase, aĉeti.
Pure (clean), pura.
Pure (morals), virta.
Purée, pistaĵo.
Purgative, laksilo,
laksigilo.
Purgatory, purgatorio.
Purge, laksigi.
Purify, purigi.
Puritan, Puritano.
Purity, pureco.
Purloin, ŝteli.
Purple, purpura.
Purpose, celi, intenci.
Purpose (end, aim),
celo.
Purr, bleketi,
murmureti.
Purse, monujo.
Pursue, forpeladi,
postesekvi.
Purveyor, liveranto.
Pus, puso—aĵo.
Push, puŝi.
Push through, trapuŝi.
Pusillanimous,
timema.
Pustule, pustulo.
Put, meti.
Put aside, apartigi.
Put on airs, afekti.
Put away, formeti,
forigi.
Put down, demeti.
Put instead of,
anstataŭigi.
Put in order, reguligi,
ordigi.
Put right, rektigi.

Put up with, suferi,
toleri.
Putrefaction, putraĵo.
Putrescence, putro—
eco.
Putrify, putrigi.
Putty, mastiko.
Puzzle, enigmo.
Pyramid, piramido.
Python, serpentego,
pitono.

Q

Quack (duck),
anasbleki.
Quack, ĉarlatano.
Quackery,
ĉarlatanismo.
Quadrangle,
kvarangulaĵo.
Quadrant, kvadranto.
Quadrate, kvadrato.
Quadrate, kvadrata.
Quadratic, kvadrata.
Quadrature,
kvadrato.
Quadrille, kvadrilo.
Quadruped,
kvarpieda.
Quadruple, kvarobla.
Quaff, glutegi.
Quaggy, marĉa.
Quagmire, marĉejo.
Quail (bird), koturno.
Quail, tremi.
Quaint, stranga.
Quake, tremi—egi.
Qualification, eco,
kvaliteco.
Qualify, kvalitigi,
ecigi.
Quality, eco, kvalito.

Qualm, konscidubo.
Quandary, embaraso.
Quantity, kvanto.
Quarrel, malpaco.
Quarrel, malpaci.
Quarry, ŝtonejo.
Quarter (1/4), kvarono.
Quarter (district), kvartalo.
Quarterly, trimonata.
Quartern, kvarono, kvaronujo.
Quartet, kvarteto.
Quartz, kvarco.
Quash (repress), premegi.
Quash (annul), senigi, nuligi.
Quaver, trilo.
Quay, surbordo, bordmarŝejo.
Queen, reĝino.
Queer, stranga.
Quell, trankviligi.
Quench (extinguish), estingi.
Quench (thirst), kvietigi.
Querulous, malkontenta.
Query, demando.
Query, ĉu?
Quest, serĉo.
Quest, informiĝo.
Question, demando.
Question, demandi.
Question (doubt), dubi.
Questionable, duba.
Quibble, ĉikani.
Quick (adj.), rapida.
Quick (adv.), rapide.

Quick (living), viva.
Quicken, vivigi.
Quicken, rapidigi.
Quicksilver, hidrargo.
Quiescence, ripozo, kvieteco.
Quiet, kvieta.
Quiet, kvietigi.
Quietude, trankvileco.
Quill, plumo.
Quilt, litkovrilo.
Quintal, centfunto.
Quip, sarkasmo.
Quit, lasi.
Quit, kvita.
Quite, tute.
Quittance, kvitanco.
Quiver, sagujo.
Quoin, kojno.
Quoit, disko, luddisko.
Quorum, kvorumo.
Quota, parto, porcio.
Quotation, cito.
Quote, citi.
Quoth, diras, diris.
Quotient, dividrezultato.

R

Rabbi, Rabbin, rabeno.
Rabbit, kuniklo.
Rabble, kanajlaro.
Rabid, rabia.
Rabies, rabio.
Raccoon, prociono.
Race (species), raso.
Race, to run a, fari kurson.
Racecourse,

hipodromo.

Rack, hay, fojnujo.

Racket (noise), bruego.

Racy, sprita.

Radiant, radiluma.

Radiate, radii—igi.

Radical (grammar),
radiko.

Radical, Radikalo.

Radicalism,
radikalismo.

Radish, horse, rafano.

Radish, rafaneto.

Radius, radio.

Raffle, ludloto.

Raft, floso.

Rafter, tegmenttrabo.

Rag, ĉifono.

Rag-picker, ĉifonisto.

Ragamuffin, bubo.

Rage, to be in a,
koleregi.

Rage, kolerego.

Ragged, ĉifona.

Ragout, spicaĵo.

Rail (to scoff), moki.

Rail off, bari.

Rail (railway), relo.

Raillery, mokado.

Railroad, fervojo.

Railway, fervojo.

Railway Station,
stacidomo.

Raiment, vestaĵo.

Rain, pluvo.

Rainbow, ĉielarko.

Raise, levi, plialtigi.

Raise up, altlevi.

Raisin, sekvinbero.

Rake, rasti.

Rake (implement),
rastilo.

Rake (a profligate),

diboĉulo, malĉastulo.

Rally (gather together),
kolekti.

Rally (to banter), moki.

Ram, ŝafoviro.

Ram (a gun), ŝtopi.

Ramble, vagi.

Ramble (in speech),
paroli sensence.

Rampart, remparo,
murego.

Rancid, ranca.

Rancour, malameco.

Random, at, hazarde.

Range (put in order),
aranĝi.

Rank (a row), vico.

Rank (dignity), rango.

Ransom, reaĉeti.

Ransom, reaĉeti.

Rant, paroli sensence.

Ranunculus,
ranunkolo.

Rap, frapeti.

Rap, frapo, frapeto.

Rapacious, rabema.

Rapacity, rabemeco.

Rape, forrabo.

Rapid, rapida.

Rapidity, rapideco.

Rapidly, rapide.

Rapier, rapiro.

Rapine, rabo.

Rapt, rava, entuziasma.

Rapture, ravo,
entuziasmo.

Rare (seldom),
malofta.

Rare (curious),
kurioza.

Rare, antikva.

Rarely, malofte.

Rareness, malofteco.

Rarity, malofteco.
Rarity (dainty), frandaĵo.
Rascal, kanajlo.
Rase, disĵeti.
Rash, hazarda.
Rashness, hazardeco.
Rasp, raspi.
Rasp (a tool), raspilo.
Raspberry, frambo.
Rat, rato.
Rate, procento.
Rate of, at the, po.
Rate (estimate), taksi.
Rather, plivole.
Ratify, aprobi.
Ratio, proporcio.
Ration, porcio.
Rational, racionala.
Rationalism, racionalismo.
Rationalist, racionalisto.
Rattle (a toy), kraketilo.
Rattlesnake, sonserpento.
Raucous, raŭka.
Ravage (lay waste), ruinigi.
Rave, deliri, paroli sensence.
Ravel, maltordi.
Raven, korvo.
Ravenous, englutema.
Ravine, intermontaĵo.
Ravishing (delightful), rava.
Raw (chilly), freŝa, frosta.
Raw (uncooked), nekuirita.
Raw (without skin),
senhaŭta.
Raw material, kruda.
Ray (of light), radio.
Razor, razilo.
Re, again (prefix), re.
Reach to, atingi.
React, kontraŭbatali—agi.
Read, legi.
Reader, leganto.
Reader (for press), preskorektisto.
Readily, volonte.
Reading, legado.
Ready, preta.
Ready money, kontanto.
Real, vera, reala.
Reality, realeco.
Reality, in, vere, efektive.
Really, vere, efektive.
Realise (finan.), efektivigi.
Realise (comprehend), kompreni.
Realm, reĝolando, reglando.
Ream (paper), rismo.
Re-animate, revivigi.
Re-arrange, rearanĝi.
Re-ascend, resupreniri.
Re-assure, rekuraĝigi.
Reap, rikolti.
Rear (bring up), elnutri.
Rear (hinder part), posta parto.
Rear-guard, postgvardio.
Reason (faculty), racio.
Reason (cause), kaŭzo.
Reason, rezoni.

Reason, for some, ial.
Reason, for any, ial.
Reasonable, rezona.
Reasoning, rezonado.
Rebate—ment, rabato.
Rebel, ribelanto.
Rebel, ribeli.
Rebellion, ribelo—ado.
Rebellious, ribela.
Rebound, resalti.
Rebuff, malprospero.
Rebuke, riproĉo.
Rebut, refuti.
Recall to mind,
memorigi.
Recall (to dismiss),
eksigi.
Recant, malkonfesi.
Recapitulate, resumi,
ripeti.
Recede,
malproksimiĝi.
Receipt, kvitanco.
Receipts, enspezoj.
Receive, ricevi.
Receiver (of taxes),
kolektisto.
Receiver (recipient),
adresato, ricevanto.
Recent, nova.
Recently, antaŭ ne
longe.
Reception, ricevo.
Recess (vacation),
libertempo.
Recipe (medical),
recepto.
Recipient (of income),
rentulo.
Reciprocal, reciproka.
Reciprocity,
reciprokeco.
Recital, rakonto.

Recitation, deklamo—
ado.
Recite, deklami.
Reckless, senzorga.
Reckon, kalkuli.
Reckoner (book),
kalkullibro.
Reckoning, kalkulo.
Reclaim (land), eltiri.
Reclaim, redemandi.
Recline, kuŝi, apogi.
Recluse, ermito.
Recognition, rekono.
Recognize, rekoni.
Recoil (of gun, etc.),
repuŝo.
Recollect, memori.
Recommend,
rekomendi.
Recommendation,
rekomendo.
Recompense,
rekompenci.
Reconcile, pacigi.
Reconciled, to be,
paciĝi.
Reconciliation, pacigo.
Reconsider,
rekonsideri.
Recopy, rekopii.
Record, registri,
raporti.
Recount (relate),
rakonti.
Recourse, to have,
alkuri.
Recover (find), retrovi.
Recover (to get well),
resaniĝi.
Recreant, timulo.
Recreate, rekrei.
Recreation, ludtempo.
Recriminate,

kontraŭdiradi.
Recrimination, kontraŭdirado.
Recruit (health), resani, resanigi.
Recruit, varbi.
Recruit, varbito, rekruto.
Recruiting, varbo— ado.
Rectangle, rektangulo.
Rectify (make right), rektigi.
Rectify (purify), purigi.
Rectitude, rekteco, honesteco.
Rector, pastro, paroĥestro.
Rectory, pastrejo, pastra domo.
Recumbent, kuŝa.
Recur, reokazi.
Recurrence, reokazo.
Red, ruĝa.
Redbreast, ruĝgorĝo.
Redden, ruĝigi—iĝi.
Reddish, duberuĝa.
Redeem, reaĉeti, elaĉeti.
Redeemer, Elaĉetinto.
Redemption, elaĉeto.
Redness, ruĝeco.
Redouble, duobligi.
Redoubt (fortification), reduto.
Redoubtable, timinda.
Redress (amend), rebonigi, ripari.
Reduce (to powder), pisti.
Reduce (dissolve), solvi.
Reduce, malpliigi.

Redundance, sufiĉego.
Redundant, sufiĉega.
Reed, kano.
Reef (rocks), rifo.
Reel (stagger), ŝanceliĝi.
Re-enter, reeniri.
Re-establish, reigi.
Refection, manĝeto.
Refectory, manĝejo.
Refer to, turni sin.
Referring to, rilate al.
Refine, rafini.
Refined (manners), bonmaniera, ĝentila.
Refiner, rafinisto.
Refinery, rafinejo.
Reflect (light), rebrili.
Reflect (consider), pripensi.
Reflect (reproach), riproĉi.
Reflection (of light), rebrilo.
Reflection (thought), pripenso.
Reflector, rebrililo.
Reflection (censure), cenzuro, mallaŭdo.
Reflux, forfluo.
Refold, refaldi.
Reform, reformi, plibonigi.
Reformation, reformo, plibonigo.
Reformatory, reformejo, plibonigejo.
Refractory, ribela.
Refrain (song), rekantaĵo.
Refresh, refreŝigi.
Refreshment (food), refreŝigo.

Refreshment-room,
bufedo, restoracio.
Refuge, to take, rifuĝi.
Refuge, a, rifuĝejo.
Refund, repagi, redoni.
Refusal, rifuzo.
Refuse, rifuzi.
Refuse (rubbish),
forĵetaĵo, rubo.
Refutation, refuto.
Refute, refuti.
Regain, rericevi.
Regal, reĝa.
Regale, regali.
Regard (to look at),
rigardi.
Regardful (careful),
zorga.
Regarding, pri.
Regards (respects),
respektoj.
Regatta, ŝipkurado.
Regency, regeco.
Regenerate, refari,
renaski.
Regeneration, renasko.
Regent, reganto.
Regicide,
reĝmortiginto.
Regiment, regimento.
Region, regiono.
Register (luggage,
etc.), enskribi.
Register, registri.
Register (book),
registrolibro.
Registrar, registristo.
Registration,
registrado.
Regret, bedaŭri.
Regrettable,
bedaŭrinda.
Regular, regula.

Regulate, reguligi.
Regulation, regulo.
Rehearse, ripeti.
Reign, regi.
Reimburse, repagi.
Rein, kondukilo.
Rein in, moderigi.
Reindeer, norda cervo.
Reinforce, plifortigi.
Reinstate, reenmeti—
igi.
Reiterate, ripeti,
ripetadi.
Reject, rifuzi.
Rejection, rifuzo.
Rejoice, ĝoji.
Rejoin (to reply),
respondi.
Rejoin, rekunigi.
Rejoinder, respondo.
Rejuvenate, plijunigi.
Rekindle, rebruligi.
Relapse, refalo.
Relate, rakonti.
Related (to become),
parenciĝi.
Relation (business),
rilato.
Relation (mutual),
interrilato.
Relation (a relative),
parenco.
Relationship,
parenceco.
Relatively to, rilate—
al.
Relax, malpliigi.
Relax (speed),
malakceli.
Relay (horses),
ĉevalŝanĝo.
Release, liberigi.
Relegate, apartigi.

Relent, dolĉiĝi,
kvietiĝi.
Reliable, konfidinda.
Reliance, konfido.
Relic (sacred), sankta
restaĵo.
Relic, memorigo.
Relict (widow),
vidvino.
Relief (assistance),
helpo.
Relief (raised out),
reliefo.
Relieve, helpi.
Religion, religio.
Religious, religia.
Relinquish, forlasi.
Relish, ĝui, ŝati.
Relish (zest), gusto.
Reluctance,
malbonvolo—onto.
Reluctant,
malbonvola—onta.
Rely, konfidi.
Remain, resti.
Remainder, remains,
restaĵo.
Remains (food),
manĝrestaĵo.
Remake, refari.
Remand, reenmeti.
Remark, rimarki.
Remarkable,
rimarkinda.
Remedy (medical),
kuracilo.
Remedy, rimedo.
Remember, memori.
Remind, memorigi.
Reminder, memorigo.
Remiss, senzorga.
Remission, remeto,
pardoni.

Remit, remeti, sendi.
Remnant, restaĵo.
Remodel, reformi.
Remonstrance, averto,
kontraŭdiro.
Remonstrate, averti,
kontraŭdiri.
Remorse, memriproĉo.
Remote, malproksima.
Remotely,
malproksime.
Remove, transloki,
formovi.
Remunerate,
rekompenci.
Remunerative, gajniga,
paga.
Rend, disŝiri.
Render, redoni.
Render possible,
ebligi.
Render a service, fari
servon.
Rendezvous,
kunvenejo.
Rending, disŝiro.
Renew, renovigi.
Renewal, renovigo.
Renewable,
renovigebla.
Renounce, forlasi,
malpretendi.
Renovate, renovigi.
Renovation, renovigo.
Renown, famo.
Rent (payment),
depago, luprezo.
Rent, disŝiro, disŝiraĵo.
Renunciation, forlaso,
eksiĝo.
Repair, ripari.
Reparation, riparo.
Repartee, respondaĵo.

Repast, manĝado.
Repay, repagi.
Repeal, nuligi.
Repealable, nuligebla.
Repeat, ripeti.
Repel, repeli, repuŝi.
Repent, penti.
Repentance, pento—
ado.
Repetition, ripetado.
Repiece, fliki.
Repine, plendi,
murmuri.
Replace, anstataŭi.
Replant, replanti.
Replenish, replenigi.
Replete, plena, sata.
Repletion, pleneco,
sateco.
Reply, respondi.
Report, raporti.
Report, famo, raporto.
Report (official),
protokolo.
Report (of gun, etc.),
eksplodsono.
Repose, ripozo.
Repose, ripozi.
Repository, tenejo.
Reprehend, riproĉi.
Reprehensible,
riproĉinda.
Represent, reprezenti.
Representation,
reprezentado.
Representative,
reprezentanto.
Repress, haltigi,
subpremi.
Repression,
subpremo—ado.
Repressive, subprema.
Reprieve, pardoni.

Reprimand, riproĉi,
mallaŭdi.
Reprimand, riproĉo,
mallaŭdo.
Reprisals, revenĝo.
Reproach, riproĉo.
Reproachful, riproĉa.
Reprobate, malaprobi,
riproĉi.
Reproduce, reprodukti.
Reproduction, kopiaĵo,
reproduktaĵo.
Reproof, riproĉo.
Reprove, malaprobi,
riproĉi.
Reptile, rampaĵo.
Republic, respubliko.
Republican,
respublikano.
Repudiate, nei.
Repugnance,
antipatio—eco.
Repugnant, antipatia.
Repulse, repuŝi, repeli.
Repulsive, malbelega.
Reputable, estimebla,
ŝatinda.
Reputation, famo, ŝato,
reputacio.
Request, peti.
Require, postuli,
bezoni.
Requirement, postulo,
bezono, neceseco.
Requisite, necesa,
bezona.
Requisition, rekvizicio.
Requite, rekompenci.
Rescind, eksigi,
neniigi.
Rescue, savi.
Research, esploro,
esplorado.

Resemblance,
simileco.
Resemble, simili.
Resent, sentegi.
Resentment, kolero.
Reserve, rezervi.
Reserved (in speech),
silentema.
Reservoir, akvujo,
akvujego.
Reside, loĝi, restadi.
Residence, loĝejo,
restadejo.
Resident, loĝanto.
Residue, restaĵo.
Resign, eksiĝi.
Resign one's self,
submetiĝi.
Resignation,
rezignacio.
Resignation (giving
up), eksiĝo.
Resin, rezino,
kolofono.
Resin-wood, keno
Resinous, rezina.
Resist, kontraŭbatali,
kontraŭstari.
Re-sole (boots, etc.),
replandumi.
Resolute, decida.
Resolution, decideco.
Resolve, decidi.
Resonant, resona.
Resort, kunvenejo.
Resound, resoni.
Resource, rimedo.
Respect, respekti.
Respect, respekto.
Respectable,
respektinda.
Respectful, respekta.
Respecting (concernin

g), pri.
Respirable, spirebla.
Respiration, spirado.
Respire, spiri.
Resplendent, to
become, briliĝi.
Respond, respondi.
Response, respondo.
Responsible for, to be,
garantii, respondi pri.
Responsible, responda.
Responsibility,
respondeco.
Resuscitate, revivigi.
Rest (pause), paŭzo.
Rest (remainder),
restaĵo.
Rest (quietude),
kvieteco, ripozeco.
Rest (lean on), apogi.
Rest one's self, ripozi,
kuŝi.
Restaurant, restoracio.
Restitution, redonado.
Restless, restive,
maltrankvila.
Restoration, redoneco,
ripareco.
Restorative, fortigilo,
refortigilo.
Restore (give back),
redoni.
Restore, refari, ripari.
Restrain, haltigi,
deteni.
Restrict, malvastigi,
malgrandigi.
Result, rezulti.
Result, sekvo,
rezultato.
Resume (continue),
daŭrigi.
Résumé (précis),

resumo.
Resurrection,
revivigo—iĝo.
Retail, to sell by, detale
vendi.
Retail, by,
pomalgrande, detale.
Retail (trade), detala.
Retailer, revendisto.
Retain, gardi, teni.
Retainer, vasalo.
Retaliate, revenĝi.
Retaliation, revenĝo.
Retard, prokrasti,
malhelpi.
Retardation, prokrasto,
malhelpo.
Retentive, persista,
premorebla.
Retina, retino.
Retinue, sekvantaro.
Retire, reeniri.
Retirement, kvieteco.
Retort, respondi,
reparoli.
Retort (chem. vessel),
retorto.
Retouch (revise),
korekti.
Retrace, reveni, repaŝi.
Retract, malkonfesi.
Retreat (place),
rifuĝejo.
Retreat, foriri, remarŝi.
Retribution, repago.
Retrieve, trovi, gajni,
re—.
Retrograde,
malprogresi.
Retrospect,
retrospekto.
Retrospective,
retrospektiva.

Return (give back),
redoni.
Return (come back),
reveni.
Return, to make a,
raporti.
Return (report),
raporto.
Return, in, reciproke.
Reunion, rekunigo.
Re-unite, rekunigi.
Reveal, malkaŝi.
Revel, festenego.
Revenge, revenĝo.
Revenue, rento,
enspezo.
Revere, respektegi.
Reverence, to make a,
riverenci.
Reverence, respektegi.
Reverence (salutation),
riverenco.
Reverie, revado.
Reverse, renversi.
Reverse (a loss),
malprospero.
Reverse side, posta
flanko.
Revert, reveni.
Review (journal),
revuo.
Review (milit.),
parado.
Revile, mallaŭdegi.
Revise, korekti,
ekzameni.
Revival, revivigo.
Revive, revivigi.
Revocable, nuligebla.
Revocation, nuligo.
Revoke, nuligi.
Revolt, ribelo.
Revolution, revolucio.

Revolve, turniĝi,
pivoti.
Revulsion, antipatio.
Reward, premio,
rekompenco.
Rhapsodist,
rapsodiisto.
Rhapsody, rapsodio.
Rhetoric, parolarto,
retoriko.
Rhetorical, elokventa,
retorika.
Rheumatic,
reŭmatisma.
Rheumatism,
reŭmatismo.
Rhinoceros, rinocero.
Rhomb, rombo.
Rhombus, rombo.
Rhubarb, rabarbo.
Rhyme, rimi.
Rhythm, ritmo.
Rib, ripo.
Ribald, malĉasta,
diboĉa.
Ribaldry, diboĉo—aĵo.
Ribbon, rubando.
Rice, rizo.
Rich, to grow, riĉiĝi.
Rich, riĉa.
Riches, riĉeco.
Rid, malembarasi,
liberigi.
Riddle (sieve), kribrilo.
Riddle, enigmo,
logogrifo.
Ride, rajdi.
Ridge, supro, pinto.
Ridge (agricul.), sulko.
Ridicule, moki.
Ridiculous, ridinda.
Riding-master,
ĉevalestro, rajdmastro.

Riding-school, rajdejo.
Rife, ĝenerala.
Riff-raff, forĵetaĵo.
Rifle, pafilo.
Rifle (plunder), rabi.
Rift, fendo.
Rig, ŝnurarmi.
Rigging, ŝnurarmilaro.
Right, dekstra.
Right (justice), rajto.
Right (straight), rekta.
Right (correct), prava.
Righteous, justa, pia.
Rightful, rajta.
Rightly, rajte, prave,
juste.
Rigid, rigida, severa.
Rigid (exact), preciza.
Rigidity, rigideco.
Rigidly, severe.
Rigour, severeco.
Rigorous, severa,
severega.
Rill, rivereto.
Rim, rando.
Rime, prujno.
Rind, ŝelo, ŝelaĵo.
Ring (intrans.), sonori.
Ring, ringo.
Ring (a circle), rondo.
Ringleader, instigulo,
instiganto.
Ringlet, buklo, harleto.
Ringworm, favo.
Rinse, laveti, gargari.
Riot, tumulto, ribelo.
Riotous, tumulta,
ribela.
Rip, ŝiri.
Ripe, matura.
Ripen (intrans.),
maturiĝi.
Ripple, ondeto.

Rise (ascent), altaĵo.
Rise (origin), deveno.
Rise (in price), plikariĝo.
Rise (get up), leviĝi.
Risible, ridinda.
Risibility, ridindeco.
Rising (revolt), ribelo.
Risk, riski.
Rite, ceremoniaro.
Rival, konkuri.
Rival, konkuranto.
Rivalry, konkuro—eco.
River, rivero.
Rivulet, rivereto.
Roach, ploto.
Road, vojo, strato.
Road-labourer, stratlaboristo.
Roadstead, rodo.
Roam, vagi.
Roar (of wind), muĝi.
Roar (of animals), blekegi.
Roar (cry out), kriegi.
Roast, rosti.
Roast (meat), rostaĵo.
Rob, ŝteli, rabi.
Robber, ŝtelisto, rabisto.
Robbery, rabado.
Robe, vesti, robi.
Robe, robo.
Robing-room, vestejo, robĉambro.
Robust, fortika.
Robustness, fortikeco.
Rock, ŝtonego.
Rock (to move to and fro), luli.
Rock (reef), rifo.
Rocking, lulado.

Rocket, raketo.
Rock-oil, petrolo.
Rocky, ŝtonegplena.
Rod (switch), vergo.
Rod (for stairs, etc.), metalvergo.
Rod (fishing), hokfadeno.
Roebuck, kapreolo.
Rogue, fripono.
Roguish, fripona.
Rôle (play), rolo.
Roll (paper, etc.), kunvolvaĵo.
Roll, ruli.
Roll one's self, ruliĝi.
Roll (bread), bulko.
Roll (of drum), tamburado.
Roll (a list), registro.
Roller (caster), radeto.
Rolling (of ships), marrulado.
Roll-book, registrolibro.
Roman, a, Romano.
Roman, Roma.
Romance (a novel), romano.
Romance (music), romanco.
Romantic, sentimentala.
Romp, ludegi.
Romp, bubino, petolulo.
Rood (crucifix), krucifikso, kruco.
Roof, tegmento.
Roofing (material), tegmentaĵo.
Rook, frugilego.
Room, ĉambro.

170

Room (space), spaco.
Roomy, vasta.
Roost, stangiĝi.
Rooster, koko.
Root, to take, enradiki.
Root-word, radikvorto.
Root (of trees, etc.),
radiko.
Root up, elradiki.
Rope, ŝnurego.
Rosary, rozario.
Rose, rozo.
Rosebush, rozarbeto.
Rose-coloured,
rozkolora.
Rosette, banto.
Rosemary, rosmareno.
Rosewood, palisandro.
Rosin, kolofono.
Rostrum, tribuno.
Rosy, roza, ruĝa.
Rot, putri, putriĝi.
Rotate, turniĝi.
Rotation, turniĝado.
Rotation, in, laŭ vico,
laŭvice.
Rottenness, putreco,
putro—aĵo.
Rotunda, rotondo.
Rouble, rublo.
Rough (surface),
malglata, malebena.
Rough (rugged),
ŝtonplena.
Rough (manner),
malafabla.
Rough, in the, krude.
Rough draft, malneto.
Roughen, malglatigi.
Roughness,
malglateco.
Round, rondigi.
Round, to turn, turni,

turnigi.
Round (form), ronda,
rondforma.
Round (of ladder),
ŝtupeto.
Round (sentry),
patrolo.
Rouse, eksciti.
Rouse (waken), veki—
igi.
Rout, malvenkego.
Route, vojo.
Routine, kutimo.
Rove, vagi.
Row (noise), bruego,
tumulto.
Row (line, rank), vico.
Row (boat), remi.
Royal, reĝa.
Royalty, reĝeco.
Rub, froti—adi.
Rubbish, rubo,
forĵetaĵo.
Rubric, rubriko.
Ruby, rubeno.
Ruby-color, ruĝa.
Rudder, direktilo.
Rude, malĝentila.
Rudeness,
malrespekto.
Ruddiness, ruĝeco.
Ruddy, ruĝa.
Rudiment (embryo),
embrio.
Rudiment (elements),
elementaĵo.
Rue (botan.), ruto.
Rue (to grieve),
bedaŭregi.
Ruff, krispo.
Ruffian, malbonulo.
Ruffle (agitate),
malkvietigi.

Rug, tapiŝeto.
Rugged, ŝtonplena, malebena.
Ruin (remains), restaĵo, ruinaĵo.
Ruin, ruino, ruinoj.
Ruin, ruinigi.
Ruinous, ruina.
Rule (to govern), regi.
Rule, or ruler, liniilo.
Rule (to regulate), reguligi.
Rule, regulo.
Ruler, regnestro.
Rum, rumo.
Rumble, bruegadi.
Ruminate (to chew the cud), remaĉadi.
Ruminate, pripensi.
Rumour, famo.
Rumple, ĉifi.
Run, kuri.
Run (flow), flui.
Run against, ektuŝegi.
Run away, forkuri.
Run to, alkuri.
Run off rails, elreliĝi.
Runaway, forkuranto.
Rung (of ladder), ŝtupeto.
Rupture, rompo.
Rupture (med.), hernio.
Rural, kampa.
Ruse, ruzo.
Rush, ĵeti sin sur, kuregi.
Rush, junko.
Russet, flavruĝa.
Russia, Rusujo.
Russian, Ruso.
Rust, rusti, rustiĝi.
Rust, rustaĵo.

Rut, radkavo, radsigno.
Ruthless, kruelega.
Rye, sekalo.

S

Sabbath, dimanĉo.
Sable (animal), zibelo.
Sabot, ligna ŝuo.
Sabre, hakglavo, sabro.
Sacerdotal, pastra.
Sack, sako.
Sack (pillage), rabadi.
Sackcloth, ŝtofego.
Sacrament, sakramento.
Sacred, sankta.
Sacredness, sankteco.
Sacrifice, oferi.
Sacrilege, malpiaĵo.
Sad, malĝoja.
Sadden, malĝojigi.
Saddle, selo.
Sadness, malĝojeco.
Safe (money), monkesto.
Safe, sendanĝera.
Safety, sendanĝereco.
Saffron, safrano.
Sagacious, sagaca.
Sagacity, sagaceco.
Sage, saĝa.
Sage (botany), salvio.
Sail (of a ship), velo.
Sail, surnaĝi.
Sailing-ship, velŝipo.
Sailor, maristo.
Sails, velaro.
Sainfoin, sanfojno.
Saint, sanktulo.
Saintly, sankta.
Sake of, for the, pro.

Salad, salato.
Salamander, salamandro.
Sal-ammoniac, salamoniako.
Salary, salajro.
Sale, vendo.
Saleable, vendebla.
Salesman, vendisto.
Saline, sala.
Saliva, kraĉaĵo.
Sally (of wit), spritaĵo.
Salmon, salmo.
Saloon, salono.
Salt, salo.
Salt-cellar, salujo.
Salt-meat, peklaĵo.
Saltpetre, salpetro.
Salubrious, saniga.
Salutation, saluto.
Salutary, sanplena.
Salute, saluti.
Salvage, savado.
Salvation, savo.
Salve, ŝmiraĵo.
Salver, pladeto.
Same, sama.
Same time, at the, samtempe.
Sameness, sameco.
Sample, specimeno.
Sanctify, sanktigi.
Sanction, sankcii.
Sanctity, sankteco.
Sanctuary, sanktejo.
Sand, sablo.
Sand, a grain of, sablero.
Sandbank, sablaĵo.
Sandal, pantofleto.
Sandwich, vianda bulko.
Sane, racia.

Sanguinary, sangavida.
Sanguine, esperplena.
Sanhedrim, sinedrio.
Sanitary, higiena.
Sanity, racieco.
Sanscrit, Sanskrito.
Sap, suko.
Sap (undermine), subfosi.
Sapling, juna arbo.
Sapphire, safiro.
Sarcasm, sarkasmo.
Sarcastic, sarkasma.
Sardine, sardelo.
Sardinian, Sardo.
Sarsaparilla, smilako.
Sash, zono.
Satan, Satano.
Satanic, satana, diabla.
Satchel, saketo.
Sate, sati.
Satellite, sekvulo, sekvanto.
Satiate, satigi.
Satiety, sato.
Satin, atlaso.
Satire, satiro.
Satisfaction, kontentigo.
Satisfactory, kontentiga.
Satisfied, to be, kontentiĝi.
Satisfied, kontenta.
Satisfy, kontentigi.
Satisfy (hunger), satigi.
Satrap, satrapo.
Saturate, saturi.
Saturday, Sabato.
Sauce, saŭco.
Saucer, subtaso, telereto.
Saucepan, kaserolo.

Saucy, insultema, petola.
Saunter, malrapidiri.
Sausage, kolbaseto.
Sausage, German, kolbaso.
Savage, sovaĝa.
Savage, a, sovaĝulo.
Savant, scienculo.
Save (prep.), krom.
Save (rescue), savi.
Save (economise), ŝpari.
Saveloy, kolbaseto.
Saving, ŝparema.
Saviour, Savinto.
Savour, gusto.
Savoury, bongusta.
Saw, segi.
Saw, segilo.
Saw (saying), proverbo, diro.
Sawdust, segaĵo.
Sawyer, segisto.
Say, diri.
Saying, a, proverbo, diro.
Scab, skabio.
Scabbard, glavingo.
Scaffold, eŝafodo.
Scaffold (for building), trabaĵo.
Scald, brogi.
Scale (music), skalo.
Scale (of fish), skvamo.
Scale of charges, tarifo.
Scale, surrampi.
Scales, pesilo.
Scamp, kanajlo.
Scan, elekzameni.
Scandal, skandalo.

Scandalise, skandali.
Scandinavian, Skandinavo.
Scantling, lignaĵo, trabetaĵo.
Scanty, malsufiĉega.
Scapegoat, propekulo.
Scapula, skapolo.
Scar, cikatro.
Scarabaeus, skarabo.
Scarce, malsufiĉa.
Scarcely, apenaŭ.
Scarcity, malsufiĉo.
Scare, timigi.
Scarecrow, timigilo.
Scarf, skarpo.
Scarlatina, skarlatino.
Scarlet, skarlato.
Scatter, disĵeti, dissemi.
Scene, scenejo.
Scene (painted), sceno.
Scenery, pejzaĝo.
Scent, odoro.
Scent, flari.
Sceptic, skeptikulo.
Sceptical, skeptika.
Sceptre, sceptro.
Schedule, katalogo.
Scheme, projekto.
Schism, disigo.
Schismatic, disiginta.
Scholar, lernanto.
Scholarship, klereco.
Scholastic, skolastika.
School, lernejo.
Schoolfellow, kunlernanto.
Schoolmaster, lernejestro, instruisto.
Science, scienco.
Scientific, scienca.
Scintillate, brileti.

Scissors, tondilo.
Scoff, moki.
Scold, riproĉegi.
Scoop, kulerego.
Scorbutic, skorbuta.
Scorch, bruleti.
Score, dudeko.
Scorn, malestimo.
Scorpion, skorpio.
Scotchman, Skoto.
Scoundrel, kanajlo.
Scour, frotlavi.
Scourge, skurĝi.
Scout, antaŭmarŝanto,
antaŭ rajdanto.
Scowl, sulkegiĝi.
Scramble up,
suprenrampi.
Scrap, peceto.
Scrape, skrapi.
Scrapings, skrapaĵo.
Scratch, grati.
Scratch, grataĵo.
Scratch (claw),
ungograti.
Scream, kriegi.
Screen, ŝirmilo.
Screw, ŝraŭbo.
Screw, ŝraŭbi.
Screw-driver,
ŝraŭbturnilo.
Scribble, malbonskribi.
Scribe, skribisto.
Scripture, Sankta
Skribo.
Scrofula, skrofolo.
Scroll, rulpapero.
Scrub, frotlavi.
Scruple,
konsciencdubo.
Scrupulous,
konscienca.
Scrutinize, esplori,

serĉadi.
Scrutiny, serĉado.
Scuffle, interpuŝo.
Scull (oar), remilo.
Scullery, lavejo,
potlavejo.
Sculptor, skulptisto.
Sculpture (art),
skulptarto.
Sculpture (statuary),
skulptaĵo.
Sculpture (to carve),
skulpti.
Scum, ŝaŭmo.
Scurf, favo.
Scurrilous, maldeca,
maldelikata.
Scurvy, skorbuto.
Scuttle, coal,
karbujo—eto.
Scythe, falĉilo.
Sea, maro.
Seafaring, mara.
Sea-gull, mevo.
Sea-horse (walrus),
rosmaro.
Seal, sigeli.
Seal, sigelo—ilo.
Seal (animal), foko.
Sealing-wax,
sigelvakso.
Seam, kunkudro.
Seaman, maristo,
marano.
Seamanship,
marveturarto.
Seamstress, kudristino.
Sear, kaŭterizi, bruligi.
Search, serĉi.
Search-warrant,
traserĉo.
Seaside, marbordo.
Seashore, marbordo.

175

Season (food, etc.),
spici.
Season, sezono.
Seasonable,
ĝustatempa.
Seasoning, spicaĵo.
Seaworthy, marirebla,
martaŭga.
Seat, seĝo.
Seat, sidigi.
Seated, to be, sidi.
Sebaceous, sebeca.
Seclusion, soleco.
Second (order), dua.
Second (time),
sekundo.
Second offence,
rekulpo.
Secondary school,
duagrada lernejo.
Secrecy, sekreteco,
kaŝeco.
Secret, sekreta.
Secretary, sekretario.
Secrete, kaŝi.
Sect, sekto.
Sectarian, sektano.
Section (group),
sekcio.
Section (portion),
parto.
Secular, monda.
Secure, sendanĝera.
Security,
sendanĝereco.
Security (guarantee),
garantiaĵo.
Sedan-chair, portilo.
Sedate, serioza.
Sedentary, hejmsida.
Sediment, feĉo.
Sedition, ribelo.
Seduce, delogi.

See, vidi.
See again, revidi.
See after, zorgi pri.
See to, zorgi pri.
See one's self, sin vidi.
Seesaw, balancilo.
Seed, semo.
Seedling, kreskaĵo.
Seek, serĉi.
Seem, ŝajni.
Seeming, ŝajna,
verŝajna.
Seemly, deca.
Seer, profeto.
Seethe, boli.
Seize, ekkapti.
Seldom, malofte.
Select, elekti.
Selection, elektaro.
Self, or selves, mem.
Self-conceit,
tromemfido.
Self-denial,
memforgeso.
Self-esteem,
memestimo.
Self-evident, klarega.
Self-reproach,
memriproĉo.
Self-taught,
memlerninta.
Self-willed, obstina.
Selfish, egoista.
Selfishness, egoismo.
Sell, vendi.
Selvage, ŝtofrando.
Semaphore, semaforo,
signalilo.
Semblance, ŝajneco.
Semibreve, plena noto.
Semicircle, duonrondo.
Semicolon,
punktokomo.

Seminarist,
seminariano.
Seminary, seminario.
Semolina, tritikaĵo.
Senate, senato.
Senate-house, senatejo,
senatdomo.
Senator, senatano.
Send, sendi.
Send away, forsendi.
Send back, resendi.
Senile, maljuna.
Senility, maljuneco.
Senior, plenaĝa,
pliaĝa.
Sensation, sentado.
Sensational, sensacia.
Sense, sento.
Sense (meaning),
senco.
Senseless, sensenta.
Senseless (unmeaning)
, sensenca.
Sensibility, sentemo.
Sensible (feelingo),
sentebla.
Sensible, saĝa.
Sensitive, sentema.
Sensual, voluptema.
Sensuality, volupteco.
Sentence (gram.),
frazo.
Sentence (judgment),
juĝo.
Sentence, juĝi,
kondamni.
Sentient, sentema.
Sentiment (feeling),
sento.
Sentiment, opinio.
Sentimental,
sentimentala.
Sentinel,

gardostaranto.
Sentry, gardostaranto.
Sentry-box, budeto.
Separate, apartigi,
disigi.
Separate, aparta.
Separate, malkunigi,
disigi.
Separately, malkune.
Separation, disigo.
September, Septembro.
Sepulchre, tombego.
Sequel, sekvo,
sekveco.
Seraph, serafo.
Sere, velkinta.
Serenade, serenado.
Serene, trankvila.
Serenity, trankvileco.
Serf, servutulo.
Sergeant, serĝento.
Series, serio.
Serious, serioza.
Seriousness, seriozeco.
Sermon, prediko
Serpent, serpento.
Serum, serumo.
Servant, servisto—ino.
Serve, servi.
Serve for, taŭgi.
Service, servo.
Service, table,
manĝilaro.
Service, Divine,
Diservo.
Serviceable, servema.
Serviette, buŝtuko.
Servile, sklava.
Servility, sklavemo.
Servitude, sklaveco.
Session, kunsido.
Set apart, apartigi.
Set free, liberigi.

Set out, foriri.
Set (a bone, etc.), enartikigi.
Set fire to, ekbruligi.
Set in order, ordigi.
Set (of the sun), subiri.
Set on edge, agaci.
Settle, loĝiĝi.
Settle an account, elpagi.
Settle, decidi.
Seven, sep.
Seventh (music), septimo.
Seventeen, dek-sep.
Seventy, sepdek.
Sever, disigi.
Several, diversa.
Several, multaj.
Severally, diverse.
Severe, severa.
Severity, severeco.
Sew, kudri.
Sewer, defluilego.
Sewing machine, stebilo.
Sex, sekso.
Sexton, servisto de preĝejo.
Sexual, seksa.
Shabby (worn out), eluzita.
Shabby, malnobla.
Shackles, malhelpoj, baroj, katenoj.
Shade (screen), lumŝirmilo.
Shade, ombraĵo.
Shade (tint), nuanco.
Shade, nuanci.
Shadow, ombro.
Shadowy, ĥimera.
Shaft (of vehicle), timono.
Shaggy, harplena.
Shake, ŝanceli.
Shake (jolt), skui.
Shake (tremble), tremi.
Shaking (jolting), skuo.
Shake hands, manpremi.
Shallow, malprofunda.
Sham, ŝajniĝi.
Sham, ŝajniĝo.
Shambles, buĉejo.
Shame, honto.
Shame, hontigi.
Shameful, hontinda.
Shameless, senhonta.
Shank, tibio.
Shape, formo.
Shape, formi.
Share, dividi.
Share (finance), akcio.
Share, parto, porcio.
Share, partopreni.
Shark, ŝarko.
Sharp (music), duontono supre.
Sharp (edge), akra.
Sharp (sour), acida.
Sharpen, akrigi.
Sharper (cheat), ŝtelisto.
Shatter, frakasi.
Shave, razi.
Shavings, rabotaĵo.
Shawl, ŝalo.
She, ŝi.
Sheaf, garbo.
Shear, tondi.
Shears, tondilo.
Sheath, ingo.
Shed, budo.
Shed tears, plori.

Sheep, ŝafo.
Sheepish, embarasita.
Sheepfold, ŝafejo.
Sheet, drapo.
Shelf, breto.
Shell, ŝelo.
Shell, senŝeligi.
Shell, bomb, bombo, kuglego.
Shelter (to screen), ŝirmi.
Shelter (refuge), rifuĝejo.
Shelve (slope), deklivo.
Shepherd, paŝtisto.
Shield, ŝildo.
Shield, ŝildi, ŝirmi.
Shift (garment), ĉemizo.
Shift, movi, transporti.
Shilling, ŝilingo.
Shin, tibio.
Shine, brili.
Shingle, ŝindo—eto.
Shining, brila.
Ship, ŝipo.
Ship, enŝipigi.
Shipwreck, ŝippereo.
Shipwright, ŝipfaristo.
Shire, graflando.
Shirk, eviti.
Shirt, ĉemizo.
Shiver, tremeti.
Shoal, fiŝaro.
Shock, frapo.
Shocking, terura.
Shoe, ŝuo.
Shoes, boots, etc., piedvesto.
Shoot (tree), branĉeto.
Shoot (to bud), ĝermi.
Shoot (a gun), pafi.
Shoot (to kill), mortpafi.
Shop, butiko.
Shore, marbordo.
Shore up, subteni.
Short, mallonga.
Shorten, mallongigi.
Shortly, frue.
Shortsighted, miopa.
Shortsightedness, miopeco.
Shot, pafo.
Should, devus.
Shoulder, ŝultro.
Shoulder-blade, skapolo.
Shout, kriegi.
Shove, puŝi.
Shovel, ŝoveli.
Shovel, ŝovelilo.
Show, montri.
Show, parado.
Show in, enigi.
Show goods, elmeti.
Shower, pluveto.
Shower-bath, pluvbano.
Showy, luksa.
Shred, peco, dispeco.
Shrewd, sagaca.
Shrewdness, sagaceco.
Shriek, kriegi.
Shriek (of the wind), muĝi.
Shrill, sibla.
Shrink, malpliiĝi.
Shrivel up, sulkiĝi.
Shrimp, markankreto.
Shroud, mortkitelo.
Shroud, kaŝi, protekti.
Shrub, arbeto.
Shrug, altigi.
Shudder, tremeti.

Shuffle (cards), miksi, enmiksi—igi.
Shuffle (prevaricate), ĉikani.
Shun, eviti.
Shut, fermi.
Shutter, window, fenestra kovrilo.
Shuttle, naveto.
Shy, timeta, hontema.
Shyness, timeteco, honteco.
Si (music), B.
Si (flat), Bes.
Sibilant, sibla, sibla sono.
Sick (ill), malsana.
Sick, vomema.
Sicken, malsaniĝi.
Sickle, rikoltilo.
Sickly, malsanema.
Side, flanko.
Sideboard, telermeblo.
Side face, profilo.
Siege, sieĝo.
Sieve, kribrilo.
Sift, kribri.
Sigh, ekĝemi.
Sigh after—or for, sopiri pri.
Sight, vido.
Sight (view), vidaĵo.
Sign, signi—igi.
Sign, signo.
Sign (a document, etc.), subskribi.
Signboard, elpendaĵo.
Sign-manual, subskribo—aĵo.
Sign (notice-board), surskribaĵo.
Signpost, signa fosto.
Signal, signalo.

Signal, signali.
Signal (milit.), signaldiro.
Signature, subskribo.
Signet, sigelilo.
Significant, signifa.
Signification, signifo.
Signify (to mean), signifi.
Signify (to matter), esti grava.
Signify (to make known), sciigi.
Silence, silento.
Silence, silentigi.
Silence, to keep, silentigi.
Silent, silenta.
Silent, to be, silenti.
Silent, to become, silentiĝi.
Silex, siliko.
Silhouette, profilo.
Silk, silko.
Silkworm, silkvermo.
Silken, silka.
Silky, silkeca.
Sill, sojlo.
Silliness, malsaĝeco.
Silly, naivega.
Silver, arĝento.
Silver plate, arĝenti.
Silver-fir, pinio.
Similar, simila.
Similarity, simileco.
Similitude, komparaĵo.
Simile, simileco.
Simmer, boleti.
Simper, naivegrideti.
Simple, simpla.
Simple (foolish), naivega.
Simpleton, naivegulo.

Simpleness, simpleco.
Simplicity, simpleco.
Simplify, simpligi.
Simply (adv.), simple, nur.
Simultaneous, samtempa.
Sin, peko.
Sin, peki.
Sinapis, sinapo.
Sinapism, sinapa kataplasmo.
Since (conjunction), tial ke, ĉar.
Since then, de tiu tempo.
Since (adv.), antaŭ ne longe.
Sincere, sincera.
Sincerity, sincereco.
Sinecure, senlaborofico.
Sinew, tendeno.
Sinful, pekema.
Sing, kanti.
Singing (the art), kantarto.
Single (alone), sola.
Single, unuobla.
Singe, bruleti, flameti.
Singular (gram.), ununombro.
Singular, stranga.
Sinciput, verto.
Sinister, funebra.
Sink, ŝtonlavujo.
Sink, malflosi, iĝi.
Sinner, pekulo.
Sinovia (anat), sinovio.
Sip, trinketi.
Siphon, sifono.
Sir, sinjoro.
Sire, patro.

Sire, moŝto.
Siren, sireno.
Sister, fratino.
Sister-in-law, bofratino.
Sit, sidi.
Sit on eggs, sursidi.
Site, sido, situacio.
Sitting (of assembly), kunsido.
Situation, situacio, sido.
Situation (post), oficio.
Six, ses.
Sixteen, dek-ses.
Sixty, sesdek.
Size, grandeco.
Size (of a book), formato.
Size, glueto.
Skate, gliti.
Skates, glitiloj.
Skein, fadenaro.
Skeleton, skeleto.
Sketch, skizi.
Sketch, skizo.
Skewer, trapikileto.
Skid, malakcelo.
Skiff, boateto.
Skilful, lerta.
Skill, lerteco.
Skilled, lerta.
Skim, senŝaŭmigi.
Skimmer, ŝaŭmkulero.
Skin, haŭto.
Skin (animal), felo.
Skin, senfeligi.
Skinner, felisto.
Skip, salteti.
Skirmish, bataleto.
Skirt, jupo.
Skittles, kegloj.
Skulk, kaŝiĝi.

Skull, kranio.
Sky, ĉielo.
Skylight, fenestreto.
Slack, malstreĉa.
Slacken (speed), malakceli.
Slacken (loose), malstreĉi.
Slag, metala ŝaŭmo.
Slake, sensoifigi.
Slander, kalumnii.
Slang, vulgaresprimo.
Slanting, oblikva.
Slap in the face, survango.
Slash, tranĉadi, tranĉegi.
Slate, ardezo.
Slater, tegmentisto.
Slates (roofing), tegmentaĵo.
Slaughter (animals), buĉadi.
Slaughter, mortigi.
Slaughter-house, buĉejo.
Slave, sklavo.
Slavery, sklaveco.
Slavish, sklava.
Slavishness, sklavemo.
Slay, mortigi.
Sled, sledge, glitveturilo.
Sleek, glata.
Sleep, dormi.
Sleet, hajlneĝo.
Sleeve, maniko.
Sleigh, glitveturilo.
Slender, maldika.
Slender (graceful), gracia.
Slice, tranĉaĵo.
Slide, glitejo.

Slide, gliti.
Slight, maldika.
Slip, faleti.
Slip, let, preterlasi.
Slipper, pantoflo.
Slippery, glata.
Slim, gracia.
Slime, ŝlimo.
Slimy, ŝlima.
Sling (stones), ŝtonĵetilo.
Slit, fendo.
Sloe, prunelo.
Slop, verŝeti.
Slope, deklivo.
Slope (cut out), eltranĉi.
Sloth, mallaboremo.
Slothful, mallaborema.
Slough, ŝlimejo.
Sloven, negliĝulo.
Slow, malrapida.
Slowness, malrapideco.
Slug, limako.
Sluggard, mallaborulo.
Slumber, dormeti.
Slut, negliĝulino.
Sly, ruza, kaŝema.
Small, malgranda.
Smallness, malgrandeco.
Small-pox, variolo.
Smart (to suffer), doloreti.
Smart, eleganta.
Smash, disrompi.
Smear, ŝmiri.
Smell (trans.), flari.
Smell (intrans.), odori.
Smell, odoro.
Smell (sense), flaro—ado.
Smelt, fandi.

Smile, rideto.
Smile, rideti.
Smite, frapi.
Smithy, forĝejo.
Smock, kitelo.
Smoke, fumi.
Smoke, fumo.
Smoke (fish, etc.),
fumaĵi.
Smoker, fumamanto.
Smooth, glata.
Smooth (level), ebena.
Smother, sufoki.
Smoulder, bruleti.
Smuggle, kontrabandi.
Smut, nigrigi, makuli.
Snail, limako.
Snake, serpenteto.
Snap (noise), kraki.
Snap, ataketi.
Snappish, atakema.
Snare, kaptilo.
Snatch, ekpreni.
Sneak, rampi.
Sneer, ridmoki.
Sneeze, terni.
Sniff, enflari.
Snip, tondeti.
Snivel, ploreti.
Snore, ronki.
Snort, ekronki.
Snout, nazego.
Snow, neĝi.
Snow, neĝo.
Snowflake, neĝero.
Snuff, flartabako.
Snuffle, nazparoli.
Snug, komforta.
So (adv.), tiel,
tiamaniere.
So, tia.
So many, much, tiom
da.

Soak, trempi.
Soap, sapo.
Soap, sapumi.
Soar, alte flugi.
Sob, ploregi.
Sober, sobra.
Sober (serious),
serioza.
Sobriety, sobreco.
Sobriquet, moknomo.
Sociable, societama.
Social, sociala.
Socialism, socialismo.
Socialist, socialisto.
Society, societo.
Sock, ŝtrumpeto.
Socket, ingo, tubeto.
Sod, bulo.
Soda, sodo.
Sofa, sofo.
Soft, mola.
Soft (mannered), dolĉa.
Soft (not loud),
mallaŭta.
Soften, moligi.
Softly, mallaŭte.
Softly, kviete.
Softness, moleco.
Soil, tero.
Soil, malpurigi.
Soiled, malpura.
Soirée, vesperkunveno.
Sojourn, resti.
Sol (music), G.
Solace, komforti.
Solar, suna.
Solder, luti.
Soldier, soldato.
Sole, sola.
Sole (fish), soleo.
Sole (of the foot),
plando.
Sole (of boot, etc.),

ledplando.
Solecism, solicismo.
Solely, sole.
Solemn, solena.
Solemnity, soleno.
Solemnize, solenigi.
Solfa, notkanti.
Solfeggio, notkanto.
Solicit, petegi.
Solicitor, advokato.
Solicitous, petega, zorga.
Solicitude, zorgeco.
Solid, fortika.
Solid, a, malfluido.
Solidarity, solidareco.
Solidity, fortikeco.
Solidify, malfluidiĝi.
Soliloquy, monologo.
Solitary, sola.
Solitude, soleco.
Soluble, solvebla.
Solubility, solvebleco.
Solution, solvo.
Solvable, solvebla.
Solvable (payable), pagokapabla.
Solvability (solvency), pagokapableco.
Solvability, solvebleco.
Solve, solvi.
Solvency, pagokapableco.
Solvent, pagokapablo.
Sombre, malhela.
Sombre (manner), malgaja.
Some, kelkaj.
Some (indef.), ia.
Someone, iu.
Somebody, iu.
Somebody's, ies.
Somehow, iel.

Some (quantity), iom.
Something, io.
Sometime, iam.
Sometimes, kelkfoje.
Sometimes— sometimes, jen—jen.
Some way, iel.
Somewhat, iom.
Somewhere, ie.
Son, filo.
Son-in-law, bofilo.
Sonata, sonato.
Song, kanto.
Songster, kantisto.
Sonnet, soneto.
Sonorous, sonora.
Soon, baldaŭ.
Soon (early), frue.
Soot, fulgo.
Soothe, kvietigi.
Sop, trempaĵo.
Sophism, sofismo.
Soprano, soprano.
Sorb, sorpo.
Sorcerer, sorĉisto.
Sorcery, sorĉarto.
Sordid, malpurega.
Sore, ulcereto.
Sorrel, okzalo.
Sorrow, malĝojo.
Sorry, malĝoja—eta.
Sort, speco.
Sort, dece kunmeti, disspecigi.
Sot, drinkulo.
Soul, animo.
Sound (try depth), sondi.
Sound (noise), sono.
Sound, soni.
Sound (trans.), sonigi.
Sound health, sana.
Soup, supo.

Sour, acida.
Sour (manner),
malgaja.
Sourkrout, fermentita
brasiko.
Source, fonto.
Source (origin),
deveno.
Souse, trempegi.
South, Sudo.
Southern, Suda.
Southerly, suda.
Sovereign (pound),
livro.
Sovereign, regnestro.
Sovereignty, regeco.
Sow, porkino.
Sow, semi.
Space, spaco.
Space (time), daŭro.
Spacious, vasta.
Spade, fosilo.
Spade (at cards), piko.
Spain, Hispanujo.
Spangle, briletajo.
Spanish-fly, kantarido.
Spare (extra), ekstra.
Spare, indulgi.
Sparing, to be, ŝpari.
Sparing (saving),
ŝparema.
Spark, fajrero.
Sparkle, brili.
Sparrow, pasero.
Sparrow-hawk,
akcipitro.
Sparse, maldensa.
Spasm, spasmo.
Spatter, ŝprucigi (sur).
Spawn, fiŝsemo.
Speak, paroli.
*Speak through the
nose*, nazparoli.

Speaker, parolanto.
Spear, lanco.
Special, speciala.
Specialise, specialigi.
Specialist, specialisto.
Speciality, specialo—
eco.
Specie, monero.
Species, speco.
Specimen, modelo.
Specious, verŝajna.
Speck, makuleto.
Spectacle (a sight),
vidajô.
Spectacles, okulvitroj.
Spectator, rigardanto.
Spectre, fantomo.
Spectrum, spektro.
Speculate, spekulacii.
Speculation,
spekulacio.
Speculative,
spekulativa.
Speculate (theorise),
teoriigi.
Speculative (theoretic),
teoria.
Speculum, spegulo.
Speech, parolado.
Speechless, muta.
Speed, rapido.
Speed, rapidigi.
Speedy, rapida.
Spell, silabi.
Spell, ĉarmo.
Spend, elspezi.
Spendthrift,
malŝparulo.
Sphere, sfero.
Spherical, sfera.
Sphinx, sfinkso.
Spice, spico.
Spider, araneo.

Spider's web, araneaĵo.
Spike, najlego.
Spile, ligna najlo.
Spill (liquid), disverŝi.
Spill (corn, etc.),
disŝuti.
Spin, ŝpini.
Spinage, spinaco.
Spinal, spina.
Spindle, akso.
Spine, spino.
Spinning-wheel,
radŝpinilo.
Spinning-top,
turnludilo.
Spinster, ŝpinistino
(fraŭlino).
Spiral, helikforma.
Spire, preĝeja turo,
sonorilejo.
Spirit (soul), spirito.
Spirit (energy),
energio.
Spirit (ghost),
fantomo.
Spirit, alkoholo.
Spiritual, spirita.
Spiritualism,
spiritualismo.
Spiritualist,
spiritualisto.
Spirituous, alkohola.
Spit, kraĉi.
Spit (spike), trapiko.
Spite, malamo.
Spite of, in, spite.
Spiteful, venĝema.
Spittle, kraĉaĵo.
Spittoon, kraĉujo.
Splash, ŝpruci.
Splash (with the
hands), plaŭdi.
Spleen, lieno.

Spleen (ill-humour),
ĉagreno.
Splendid, belega.
Splendour, belegeco.
Splice, kunigi.
Splinter, fendpeceto.
Split, fendi.
Spoil, difekti.
Spoil, malbonigi.
Spoil (booty), akiro.
Spoke (of wheel),
radio.
Spokesman, parolanto.
Spoliation, ruinigo.
Sponge, spongo.
Sponsor, baptopatro—
ino.
Spontaneous,
propramova.
Spoon, kulero.
Spoonful, plenkulero.
Sport (joke), ŝerci.
Sport, sporto.
Sportsman, sportisto.
Spot (place), loko.
Spot (stain), makulo.
Spotless, senmakula.
Spouse, edzo—ino.
Spout, ŝpruci.
Sprain, elartikigi.
Sprawl, sterni.
Spray (sprinkle),
surverŝi, ŝprucigi sur.
Spread (news),
disvastigi.
Spread (extend),
etendi.
Sprig, vergeto,
branĉeto.
Sprightly, sprita, viva.
Sprightliness, viveco.
Spring, salti.
Spring (season),

printempo.
Spring (of watch, etc.),
risorto.
Springy, elasta.
Sprinkle, ŝprucigi sur.
Sprinkler, ŝprucigilo.
Sprite, feino, koboldo.
Sprout (bud), elkreski.
Spue, vomi.
Spume, ŝaŭmo.
Spur, sprono.
Spurious, falsa.
Spurn, elĵeti.
Spurt, elŝpruci.
Spy, spioni.
Spy, ekvidi, esplori.
Spyglass, vidilo.
Squabble, malpaceti.
Squad, taĉmento, roto.
Squadron (milit.),
skadro.
Squadron (naval),
eskadro.
Squall, krieti.
Squall (wind),
ventego.
Squander, malŝpari.
Square, kvadrato.
Square (tool),
rektangulilo.
Square (adj.),
kvadrata.
Square (make square),
kvadratigi.
Square (math.),
kvarobligi.
Squash, premegi.
Squat, dikkorpa.
Squeak, bleketi.
Squeamish, precizema.
Squeeze, premi.
Squib, raketo.
Squint, strabi.

Squint-eyed, straba.
Squirt, elŝprucigilo.
Squirt, elŝpruci.
Squirrel, sciuro.
Stab, vundi, pikegi.
Stable, ĉevalejo.
Stable (firm), fortika.
Stability, fortikeco.
Stack (straw), garbaro.
Stadium, stadio.
Staff (pole), stango.
Staff, of officers, stabo.
Staff (managers),
estraro.
Staff, flag, flagstango.
Stag, cervo.
Stag-beetle, cerva
skarabo.
Stage, estrado.
Stage (theatre),
scenejo.
Stagger, ŝanceliĝi.
Stagnant, senmova.
Stagnation,
senmoveco.
Staid, deca, kvieta.
Stain, makuli.
Stain, makulo.
Stair, ŝtupo.
Staircase (stairs),
ŝtuparo.
Stake, paliso, fosto.
Stake (wager), veto.
Stalactite, stalaktito.
Stalagmite, stalagmito.
Stale, malfreŝa.
Stalk (plant), trunketo.
Stall (at market, etc.),
budo.
Stall (for beast), stalo.
Stallion, ĉevalviro.
Stamen (bot.), paliseto.
Stamin, stamino.

Stammer, balbuti.
Stamp (to mark), stampi.
Stamp (brand), stampaĵo.
Stamp, postage, poŝtmarko.
Stamp with foot, piedfrapadi.
Stamper (marker), stampilo.
Stanch (firm), firma, fortika.
Stanch (trusty), fidela, fervora.
Stanchion, subteno.
Stand, stari.
Stand, piedestalo.
Stand (trans.), starigi.
Standard (flag), standardo.
Standard (model), modelo.
Stanza, strofo.
Staple, komuna.
Star, stelo.
Starboard, dekstro.
Starch, amelo.
Stare, rigardegi.
Stark, rigida, tuta.
Stark (adv.), tute.
Starling, sturno.
Start (with fear), ektremi.
Start, ekiri.
Startle, ektremi.
Starve, malnutri.
State (social condition), etato.
State (condition), stato.
State, Ŝtato.
State (subject of a), Ŝtatano.

State, esprimi, diri.
Statement (report), raporto.
Statesman, politikisto.
Station (of life), situacio, stato.
Station, railway, stacidomo.
Stationary, senmova.
Stationary, senprogresa.
Stationer, papervendisto.
Stationery, paperaĵo.
Statistics, statistiko.
Statue, statuo.
Stature, kresko.
Statute, regulo.
Statutes, regularo.
Stave, in, krevi.
Stay (to remain), resti.
Stay (to stop), haltigi.
Stay (a support), subteno.
Steadfast, konstanta.
Steady, neŝancelebla.
Steak, steko, bifsteko.
Steal, ŝteli.
Stealth, by, kaŝe, sekrete.
Stealthy, kaŝa, sekreta.
Steam, vaporo.
Steamboat, vaporŝipo.
Steam-engine, vapormaŝino.
Steed, ĉevalo.
Steel, ŝtalo.
Steelyard, pesilo, pesmaŝino.
Steep, kruta.
Steep, trempi.
Steeple, preĝeja turo.
Steer, juna bovviro.

Steer, direkti.
Steerage, antaŭparto.
Steersman, direktilisto.
Stem, trunketo.
Stem of a pipe, pipa tubo.
Stem (of ship), antaŭparto.
Stench, malbonodoro.
Stenographer, stenografisto.
Stenography, stenografio.
Step, ŝtupo.
Step, paŝi.
Step by step, paŝo post paŝo, paŝo paŝe.
Step (relationship), duon.
Stepfather, duonpatro.
Steppe, stepo.
Stereotype, stereotipo.
Stereotype plate, kliŝaĵo.
Stereometry, stereometrio.
Sterile, senfrukta.
Sterility, senfrukteco.
Sterling, vera.
Stern (of ship), posta parto.
Stern, severega.
Stertorous, stertora.
Stew, boleti.
Steward (of ship), ŝipintendanto.
Steward, intendanto.
Stick, bastono.
Stick, glui.
Stick bills, afiŝi.
Sticky, gluanta.
Stiff, rigida.
Stiff neck, koldoloro.

Stifle, sufoki.
Stigma (bot.), rostreto.
Stigma, velkeco, malhonoreco.
Stigmata, vundpostsignoj.
Stigmatise, kalumnii, malhonori.
Still (distilling), distililo.
Still (calm), trankvila.
Still (adv.), tamen.
Still, senmova.
Stilts, iriloj.
Stimulant, stimulilo.
Stimulate, stimuli.
Sting, piki.
Sting, pikilo.
Stingy, avara, troŝpara.
Stink, malbonodori.
Stint, limigi.
Stipend, salajro.
Stipulate, kondiĉigi.
Stir, movi.
Stir up, eksciti, inciti.
Stir (the fire), inciti.
Stirrup, piedingo.
Stitch, stebi.
Stock, provizo.
Stock (of a wheel), aksingo.
Stockholder, rentulo.
Stocking, ŝtrumpo.
Stoical, stoika.
Stoker, hejtisto.
Stomach, stomako.
Stomachic, stomaka.
Stone, ŝtono.
Stone (of fruit), grajno.
Stone to death, ŝtonmortigi.
Stool, skabelo.
Stoop, kurbiĝi.

Stop (trans.), haltigi.
Stop (at a place), resti.
Stop (halt), halti.
Stop, full, punkto.
Stop (pause), paŭzo.
Stoppage, obstrukco.
Stopper, ŝtopilo.
Store (supply), provizo.
Store, magazeno.
Storehouse, tenejo.
Stork, cikonio.
Storm, ventego.
Storm, ataki.
Story (tale), fabelo.
Story (untruth), mensogeto.
Story (floor), etaĝo.
Stout, dika.
Stout (beer), nigra biero.
Stoutness, dikeco.
Stove, forno.
Strabism, strabeco.
Straight, rekta.
Straightforwardness, sincereco.
Straightway, tuje.
Strain, streĉi.
Strain (filter), kribri.
Strain after, celi.
Strainer, kribrilo.
Strait (geog.), markolo.
Strait (narrow), mallarĝa.
Strait (difficulty), embarasaĵo.
Straiten, mallarĝigi.
Strand, marbordo.
Strand (of rope, etc.), fadeno.
Strange, stranga.

Stranger, fremdulo, malkonulo.
Strangeness, strangeco.
Strangle, sufoki.
Strap, rimeno.
Stratagem, ruzo.
Strategy, militarto.
Stratify, tavoli.
Stratum, tavolo.
Straw, pajlo.
Strawberry, frago.
Stray, erariĝi.
Streak, streko.
Stream, rivereto.
Street, strato.
Strength, forteco.
Strengthen, plifortigi.
Strenuous, energia.
Stress, forto, premo— eco.
Stretch, streĉi.
Stretcher, portilo.
Strew, disĵeti.
Strict, severa.
Stride, paŝegi.
Strident, sibla sono.
Strife, malpaco, disputo.
Strike, frapi.
Strike (of workmen), striki.
Strike (coins), presi, monopresi.
Strike up singing, ekkanti.
Strike out (writing), surstreki.
Striking, surpriza, tuŝanta, solena.
String, ŝnureto.
Stringent, severa.
Strip, strio.

Strip off, senigi je.
Stripe, strio.
Strive, penadi.
Stroke, streko.
Stroke (a blow), bato.
Stroke (to touch),
karesi, froti.
Stroll, promeni.
Strong, forta.
Stronghold, fortikaĵo.
Strophe, strofo.
Structure, strukturo.
Struggle, barakti.
Strut, paradi.
Strut (a stay),
subtenaĵo.
Strychnine, striknino.
Stubborn, obstinega.
Stubbornness,
obstinegeco.
Stucco, stukaĵo.
Stud, butono.
Student, studento.
Studio, studĉambro.
Studious, lernema.
Study, lerni, studi.
Stuff (material), ŝtofo.
Stuff, plenigi.
Stumble, faleti.
Stump, trunkrestaĵo.
Stun, duonesvenigi.
Stupefy, malspritigi.
Stupefaction, mirego.
Stupendous,
mireginda.
Stupid, malsprita.
Stupidity, malspriteco.
Stupor, letargio.
Sturdy, harda.
Sturgeon, sturgo, huzo.
Stutter, balbuti.
Stye (pig), porkejo.
Style, stilo.

Style (fashion), fasono.
Stylish, stila.
Subaltern, subulo.
Subcutaneous,
subhaŭta.
Subdivide, redividi.
Subdue, submeti,
venki.
Subject (gram.),
subjekto.
Subject, regato,
regnano.
Subject, objekto.
Subject (lit.), temo.
Subject, submeti,
subigi.
Subjection, regateco,
submeteco.
Subjugate, submeti.
Subjunctive (gram.),
relata modo.
Sublime, altega,
belega.
Submarine, submara.
Submarine vessel,
submarŝipo.
Submerge, subakvi.
Submission,
submetiĝo.
Submissive, humila.
Submit (yield), cedi.
Submit, submetiĝi.
Subordinate, subulo.
Subordinate, suba.
Suborn, subaĉeti.
Subpœna, asigno.
Subscribe (to a
newspaper, etc.),
aboni.
Subscribe (sign),
subskribi.
Subscribe (money),
monoferi.

Subscription,
monoferado.
Subscription, abono.
Subsequent, sekva.
Subside, mallevi.
Subsidy, helpa mono.
Substance, substanco.
Substantial, fortika.
Substantiate, pruvi.
Substantive,
substantivo.
Substitute, anstataŭi.
Subterfuge, artifiko.
Subterranean, subtera.
Subterraneous,
subtera.
Subtile, maldika.
Subtle, ruza.
Subtract, elpreni.
Subtraction, elpreno.
Suburbs, ĉirkaŭurbo.
Subvention, helpa
mono.
Subversive, detruanta.
Succeed (order),
postveni, sekvi.
Succeed, sukcesi.
Success, sukceso.
Successful, sukcesa.
Succession, in, vice.
Successive, intersekva.
Successor, posteulo.
Succinct, mallonga.
Succour, helpi.
Succulent, bongusta.
Succumb, subfali.
Such a, tia.
Suck, suĉi.
Sucking-pig, porkido.
Suckle, mamnutri.
Suction, suĉado.
Sudden, subita.
Sue, procesi.

Suet, graso.
Suffer (endure), suferi.
Suffer (tolerate), toleri.
Suffering, sufero.
Suffice, sufiĉi.
Sufficiency, sufiĉeco.
Sufficient, sufiĉa.
Suffix, sufikso.
Suffocate, sufoki.
Suffrage (vote),
voĉdono.
Sugar, sukero.
Sugar basin, sukerujo.
Suggest, proponi,
inspiri.
Suicide, memmortigo.
Suicide, to commit, sin
memmortigi.
Suit, konveni.
Suitable, konvena,
taŭga.
Suite, sekvantaro.
Suitor (lover), amanto.
Suitor, plendulo.
Sulk, kolereti.
Sullen, malgaja.
Sully, malpurigi.
Sulphur, sulfuro.
Sulphuric acid,
vitriolo.
Sultan, sultano.
Sultry, varmega.
Sum, sumo.
Sum, sumi.
Sum up, resumi.
Summarise, resumi.
Summary, resumo.
Summary, mallonga.
Summer, somero.
Summerhouse, laŭbo.
Summit, supro.
Summon, asigni, citi.
Summon (a meeting),

192

kunvoki.
Summons, citato.
Sumptuous, luksa.
Sun, suno.
Sunbeam, sunradio.
Sunday, dimanĉo.
Sundry, diversa.
Sunflower, sunfloro.
Sunshade, sunombrelo.
Sunstroke, sunfrapo.
Sup, noktomanĝi.
Superb, belega.
Superficial, supraĵa.
Superficies, supraĵo.
Superfluity, superfluo.
Superfluous, superflua.
Superhuman,
superhoma.
Superintend, observi,
zorgi pri.
Superior, supera.
Superior, a, superulo.
Superiority, supereco.
Superlative (gram.),
superlativo.
Supernatural,
supernatura.
Supernumerary,
ekstrulo.
Superscription,
surskribo.
Supersede, anstataŭi.
Superstition,
superstiĉo.
Superstitious,
superstiĉa.
Supervise, observi.
Supper, noktomanĝo.
Supplant, anstataŭi,
uzurpi.
Supple, fleksebla.
Supplement, aldono.
Supplement, aldoni.

Supplementary,
aldona.
Supplicate, petegi.
Supply, provizi.
Support, subteni.
Support (prop),
subportilo.
Supporter, partiano.
Suppose, supozi,
konjekti.
Suppress, subpremi.
Supremacy,
superegeco.
Supreme, superega,
ĉefa.
Surcharge, supertakso.
Sure, certa.
Surely, certe, nepre.
Surety, garantiaĵo.
Surety, to be, garantii.
Surf, ŝaŭmo, mar—.
Surface, supraĵo.
Surfeit, supersati.
Surge, ondego.
Surgeon, ĥirurgiisto.
Surgery, ĥirurgio.
Surly, malgaja.
Surmise, konjekti.
Surmount, venki.
Surname, alnomo.
Surpass, superi.
Surprise, surprizi.
Surrender, kapitulaci.
Surreptitious, kaŝa.
Survey (land),
termezuri.
Survey, vidadi, elvidi.
Surveyor, termezuristo.
Survive, postvivi.
Susceptible, sentebla—
ema.
Susceptibility,
sentemo.

Suspect, suspekti.
Suspend, pendigi.
Suspense (uncertainty),
necerteco.
Suspicion, suspekto.
Suspicious,
suspektema.
Sustain, subteni.
Sustenance, nutrajô.
Swaddle, vindi.
Swaddling clothes,
vindotuko.
Swagger, fanfaroni.
Swallow (bird),
hirundo.
Swallow, gluti.
Swamp, marĉejo.
Swan, cigno.
Sward, herbejo.
Swarm, —aro.
Swarm of bees,
abelaro.
Swarthy, nigravizaĝa,
dube—nigra.
Swathe, envolvi, vindi.
Sway (swing), balanci.
Swear (jud.), ĵuri.
Swear, blasfemi.
Sweat, ŝviti.
Sweater (garment),
trikoto.
Swede, a, Svedo.
Sweep, balai.
Sweepings, balaajô.
Sweet (mannered),
dolĉa.
Sweet, a, sukerajô.
Sweet, malacida.
Sweetbriar, rozo
sovaĝa.
Sweetheart (m.),
amanto, fianĉo.
Sweetmeat, sukerajô.

Swell, ŝveli.
Swelling, ŝvelo.
Swerve, malrektiĝi.
Swift, rapida.
Swiftness, rapideco.
Swill, glutegi, drinkegi.
Swim, naĝi.
Swimming, naĝarto.
Swimming (in head),
kapturno.
Swindle, ŝteli.
Swindler, ŝtelisto.
Swine, porko.
Swing, balanci.
Swing, a, balancilo.
Swiss, a, Sviso.
Switch, vergo.
Swivel, turnkruco.
Swoon, sveni.
Sword, glavo.
Syllable, silabo.
Syllogism, silogismo.
Symbol, simbolo.
Symmetry, simetrio.
Sympathetic, simpatia.
Sympathise, simpatii.
Sympathy, simpatio.
Symphony, simfonio.
Symptom, simptomo.
Synagogue, sinagogo.
Syncope, sveno.
Syndicate, sindikato.
Synod, sinodo.
Synonym, sinonimo,
egalsenco.
Synonymous,
sinonima, egalsenca.
Synopsis, resumo,
sinopsiso.
Syntax, sintakso.
Synthesis, sintezo.
Syphilis, sifiliso.
Syringe, enŝprucigi.

Syrup, siropo.
System, sistemo.

T

Tabernacle, sanktejo, tendo.
Table, tablo.
Table (index), tabelo.
Table cloth, tablotuko.
Table requisites, teleraro, manĝelaro.
Tacit, neesprimita, silenta.
Taciturn, silentema.
Tack, najleto.
Tack, najleti.
Tackle (apparatus), ilaro.
Tact, delikateco.
Tactics, taktiko.
Tadpole, ranido.
Taffeta, tafto.
Tail, vosto.
Tailor, tajloro.
Taint, difekti.
Take, preni.
Take away, forpreni.
Take away (by force), rabi.
Take care! atentu!
Take care of, zorgi pri.
Take care (of a child), varti.
Take from, depreni.
Take notice of, observi.
Take off (undress), senvestigi, senvestiĝi.
Take part, partopreni.
Take place (happen), okazi.
Take refuge, rifuĝi.
Take snuff, flari

tabakon.
Take supper, noktomanĝi.
Taking (attractive), ĉarmeta, beleta.
Tale, rakonto, fabelo.
Talent, talento.
Talented, lerta, klera.
Talisman, talismano.
Talk, paroli.
Talk foolishly, paroli sensence.
Tall, granda.
Tallow, sebo.
Tally, egali, kunegali.
Talmud, Talmudo.
Talon, ungego.
Tame, malsovaĝigi, kvietigi.
Tame, malsovaĝa.
Tamely, kviete.
Tamper, intrigi, enmiksiĝi pri.
Tan, tani.
Tan, tanilo.
Tan (the skin), brunigi.
Tangent, tangento.
Tangible, palpebla.
Tangle (entangle), enmiksigi.
Tank, akvujo.
Tankard, pokalo, kaliko.
Tanner, tanisto.
Tannin, tanino.
Tantamount to, egalvalora al.
Tap, bateti, frapeti.
Tap, krano.
Tape, kotonrubando.
Tape worm, solitero.
Taper, kandeleto.
Taper, maldikigi.

Tapestry, to hang with, tapeti.
Tapestry, tapeto.
Tar, gudri.
Tar, gudro.
Tardy, malfrua, malrapida.
Target, celtabulo.
Tariff, tarifo.
Tarnish, malheligo.
Tarnish, malheligi.
Tarry, malfrui.
Tarry (to stay in a place), resti.
Tart (pastry), torto.
Tart, acida.
Task, tasko.
Taskwork, tasklaboro.
Tassel, drappendajô.
Taste, gustumi.
Taste, gusto.
Tasty (palatable), bongusta.
Tatter, ĉifonajô.
Tattle, babilajô, babilado.
Tattoo, tatui.
Taunt, sarkasmo.
Taut, streĉa.
Tautology, ripetado, taŭtologio.
Tavern, drinkejo.
Taw, felpreparadi.
Tawdry, falsluksa.
Tawny, dubeflava.
Tax, taksi.
Tax, takso, imposto.
Tea, teo.
Tea canister, teujo.
Tea caddy, teujo.
Tea plant, tearbeto.
Teapot, tekruĉo.
Teach, instrui.

Teacher, instruisto.
Teaching, instruo— ado.
Tear, ŝiri.
Tear in pieces, dispecigi, disŝiri.
Tear (a rent), deŝirajô.
Tear, larmo.
Tease, inciteti, tedi.
Teat, mampinto.
Technical, teknika.
Tedious, teda.
Tediousness, tedeco.
Teem, sufiĉegi.
Teeth, dentoj.
Telegram, telegramo.
Telegraph, telegrafi.
Telegraph (instrument) , telegrafilo.
Telegraphic, telegrafa.
Telegraphist, telegrafisto.
Telegraphy, telegrafo.
Telephone, telefoni.
Telephonic, telefona.
Telescope, teleskopo.
Tell (to relate), rakonti.
Tell, diri.
Temerity, bravegeco.
Temper, karaktero, humoro.
Temperance, sobreco.
Temperate, sobra.
Temperate, modera.
Temperature, temperaturo.
Tempest, ventego, uragano.
Temple (forehead), tempio.
Temple (edifice), templo.
Temporal, monda.

Temporary, kelkatempa, provizora.
Temporize, prokrasti.
Tempt, tenti.
Temptation, tento—ado.
Tempter, tentanto.
Ten, dek.
Tenacity, persisteco.
Tenant, luanto.
Tench, tinko.
Tendency, emo, inklino.
Tender (to become), kortuŝiĝi.
Tender (offer), proponi, prezenti.
Tender (affectionate), amema.
Tenderness, ameco.
Tendon, tendeno.
Tenement, loĝejo, apartamento.
Tenet, dogmo, kredo.
Tenor, tenoro.
Tension, streĉo.
Tent, tendo.
Tentative, prova.
Tepid, varmeta.
Term (time), templimo.
Term (expression), termino.
Termagant, kriegulino.
Terminate, fini.
Terminology, terminaro.
Termite, termito.
Terrace, teraso.
Terrestrial, tera.
Terrible, terrific, terura.
Terrify, timegigi.

Territory, teritorio.
Terror, teruro.
Terrorise, terurigi.
Test, provi.
Testament, testamento.
Testator, testamentanto.
Testify, atesti.
Testimonial, atesto, rekomendo.
Testy, kolerema.
Tetanus, tetano.
Tether, ligilo.
Text, teksto.
Textile, teksa.
Textual, laŭteksta.
Texture, teksaĵo.
Thaler, talero.
Than, ol.
Thank, danki.
Thankfully, danke.
Thankfulness, dankeco.
Thankless, sendanka.
Thanks, dankon.
That, tio.
That (demon. adj.), tiu.
That (rel. pron.), kiu.
That (conjn.), ke.
Thatch, pajla tegmento.
Thaw, degeli.
Thaw, degelado.
The, la.
The more...the more, ju pli...des pli.
Theatre, teatro.
Theatrical, teatra.
Theft, ŝtelo.
Their, theirs, ilia, sia.
Them, ilin.
Theme, temo.
Then, tiam.
Then (after that), poste.

Then (therefore), do.
Theologian, teologisto.
Theology, teologio.
Theorem, teoremo.
Theory, teorio.
Theoretic, teoria.
Therapeutics,
kuracarto.
There (adverb), tie.
There is, jen estas,
estas.
There are, jen estas,
estas.
Therefore, tial.
Thermometer,
termometro.
Thesis, tezo.
They, ili.
Thick, dika.
Thick (dense), densa.
Thicket, arbetaĵo,
arbetaro.
Thickness, dikeco.
Thickset, dikkorpa.
Thickskinned,
dikhaŭta.
Thief, ŝtelisto.
Thieve, ŝteli.
Thievish, ŝtelema.
Thigh, femuro.
Thigh bone, femurosto.
Thimble, fingringo.
Thin (slender),
maldika.
Thine, cia, via.
Thing (matter), afero.
Thing, some, io.
Thing, any, io.
Think, pensi.
Thinker, pensulo.
Think over, pripensi.
Thirst, soifo.
Thirsty, to be, soifi.

This, tio ĉi.
This (demon, pron.),
tiu ĉi.
Thistle, kardo.
Thong, ledrimeno.
Thorax, brustkesto.
Thorn, dorno.
Thorough, plenega.
Thoroughfare, trairejo.
Thou, ci, vi.
Though, kvankam.
Thought, penso,
pensado.
Thoughtful, pripensa.
Thoughtless,
senpripensa.
Thraldom, servuto.
Thrash, draŝi, bategi.
Thread, fadeno.
Threadbare, eluza,
eluzita.
Threat, minaco.
Threatening, minaca.
Three, tri.
Threshold, sojlo.
Thrift, ŝpareco.
Thrifty, ŝparema.
Thrill, vibri, eksciti.
Thrive, prosperi.
Throat, gorĝo.
Throb, bati, palpiti.
Throbbing, bato—ado,
ekbato.
Throe, agonio.
Throne, trono.
Throng (crowd),
amaso.
Throttle, sufoki.
Through, tra.
Throw, ĵeti.
Throw across,
transĵeti.
Throw out, elĵeti.

Thrush, turdo.
Thrust, puŝegi, enpuŝi.
Thumb, dika fingro.
Thump, frapegi, bategi.
Thunder, tondri.
Thunderstorm, fulmotondro.
Thunderstruck, fulmofrapa.
Thursday, ĵaŭdo.
Thus, tiel, tiamaniere.
Thwart, malhelpi.
Thy, cia, via.
Thyme, timiano.
Tibia, tibio.
Tick, bateti, frapeti.
Ticket, bileto.
Tickle, tikli.
Ticklish, tiklosentema.
Tidal, marmova.
Tide, incoming, alfluo.
Tide, receding, forfluo.
Tidings, sciigo.
Tidiness, malnegliĝeco.
Tidy, malnegliĝa.
Tie, ligi.
Tie together (unite), kunligi.
Tie (cravat), kravato.
Tier (row), vico.
Tier (string, etc.), ligilo.
Tiger, tigro.
Tight, prema, troprema.
Tile, tegmenta briko.
Till (money-box), monujo, monokesteto.
Till, until, ĝis.
Till (cultivate), kulturi.
Tillage, kulturaĵo, terkulturo.

Tiller (of boat), direktilo.
Tilt, klini—igi, duonlevi.
Tilt (an awning), kovrilego.
Timber, ligno, lignaĵo.
Time, tempo.
Timely, ĝustatempa.
Timepiece, horloĝo.
Timid, timema.
Timidity, timeco.
Timorous, timema.
Tin, stani.
Tin, stano.
Tinder, fajrfungo.
Tinfoil, hidrargaĵo.
Tinge, koloretigi.
Tingle, vibreti, soneti.
Tinkle, tinti.
Tint, koloretigi.
Tiny, malgrandeta.
Tip, pinto.
Tip (gratuity), trinkmono.
Tippet, manteleto.
Tipple, drinki.
Tippler, drinkemulo.
Tipsy, ebria.
Tirade, denuncado, mallaŭdegado.
Tire, lacigi.
Tire (bore), tedi, enui.
Tired, laca.
Tiresome, teda, enua.
Tissue, teksaĵo.
Tithe (a tenth part), dekono.
Tithing, dekoneco.
Title, titolo.
Titmouse, paruo.
Titter, rideti, ekrideti.
To, al.

Toad, bufo.
Toast (a health), toasto.
Tobacco, tabako.
Tobacco box, tabakujo, tabakskatolo.
Tobacco pouch, tabakujo.
Tobacco shop, tabakbutiko.
Toboggan, glitveturilo.
Tocsin, tumultsonorilo.
To-day, hodiaŭ.
Toe, great, piedfingrego.
Toe, piedfingro.
Together, kune.
Toil, laboro, penado.
Toilet, tualeto.
Toilsome, labora.
Token, signo.
Tolerable, tolerebla.
Tolerably, tolereble.
Tolerance, toleration, tolereco, toleremo.
Tolerant, tolera—ema.
Tolerate, toleri.
Toll, takso, depago.
Toll (bell), sonoradi.
Tomato, tomato.
Tomb, tombo.
Tom cat, katviro.
Tome, volumo.
To-morrow, morgaŭ.
To-morrow, the day after, postmorgaŭ.
Tone (music), tono.
Tongs, prenilo.
Tongs, fire, fajrprenilo.
Tongue, lango.
Tonic, fortigilo.
Tonic accent, tonakcento.

Tonnage, enhavebleco.
Tonsure, tonsuro.
Too (much), tro.
Tool, ilo.
Tooth, dento.
Toothless, sendenta.
Top (summit), supro.
Top (peak), pinto.
Top (of head), verto.
Topaz, topazo.
Topic, subjekto.
Topmost, plejsupra.
Topography, topografio.
Topple, fali.
Topsy-turvy, to turn, renversi.
Topsy-turvy, renversita—ite.
Toque, ĉapo.
Torch, torĉo.
Toreador, toreadoro.
Torment, turmenti.
Torment, turmento—ado.
Torpedo, torpedo.
Torpedo boat, torpedboato.
Torpid, sensenta.
Torpidity, sensenteco.
Torpor, sensento.
Torrent, torento.
Torrid, varmega.
Torsion, tordo.
Torso, torso.
Tortoise, testudo.
Tortuous, torda.
Torture, turmentego.
Torture, turmentegi.
Tory, konservativulo.
Toss, skui.
Toss (throw), ĵeti.
Total, tuto, a.

Totality, tuteco.
Totter, ŝanceli.
Touch, tuŝi.
Touch (feel), palpi.
Touch lightly, tuŝeti.
Touch up (improve), korekti.
Touch, palpo.
Touchiness, ofendsenteco.
Touching, tuŝanta.
Touching (emotion), kortuŝanta.
Touchy, ofendsentema.
Tough, malmola.
Tour, vojaĝo.
Tourism, turismo.
Tourist, turisto.
Touring club, turisma klubo.
Tow, posttreni.
Tow, stupo.
Toward, al.
Towel, viŝilo.
Tower, turo.
Towing-vessel, trenŝipo.
Town, urbo.
Township, urbeto.
Toy, ludilo.
Trace (plan), desegni.
Trace, postsigno.
Track (path), vojo, vojeto.
Tract (of land), regiono.
Tract (pamphlet), traktato.
Traction, tiro—ado.
Trade, negoci, komerci.
Trade (business, etc.), negoco, komerco.

Trade (profession, etc.), metio.
Trade, free, libera interŝanĝado.
Tradesman, butikisto, komercisto.
Tradition, tradicio.
Traduce, mallaŭdegi.
Traffic (commerce, etc.), negoco, komerco.
Tragedian, tragediisto.
Tragedy, tragedio.
Tragic, tragical, tragedia.
Trail (to draw along), treni.
Train, instrui, dresi.
Train (railway), vagonaro.
Train (retinue), sekvantaro.
Train (of carriages), veturilaro.
Train (of a dress), trenaĵo.
Train (to drag), treni.
Trait, trajto.
Traitor, perfidulo.
Traitorous, perfida.
Tramcar, tramveturilo.
Tramway, tramvojo.
Trammel, malhelpi, embarasi.
Tramp, vagisto.
Trample, trabati per la piedoj.
Trance, katalepsio, svenadego.
Tranquil, trankvila.
Tranquilise, trankviligi.
Tranquility,

trankvileco.
Transaction,
interkonsento.
Transcribe, transskribi.
Transfer, transloki,
transporti.
Transfigure,
aliformigi.
Transfix, trabori,
trapiki.
Transform,
aliformigi—iĝo.
Transformed, to be,
aliformiĝi.
Transformation,
aliformigo.
Transfuse, transverŝi.
Transgress, peki,
ofendi.
Transgression, ofendo,
transpaŝo.
Transgressor,
ofendanto, pekanto.
Transit, pasado.
Transition, transiro.
Transitory, rapida.
Translate, traduki.
Translation, traduko.
Translator, tradukisto.
Transmarine,
transmara.
Transmission, transigo.
Transmit, transigi.
Transmitter,
transiganto.
Transmute, aliformigi.
Transparent,
travidebla, diafana.
Transparency,
diafaneco.
Transpire, konigi,
okazi.
Transplant, transloki.

Transport (to delight),
ravi.
Transport (by vehicle),
veturigi.
Transport, transporti.
Transportation,
transportado.
Transpose, transloki.
Transverse, laŭlarĝa,
diagonala.
Trap (snare), kaptilo,
enfalujo.
Trap, kapti.
Trapdoor, plankpordo.
Trapezium, trapezo.
Trash (rubbish),
forĵetaĵo.
Travail, nasklaboro,
naskdoloro.
Travel (by car), veturi.
Travel, vojiri, vojaĝi.
Traveller, vojaĝanto.
Traverse, trapasi,
trairi.
Travesty, maskaĵo.
Tray, pleto.
Treacherous,
perfida—ema.
Treachery, perfideco.
Treacle, mielsiropo.
Tread, premi,
subpremi, marŝi, paŝi.
Treadle, pedalo.
Treason, perfido.
Treasure, trezoro.
Treasurer, kasisto.
Treat (to feast), regali.
Treat (medicinally),
kuraci.
Treat (to discuss),
trakti.
Treatise, traktato.
Treatment (medical),

kuracado.
Treaty, kontrakto, traktaĵo.
Tree, arbo.
Trefoil, trifolio.
Trellis, palisplektaĵo.
Tremble, tremi.
Trembling, tremo—ado.
Tremendous, grandega.
Tremor, tremeto, skueto.
Tremulous, trema, skueta.
Trench, fosaĵo.
Trenchant, akra.
Trencher, lignotelero.
Trepidation, tremeco, tremado.
Trespass, transpaŝo, ofendo.
Tress (hair), harligo.
Tress, plektaĵo.
Trestle (bench), stablo.
Trial (an attempt), provo—aĵo—ado.
Triangle, triangulo.
Tribe, gento.
Tribulation, doloro, malĝojo, suferado.
Tribunal (place), juĝejo.
Tribunal (judges), juĝistaro.
Tributary, depaganta.
Tribute, depago.
Trice, in a, momente.
Trick, friponi.
Trick, malbonfaraĵo.
Trick (at cards), preno.
Trickle, guteti.
Tri-coloured, trikolora.
Tricycle, triciklo.

Trident, tridento.
Triennial, trijara.
Trifle, bagatelo, trivialaĵo.
Trifling, triviala.
Trigger, tirilo.
Trigonometry, trigonometrio.
Trill (mus.), trili.
Trinity, the, Triunuo.
Trinket, juvelo—eto.
Trio, trio.
Trip, faleti.
Trip, vojaĝo—eto.
Tripe, tripo.
Triple, triobla.
Tripod, tripiedo.
Trisyllable, trisilabo.
Trite, komuna, eluzita.
Triturate, pisti.
Triumph, triumfi.
Triumphal, triumfa.
Trivial, triviala.
Triviality, trivialaĵo.
Trombone, trombone.
Troop (people), bando, amaso.
Trooper, rajdistarano.
Trophy, venksigno.
Tropics, tropiko.
Tropical, tropika.
Trot, troti.
Trot, troto—ado.
Trouble, konfuzi, ĉagreni.
Troublesome, malfacila.
Trough, trogo.
Trousers, pantalono.
Trousseau, vestaro.
Trout, truto.
Trowel, trulo.
Truant, kuŝemulo,

forkuranteto.
Truce, interpaco.
Truck, manveturilo.
Truculent, kruelega.
True, vera.
Truffle, trufo.
Truly, vere.
Trump (cards), atuto.
Trumpery, ĉifaĵo
senvalora.
Trumpet, trumpetadi.
Trumpet, trumpeto.
Trumpeter,
trumpetisto.
Trunk (animal or
insect), rostro.
Trunk (tree), trunko.
Trunk (box), kesto,
vojaĝkesto.
Trunk (of body), torso.
Truss (bandage),
bandaĝo.
Truss (a pack), pakaĵo,
ilaro.
Trust, konfidi.
Trustful, konfidema.
Trustworthy, fidinda.
Trusty, fidinda.
Truth, vero—eco.
Truthful, verema.
Truth, in, vere.
Try (attempt), peni.
Try (test), provi.
Tsar, Caro.
Tub, kuvo—eto.
Tube, tubo.
Tuber, tubero.
Tubercle (med.),
tuberkulo.
Tuberosity, tubero.
Tubular, tubforma.
Tuck up, alfaldi.
Tuesday, mardo.

Tuft, tufo.
Tuft (hair), hartufo.
Tug, posttreni.
Tug boat, trenŝipo.
Tulip, tulipo.
Tulle, tulo.
Tumble, elrenversi.
Tumbler, glaso.
Tumbrel,
ŝarĝoveturilo.
Tumour, ŝvelabsceso.
Tumult, tumulto.
Tumultuous, tumulta.
Tun, barelego.
Tune, agordi.
Tuneful, belsona.
Tunic, ĵako.
Tuning-fork,
tonforketo.
Tunnel, subtervojo.
Turban, turbano.
Turbid, ŝlima.
Turbot, rombfiŝo.
Turbulent, tumulta.
Tureen, supujo.
Turf, torfo.
Turk, Turko.
Turkey, Turkujo.
Turkey (bird),
meleagro.
Turmoil, bruego,
tumulto.
Turn, turni.
Turn (on a lathe),
torni.
Turn, vico.
Turner, tornisto.
Turnip, napo.
Turnscrew,
ŝraŭbturnilo.
Turnspit, turnrostilo.
Turnstile, turnkruco.
Turpentine, terebinto.

Turpitude, hontindaĵo.
Turquoise, turkiso.
Turret, tureto.
Turtle-dove, turto.
Tusk, dentego.
Tutor, guvernisto.
Twain, du.
Tweezers, prenileto.
Twelve, dekdu.
Twig, branĉeto.
Twilight, vespera krepusko.
Twin, dunaskito.
Twine, ŝnureto.
Twinkle, brileti.
Twist, tordi.
Twitter, pepi.
Two, du.
Tympanum, oreltamburo.
Type (model), modelo.
Type, tipo, preslitero.
Typhoid (fever), tifa febro.
Typhus, tifo.
Typical, modela.
Typographist, preslaboristo.
Typography, tipografio.
Tyrannical, tirana—ema.
Tyranny, tiraneco.
Tyrant, tirano.
Tyro, novico.

U

Ubiquity, ĉieesto.
Udder, mamo.
Ugliness, malbeleco.
Ugly, malbela.
Ukase, ukazo.

Ulcer, ulcero.
Ulterior, posta, nekonata.
Ultimate, lasta, ultimata.
Ultimately, laste, ultimate.
Ultimatum, ultimatumo.
Ultramarine, ultramarino.
Umbra, ombro.
Umbrage, ombraĵo.
Umbrella, ombrelo.
Umpire, juĝanto—isto.
Unaccountable, neklarigebla.
Unadorned, senornama.
Unadvisedly, malprudente.
Unadulterated, nefalsita, pura.
Unaffected, neafekta, naiva, simpla.
Unalloyed, nemiksita.
Unalterable, neŝanĝebla.
Unanimity, unuanimeco.
Unanimous, unuvoĉa, unuanima.
Unanimously, unuvoĉe, unuanime.
Unassuming, neafektema, modesta.
Unavailing, malutila.
Unawares, senatente.
Unbar, malbari, malfermi.
Unbearable, netolerebla.
Unbecoming,

malkonvena.
Unbelief, malkredeco.
Unbeliever,
malkredulo.
Unbend (relax), distri,
amuzi, cedi.
Unbending (resolute),
decidega, neceda.
Unbiased, senpartia.
Unblushing (shameless
), senhonta.
Unbosom (to disclose),
malkaŝi.
Unbound (of books,
etc.), nebindita.
Unbounded, senlima.
Unbridle, senbridigi.
Unbroken,
senintermanka.
Unburden (reveal,
tell), malkovri.
Unbutton, debutonumi.
Unceremonious,
senceremonia.
Uncertain, necerta.
Unchain, elĉenigi.
Unchangeable,
neŝanĝebla.
Uncivil, malĝentila.
Uncivilized,
necivilizita.
Uncle, onklo.
Unclean, malpura.
Uncleanness,
malpureco.
*Uncomfortable, to
make*, ĝeni.
Uncommon,
nekomuna.
Uncommunicative,
nekomunikema,
silentema.
Unconcerned,

nezorgema.
Unconditional,
nekondiĉa, absoluta.
Unconnected,
nekunigita.
Unconscious,
nekonscia.
Uncork, malŝtopi.
Uncorrupted (phys.),
neputrigita.
Uncorrupted (moral),
neaĉetita.
Uncouth, malĝentila.
Uncover, malkovri.
Unction, ŝmiraĵo.
Uncious, grasa.
Uncultivated,
senkultura.
Undaunted,
neintimigita.
Under (prep.), sub.
Under (adv.), sube.
Underbred (rude),
vulgara.
Undergo, suferi.
Underground, subtera.
Underhand, sekreta,
kaŝema.
Underlie, subtavoli,
subteni.
Underline, substreki.
Undermaster,
submajstro.
Undermine (to dig),
subfosi.
Undermost (adv.), la
plej sube.
Underneath (prep.),
sub.
Underneath (adv.),
sube.
Underrate, malestimi.
Underscore, substreki.

Understand, kompreni.
Understanding,
intelekto.
Understanding, to
have an, interkonsenti
pri.
Undertake, entrepreni.
Undertaking,
entrepreno.
Underwrite, garantii.
Undesigned, senvola,
senintenca.
Undignified, malinda.
Undisciplined,
malobeema.
Undo, malfari.
Undo (the hair),
malligi.
Undress (one's self),
malvesti, senvestigi.
Undulate, ondolinii.
Undulating, ondolinia.
Undulation, ondolinio.
Unearthly,
supernatura.
Uneasiness,
maltrankvileco.
Uneasy, maltrankvila.
Unemployed,
senokupa.
Unendurable,
nesuferebla.
Unequal, neegala.
Unerring, neerara,
certa.
Uneven, neebena,
malglata.
Unexpected,
neatendita.
Unexpectedly,
neatendite.
Unexpressed,
neesprimita.

Unfair (dishonest),
malhonesta, malrajta.
Unfaithful, malfidela.
Unfasten, malligi.
Unfavourable,
malfavora.
Unfeeling, sensenta.
Unfeigned, sincera.
Unfilial, nefila.
Unfold (open),
malfaldi, malvolvi.
Unfold (disclose),
malkovri, malkaŝi.
Unfold (relate, tell),
rakontadi.
Unforeseen,
neantaŭvidita.
Unfortunate, malfeliĉa.
Unfrequently, malofte.
Unfruitful, senfrukta.
Unfurl, malfaldi,
malvolvi.
Unfurnish, senmebligi.
Ungainly, mallerta.
Ungodly, malpia.
Ungrateful, nedanka,
nedankema.
Unguent, ŝmiraĵo.
Unhandy, mallerta.
Unhappy, malfeliĉa.
Unhappiness,
malfeliĉeco.
Unhealthy, malsana.
Unheeded, nezorgita.
Unhook, malkroĉi.
Unhurt, sendifekta.
Unicorn, unukornulo.
Unification, unuigo.
Uniform (dress),
uniformo.
Uniform, unuforma.
Uniformity, simileco,
unuformeco.

Unify, unuigi.
Uninhabited, senhoma.
Union, unuigo, kunigo.
Unique, sola, senegala.
Unison, in (mus.),
agorde.
Unit, unuo.
Unite, unuigi, kunigi.
Universal, universala.
Universe, universo.
University,
universitato.
Unjust, maljusta.
Unknown, nekonata—
ita.
Unlawful,
malpermesita,
nelaŭleĝa.
Unless, esceptinte ke.
Unlikely, neverŝajna.
Unlimited, senlima.
Unload, senŝarĝi.
Unman, malkuraĝigi.
Unmask, senmaskigi.
Unnatural,
kontraŭnatura.
Unnerve, malkuraĝigi.
Unoccupied,
neokupata, senokupa.
Unpack, elpaki.
Unpardonable,
nepardonebla.
Unpleasant, malplaĉa.
Unpolished (surface),
malglata.
Unpretending,
neafektema, simpla.
Unprincipled,
malhonesta,
senprincipa.
Unproductive,
senfrukta.
Unpublished,

neeldonita.
Unquiet, malkvieta.
Unravel, maltordi.
Unrecognisable,
nerekonebla.
Unremitting, senĉesa.
Unreserved, nerezerva.
Unrestrained,
nedetena, libera.
Unroll, malruli,
malfaldi.
Unroof, maltegmenti.
Unruffled, trankvila,
nemaltrankvila.
Unruly, malĝentila.
Unsaddle, senseligi.
Unsafe, danĝerhava.
Unsalable,
nevendebla.
Unseal, sensigeligi.
Unsearchable,
neserĉebla.
Unseemly,
malkonvena.
Unsettle (disturb),
malordigi, konfuzi.
Unshaken, firma,
neŝanceliĝa.
Unsightly, malbelega.
Unskilful, mallerta.
Unsociableness,
nesocietamo—emo.
Unspotted (stainless),
senmakula.
Unstable, ŝanĝema.
Untamed, sovaĝa.
Untidy (dress),
negliĝa.
Untie, malligi.
Until, ĝis.
Untimely, antaŭtempa,
trofrua.
Untiring, senlaciĝa.

Untoward, kontraŭa.
Unto (prep.), al.
Untrammeled, libera.
Untrue, malvera.
Unused, neuzita.
Unusual, neordinara, malofta.
Unvarnished (plain), simpla, neafektema.
Unveil, malkovri.
Unwary, malsingardema.
Unwavering, neŝanceliĝa.
Unwell, malsana.
Unwholesome, malsana, malsaniga.
Unwieldy, multepeza, nemanregebla.
Unwillingly, kontraŭvole, malbonvole.
Unwise, malsaĝa.
Unwittingly, senintence.
Unwonted, nekutima.
Unworthy, malinda.
Unyoke, maljungi.
Up (adv.), supre.
Upbraid, mallaŭdi, riproĉi.
Uphill (fig.), malfacila.
Uphill, to go, supreniri.
Uphold, subteni.
Upholsterer, meblisto, meblofaristo.
Uplift, altlevi.
Upon (prep.), sur.
Upper (adj.), plisupra.
Uppermost (adj.), la plej supra.
Upright (erect),

vertikala, rekta.
Upright (honest), honesta.
Upright (post), fosto.
Uprightly, rekte, honeste.
Uprightness, rekteco, honesteco.
Uproar, bruego, tumulto.
Uproot, elradikigi.
Upset, renversi, renversiĝi.
Upshot, rezultato.
Upside down, renversite.
Upstairs, supre.
Upstart, elsaltulo.
Up to (until), ĝis.
Up to now, ĝis nun.
Urban, urba.
Urbane, ĝentila.
Urchin, bubo.
Urge, urĝi.
Urgent, urĝa.
Urine, urino.
Urinal, urinejo.
Urn, urno.
Us, nin.
Usage, uzo—ado.
Use, uzi.
Use (employment), uzo.
Use (custom), kutimo.
Use, to be of, utili.
Use up (wear out), eluzi.
Useful, utila.
Useless, senutila.
Uselessness, senutileco.
Usher (school), submajstro.

Usher (beadle), pedelo.
Usual, ordinara, kutima.
Usually, kutime.
Usufruct, ĝuado.
Usurer, procentegisto.
Usurp, uzurpi.
Usurpation, uzurpo—ado.
Usurper, uzurpulo.
Usury, procentego.
Utensil, uzaĵo, ilo, ujo.
Utilise, utiligi.
Utility, utilo—eco.
Utmost, ekstrema.
Utopia, utopio.
Utopian, utopia.
Utter, ekparoli.
Utterance, ekparolo.
Utterly, tute.
Uttermost, ekstrema, la plej.

V

Vacancy, malplenaĵo.
Vacant, neokupata.
Vacate, forlasi.
Vacation, libertempo.
Vaccinate, inokuli.
Vacillate, ŝanceliĝi.
Vacillating, ŝanceliĝa.
Vacuous, malplena.
Vacuum, malplenaĵo.
Vagabond, sentaŭgulo, vagisto.
Vagary, kaprico.
Vagrant, vagisto.

Vague, malpreciza.
Vain (fruitless), vana.
Vain (conceited), vanta.
Vain, in, vane.
Vainly, vane.
Vale, valeto.
Valet, lakeo, servisto.
Valiant, brava.
Valid, leĝa.
Valise, valizo.
Valley, valo.
Valorous, brava.
Valour, braveco.
Valse, valso.
Value (appraise), taksi.
Value (esteem), ŝati.
Value, valoro.
Valuable, multekosta.
Valuation, takso, taksado.
Valueless, senvalora.
Valve, klapo.
Van, veturilego.
Van (of army), antaŭgvardio.
Vane, ventoflago.
Vanguard, antaŭgvardio.
Vanilla, vanilo.
Vanish, neniiĝi.
Vanity, vaneco.
Vanquish, venki.
Vanquisher, venkanto.
Vapid, sengusta.
Vaporisation,

vaporigo.
Vaporise, vaporigi.
Vapour, vaporo.
Vapour-
bath (place),
ŝvitbanejo.
Vapourous, vapora.
Variable, ŝanĝebla.
Variance, to set at,
malpacigi.
Variation,
diverseco, ŝanĝo.
Varicose vein,
vejnego.
Variegate,
multkolorigi.
Variegated,
multkolora.
Variety, diverseco.
Variola, variolo.
Various, diversa.
Varnish, laki.
Varnish, lako—aĵo.
Vary, diversi.
Vase, vazo.
Vaseline, vazelino.
Vassal, vasalo.
Vassalage,
vasaleco.
Vast, vasta.
Vat, kuvego.
Vault (leap), salti.
Vault, arkaĵo.
Vaunt, fanfaroni.
Veal, bovidviando,
bovidaĵo.
Veer, turni, iĝi.
Vegetable, legomo.
Vegetable-garden,
legoma ĝardeno.
Vegetate, vegeti.
Vegetation,
kreskaĵado.

Vehemence,
perforteco.
Vehement, perforta.
Vehicle, veturilo.
Veil (for face),
vualo.
Veil, vuali, kovri.
Veil (conceal), kaŝi.
Vein, vejno.
Veined, vejna.
Vellum, veleno.
Velocipede,
velocipedo.
Velocity, rapideco.
Velvet, veluro.
Venal, aĉetebla.
Vend, vendi.
Venerable,
respektinda.
Venerable (aged),
maljuna.
Venerate,
respektegi.
Veneration,
respektego.
Vengeance, venĝo.
Venial, pardonebla.
Venison, ĉasaĵo.
Venom, veneno.
Venomous, venena.
Vent, ellaso.
Vent-hole,
ellastruo.
Ventilate, ventoli.
Ventilator,
ventolilo.
Ventriloquist,
ventroparolisto.
Venture, riski.
Venture, risko.
Venturous, riska.
Veracious, verema.
Veracity, vereco.

Verandah, balkono.
Verb, verbo.
Verbal, parola.
Verbena, verbeno.
Verbatim (adv.),
laŭvorte.
Verbiage, babilaĵo.
Verbose,
parolegema.
Verbosity,
parolegeco.
Verdant, verdanta.
Verdict, juĝo.
Verdigris, verdigro.
Verdure, verdaĵo.
Verger, pedelo.
Verify, verigi,
ekzameni.
Verily, vere.
Veritable, vera.
Verity, vereco.
Vermicelli,
vermiĉelo.
Vermifuge,
kontraŭvermaĵo.
Vermilion, cinabro.
Vermin, insektoj.
Vermouth, vermuto.
Verse, verso.
Verses, to make,
versi.
Versed (learned),
klera.
Versifier, versisto.
Version, traduko.
Verst, versto.
Vertebra, vertebro.
Vertebral, vertebra.
Vertex, supro,
pinto.
Vertical, vertikala.
Vertigo, kapturno.
Very, tre.

Vesicle, veziketo.
Vespers, Vespera
Diservo.
Vessel (ship), ŝipo,
boato.
Vessel, vazo, ujo.
Vest, veŝto, jaketo.
Vestibule, vestiblo.
Vestige, postsigno.
Vestment, vestaĵo.
Vestry,
preĝejoĉambro.
Veteran,
malnovulo.
Veterinary surgeon,
bestokuracisto.
Veto, vetoo,
malpermeso.
Vex, ĉagreni.
Vexation, ĉagreno.
Viaduct, vojponto.
Vial, boteleto.
Viands, viando,
manĝaĵo.
Vibrant, multesona.
Vibrate, vibri.
Viburnum, viburno.
Vicar, paroĥestro.
Vicarage,
paroĥestrejo.
Vice, malvirto.
Vice (screw press),
prenilego.
Viceroy, vicreĝo.
Vice versa,
kontraŭe, male.
Vicinity,
proksimeco,
najbareco.
Vicious, malvirta.
Vicissitude,
sortovico.
Victim, suferanto.

Victimise, suferigi.
Victor, venkanto.
Victorious, venkinta.
Victory, venko.
Victuals, manĝaĵo, provizaĵo.
Vie, konkuri.
View, vidi.
Vigil (watch), viglo, gardo.
Vigilant, vigla.
Vignette, vinjeto.
Vigorous, fortega.
Vigour, fortegeco.
Vile, malnobla.
Vileness, hontindaĵo.
Villa, domo, kampodometo.
Village, vilaĝo.
Villager, vilaĝano.
Villain, kanajlo.
Villainous, malbonega.
Vindicate, pravigi.
Vindication, pravigeco.
Vindictive, venĝema.
Vine, vinberujo— arbo.
Vine-culture, vinberkulturo.
Vinegar, vinagro.
Vinery, vinberejo.
Vine-branch, vinberbranĉo.
Vine-stock, vinbertrunko.
Vineyard, vinberejo.
Vintage, vinrikolto.

Vintner, vinvendisto.
Violate, malrespekti.
Violation, malrespekto.
Violence, perforto.
Violent, perforta.
Violet, violo.
Violet color, violkoloro.
Violin, violono.
Violinist, violonisto.
Violoncello, violonĉelo.
Violoncellist, violonĉelisto.
Viper, vipero.
Virago (fig.), drakino.
Virgin, virgulino.
Virginal, virga.
Virginity, virgeco.
Virgin, The Blessed, La Sankta Virgulino, Dipatrino.
Virile, vira.
Virility, vireco.
Virtue, virto.
Virtuous, virta.
Virtuoso, virtuozo.
Virulent, venena, malboniga.
Virus, veneno.
Visage, vizaĝo.
Vis-a-vis, kontraŭulo.
Viscera, internaĵo.
Viscuous, gluanta.
Visible, videbla.
Visibly, videble.

Vision (sense),
vido.
Vision (apparition),
aperaĵo.
Visit, viziti.
Visiting-card,
vizitkarto.
Visitor, vizitanto.
Visor, viziero.
Visual, vida.
Vital, vivema.
Vital, necesega.
Vitality, vivemo.
Vitiate, difekti.
Vitreous, vitreca.
Vitrify, vitrigi.
Vitriol, vitriolo.
Vivacity, viveco.
Vivid (color), hela.
Vivifying, viviga.
Vixen, vulpino.
Viz, nome, tio estas,
t.e.
Vizier, veziro.
Vocabulary,
vortareto.
Vocal, voĉa.
Vocalist, kantisto.
Vocation, profesio,
inklino, emo.
Voice, voĉo.
Voice (vote),
voĉdono.
Void (empty),
malplena.
Void (null), nuliga.
Void (emptiness),
malplenaĵo.
Volatile (fickle),
flirtema.
Volatilise, vaporigi.
Vol-au-vent,
pasteĉo.

Volcano, vulkano.
Volcanic, vulkana.
Volley (gun firing),
pafilado.
Voluble, babilema,
fluantparola.
Volume (book),
volumo.
Volume (size),
dikeco.
Voluminous,
multdika.
Voluntary,
memvola,
propramova.
Volunteer,
memvolulo.
Voluptuous,
voluptema.
Voluptuousness,
volupteco.
Vomit, vomi.
Vomiting, vomado.
Vomitory, vomilo.
Voracious,
englutema.
Voracity,
engluteco.
Vortex, turnakvo,
turniĝado.
Vote, voĉdoni,
baloti.
Vouch, garantii,
atesti.
Voucher, garantio,
garantianto, atesto.
Vow, dediĉi,
promesi.
Vow (religious),
religia promeso.
Vowel, vokala.
Voyage, vojaĝo,
vojiro.

Vulgar, vulgara.
Vulgarise,
vulgarigi.
Vulgarity,
vulgareco.
Vulgate, Latina
Biblio.
Vulnerable,
vundebla.
Vulture, vulturo.

W

Wobble, ŝanceli—iĝi.
Wadding, vato, vataĵo.
Waddle, balanciĝi,
ŝanceliĝi.
Wade, akvotrairi.
Wafer, oblato.
Waft, flugporti.
Wag, ŝerculo.
Wage (make, carry
on), fari.
Wager, veto.
Wages, salajro.
Waggish, ŝerca.
Waggon (cart),
ŝarĝveturilo.
Waggon (of train),
vagono.
Waggoner,
veturigisto, veturisto.
Wail, ploregi, ĝemegi.
Wain, ŝarĝveturilo.
Waist, talio.
Waistcoat, veŝto.
Wait, atendi.
Wait on (serve), servi.
Waiter, kelnero.
Waive (abandon),
forlasi.
Wake, veki.
Wake of ship,

ŝippostsigno.
Waking
time (reveille),
vekiĝo.
Walk, marŝi, promeni.
Walk (path), aleo.
Walking stick,
bastono.
Wall, muro.
Wallet, sako,
tornistro.
Wallow, ruliĝi,
enŝlimiĝi.
Walnut, juglando.
Walrus, rosmaro.
Waltz, valso.
Wan, pala, palega.
Wand, vergo,
vergego.
Wander, erari, vagi.
Wander (be delirious),
deliri.
Wanderer, nomadulo,
vagisto.
Wandering, nomada,
eraranta.
Wane, ekfiniĝi.
Wanness, paleco.
Want, seneco,
mizerego.
Want (need, require),
bezoni.
Wanton, malica.
War, milito—ado.
Warble, pepi.
Warbler, pepulo,
silvio.
Ward (guard), gardi,
prizorgi.
Ward (turn aside),
deklinigi, evitigi.
Ward (a person),
zorgatulo.

Ward (care), gardeco,
zorgateco.
Ward (district),
kvartalo.
Ward off, deturni.
Warder, gardanto.
Wardrobe,
vestotenejo.
Warehouse, provizejo,
tenejo.
Wares (merchandise),
komercaĵo.
Warfare, batalado.
Warlike, militama.
Warm, varmigi.
Warm, varma.
Warm (zealous),
fervora.
Warm bath,
varmbano.
Warm up, revarmigi.
Warmth, varmeco.
Warn, averti.
Warning, averto.
Warp (twist), tordi.
Warrant (money),
mandato,
monmandato.
Warrant (justify),
pravigi.
Warrant (assure),
certigi.
Warrantable,
pravigebla.
Warren, kuniklejo.
Warrior, militisto.
Wart, veruko.
Wary, atenta,
singardema.
Wash, lavi.
Wash one's self, sin
lavi.
Washerwoman,

lavistino.
Wash-house, lavejo.
Washstand, lavtablo.
Wasp, vespo.
Wasp's nest, vespejo.
Waspish, malĝentila,
ekkolerema.
Waste (squander),
malŝpari.
Waste (grow thin),
konsumiĝi,
malgrasiĝi.
Waste (rubbish),
forĵetaĵo, difektaĵo.
Waste (untilled),
senkultura.
Wasteful,
malŝparema.
Watch, observi,
spioni.
Watch (guard), gardi.
Watch (timepiece),
poŝhorloĝo.
Watch (a look out),
observisto.
Watchful, atentema,
zorgema, vigla.
Watchman,
observisto.
Watchword,
signaldiro.
Water, akvo.
Water (plants, etc.),
surverŝi.
Watery, akva.
Water-closet,
necesejo.
Water-colour,
akvopentraĵo.
Waterfall, akvofalo.
Water-spout, trombo.
Water-tank, akvujo.
Watering-pot, verŝilo.

Waterproof, nepenetrebla.
Wave, ondo.
Wave, agiti, svingeti.
Wavelet, ondeto.
Waver, ŝanceliĝi, ŝanceli.
Wax (bees), vakso.
Wax (shoemaker's), peĉo.
Wax, sealing, sigelvakso.
Wax candle, vakskandelo.
Way (road), vojo.
Way (sea), marrodo.
Way (manner), kutimo, maniero.
Way, Milky, lakta vojo.
Way, in that, tiel, tiamaniere.
Way out (exit), eliro.
Wayfarer, vojiranto.
Waylay, inside ataki.
Wayward, memvola.
We, ni.
Weak, malforta.
Weak (to become), malfortiĝi.
Weaken, malfortigi.
Weakness, malforteco.
Weal, feliĉeco.
Wealth, riĉeco.
Wealthy, riĉega.
Wean (a child), debrustigi.
Wean (alienate), forigi, foriĝi.
Weapon, batalilo.
Wear (use as clothes), porti.
Wear away (decay by use), eluzi.
Wear away (to decline), konsumiĝi.
Weariness, enuo, laceco.
Wearisome, enua, enuiga.
Weary, to, enui.
Weary, laca, enua.
Weather, vetero.
Weather, to, kontraŭstari.
Weathercock, ventoflago.
Weave, teksi, plekti.
Weaver, teksisto, plektisto.
Web (tissue), teksaĵo.
Wed (cf. marry), edziĝi.
Wedding (cf. marry), edziĝo.
Wedge, kojno.
Wedlock, edzeco.
Wednesday, merkredo.
Weed, malbonherbo.
Weed, sarki.
Weeding hook, sarkilo.
Week, semajno.
Weekly (adj.), semajna, ĉiusemajna.
Weep, plori.
Weft, teksaĵo.
Weigh, pezi.
Weigh (trans.), pesi.
Weigh (ponder), pripensi.
Weight, pezo.
Weight, pezilo.
Weight (importance), graveco.

Weighty, peza.
Weigh-bridge, pesilego.
Weir, akvoŝtopilo. [E
Welcome, to, bonveni, bonvoli.
Welcome, bonveno.
Weld, kunforĝi.
Welfare, bonstato.
Well, nu.
Well (pit), puto.
Well, to be, sani.
Well (adv.), bone.
Well-mannered, bonmaniera.
Well-nigh, preskaŭ.
Well-spring, fonto, akvoputo.
Well-wishing, bonvola, bonvolanta.
Welter, enŝlimiĝi.
Wen, tubero.
Wench, knabulino.
West, okcidento.
Westerly, okcidenta.
Westward (adv.), okcidente.
Wet, malsekigi.
Wet, malseka.
Whale, baleno.
Whalebone, balenosto.
Wharf, enŝipigejo.
What, what a? kia?
What? kio, kion?
Whatever, kia ajn.
Whatsoever, kia ajn.
Wheat, tritiko.
Wheedle, karesi, delogi.
Wheedling, karesa, deloga.
Wheeler, delogisto.

Wheel (turn), turnigi.
Wheel, rado.
Wheelbarrow, puŝveturilo.
Wheelwork, radaro.
Wheelwright, radfaristo.
Whelp, ido, hundido, bestido.
When, kiam.
Whenever, kiam ajn.
Where, kie.
Wherefore, kial.
Wherever, kie ajn.
Wherry, barketo.
Whet, akrigi.
Whether, ĉu.
Whey, selakto.
Which (rel. pron.), kiu, kiun.
Which, kio, kion, kiu, kiun.
Whiff, subitventeto.
While, dum.
Whim, kaprico.
Whimper, ploreti.
Whimsical, kaprica.
Whine, ploreti, bleketi.
Whinny, ĉevalbleketo.
Whip, vipi.
Whip, vipo.
Whip, riding, vipeto.
Whir, turniĝadi.
Whirl, turniĝadi.
Whirlpool, turnakvo.
Whirlwind, turnovento.
Whisk, fojnbalao.
Whiskers, vangharoj.
Whisper, paroleti, murmuri.
Whisper, murmuro.

Whistle (of wind),
sibli.
Whistle, fajfilo.
Whistle, fajfi.
Whist, visto.
Whit, porcieto.
White, blanka.
White of egg,
albumeno.
Whiten, blankigi.
Whiting, merlango.
Whitish, dubeblanka.
Whither, kien.
Whitsuntide,
Pentekosto.
Whizz, sibli.
Who, kiu.
Whoever, kiu ajn.
Whole, tuta.
Whole, tuto.
Wholesale, pogrande.
Wholesome, saniga.
Whom, kiun.
Whooping cough,
kokluŝo.
Whosoever, kiu ajn.
Whose, kies.
Why, kial.
Wick, meĉo—aĵo.
Wicked, malvirta,
malbona.
Wickedness,
malvirteco,
malboneco.
Wicket, pordeto.
Wicker, salikaĵo.
Wide, larĝa.
Widen, plilarĝigi.
Widow, vidvino.
Widower, vidvo.
Widowhood, vidveco.
Width, larĝeco.
Width, in, laŭlarĝe.

Wield, manpreni,
manregi.
Wife, edzino.
Wig, peruko.
Wild, sovaĝa.
Wilderness, dezerto.
Wile, ruzo.
Wilful, obstina.
Will, to make,
testamenti.
Will (bequeath),
testamenti.
Will, testamento.
Will-o'-the-wisp,
erarlumo.
Willing, to be, voli.
Willingly, volonte.
Willow, saliko.
Willy-nilly, vole-
nevole.
Wily, ruza.
Win, gajni.
Wince, ektremi.
Winch, turnilo.
Wind (air), vento.
Wind (coil), vindi.
Wind (twist), tordi.
Wind (on spool),
bobenumi.
Wind up (watch, etc.),
streĉi.
Winding sheet,
morttuko, mortkitelo.
Windlass, turnilo.
Window, fenestro.
Window blind,
rulkurteno.
Windpipe, traĥeo.
Windy, venta.
Wine, vino.
Wine making,
vinfarado.
Wine merchant,

vinvendisto.
Wing, flugilo.
Wing (building),
flankaĵo.
Wink, palpebrumi.
Winning (pleasing),
ĉarma, plaĉa.
Winnow, ventoli.
Winter, travintri.
Winter, vintro.
Wintry, vintra.
Wipe, viŝi.
Wire, metalfadeno.
Wisdom, saĝo, saĝeco.
Wise, saĝa, saĝema.
Wish, want, deziri,
voli.
Wish, volo, deziro.
Wistful, pensanta.
Wit, sprito.
Wit, spritulo.
Witch, sorĉistino.
Witchcraft, sorĉo—
arto.
With, kun, per, je, de.
With reference to,
rilate al.
With regard to, rilate
al.
With respect to, rilate
al.
Withdraw, eliĝi.
Withdrawal, reenpaŝo.
Wither, velki,
sensukiĝi.
Withhold, fortiri.
Within, en, interne
(adv.).
Without, sen.
Withstand,
kontraŭstari,
kontraŭbatali.
Witness, atesti.

Witness, atestanto.
Witness, eye,
okulvidanto.
Witticism, spritaĵo.
Wittiness, spriteco.
Witty, sprita, spritema.
Wizard, sorĉisto.
Woe, ve.
Woful, ĉagrenega,
malĝoja.
Wolf, lupo.
Woman, virino.
Womb, utero.
Wonder, miri.
Wonder, mirego,
miro.
Wonder, a, mirindaĵo.
Wonderful, mirinda—
ega.
Wonted, kutima.
Woo, amindumi.
Wood (material),
ligno.
Wood, arbareto.
Woodcock, skolopo.
Woodcutter,
arbohakisto.
Wood
flooring (parquetry),
pargeto.
Woodhouse, lignejo.
Woodpecker, pego.
Wooer, amisto,
amindumisto.
Woof, teksaĵo.
Wool, lano.
Woollen stuff, lanaĵo,
drapo.
Woolly, laneca.
Word (spoken),
parolo.
Word (written), vorto.
Wordiness, babilaĵo.

Word for word,
laŭvorte.
Work, labori.
Work (physical),
laboro—ado.
Work (literary), verko.
Worker, laboristo.
Worker (literary),
verkisto.
Workman, laboristo,
metiisto.
Works (place),
fabrikejo.
Workbox, necesujo.
Working day, simpla
tago.
Workshop, metiejo,
laborejo.
Workmanlike, lerta.
Workmanship,
metiistarto.
World, mondo.
Worldly, monda.
Worm, vermo.
Worm-shaped,
vermoforma.
Wormwood, absinto.
Worn out, eluzita.
Worry (vex), inciteti,
enuigi.
Worry (importune),
trudpeti.
Worry, enuo, ĉagreno.
Worse (adj.),
plimalbona.
Worse (adv.),
plimalbone.
Worship, adori.
Worship, adoro—ado.
Worst (adj.),
plejmalbona.
Worst (adv.),
plejmalbone.

Worsted, malvenkita.
Wort, mosto.
Worth, to be, valori.
Worth (value), valoro.
Worth (esteem), indo.
Worthless (morals),
malnobla.
Worthless, senvalora.
Worthy (of), inda (je).
Wound, vundi.
Wrack, fuko.
Wrangle, disputi,
malpaci.
Wrangle, disputado,
malpacado.
Wrap, faldi, kovri.
Wrapper, kovrilo.
Wrath, kolerego.
Wrathful, kolerega.
Wreath, garlando.
Wreathe, plekti,
girlandi.
Wreck (ship),
ŝippereo.
Wreckage, derompaĵo.
Wren, regolo.
Wrench, ektiregi.
Wrest, tiregi.
Wrestle, barakti.
Wrestler, baraktisto.
Wretch, malbonulo,
krimulo.
Wretched, mizera.
Wriggle, tordi, tordeti.
Wring (twist), tordi,
premegi.
Wring (the hand),
premi.
Wrinkle, sulkigi.
Wrinkle (facial),
sulko.
Wrist, manradiko.
Write, skribi.

221

Writer (author),
verkisto.
Writer, skribisto.
Writing, skribaĵo.
Writing-table,
skribotablo.
Wrong, malpraveco.
Wrong, malprava.
Wrongfully, malrajte.
Wrongly, malrajte,
malprave.
Wroth, kolerega.
Wry, torda.

Y

Yacht, ŝipeto.
Yard, korto.
Yard (of ship),
velstango.
Yarn, lanfadenaĵo.
Yawn, oscedi.
Yawn, oscedo—ado.
Ye, vi.
Yea, jes, vere.
Year, jaro.
Yearly, ĉiujara.
Yearn, deziregi.
Yearning,
dezirego—ado.
Yeast,
panfermentilo.
Yell, kriegi.
Yell, kriego.
Yellow, flava.
Yellowish,
dubeflava.
Yelp, hundbleki.
Yeoman (farmer),
farmisto.
Yes, jes.
Yes, truly, jes, vere.
Yesterday, hieraŭ.

*Yesterday, the day
before*, antaŭhieraŭ.
Yet, tamen.
Yet (adv.), ankoraŭ.
Yew, taksuso.
Yield (surrender),
kapitulaci, cedi.
Yield (produce),
produktaĵo.
Yoke, jugo.
Yolk of egg,
ovoflavo.
Yonder, tie, tien.
You, vi, vin.
Young, juna.
Young (offspring),
ido, idaro.
*Young
lady* (unmarried),
fraŭlino.
*Young
man* (unmarried),
fraŭlo.
Younger, plijuna.
Youngest, la plej
juna.
Youngster, junulo—
ino.
Your, yours, via.
Youth, junulo.
Youth (collectively),
junularo.
Youth (state of),
juneco.
Youthful, juna.
Youthfulness,
juneco.
Yule, kristnasko.

Z

Zany,
ŝercemulo.

Zeal,
fervoro.
Zealot,
fervorulo.
Zealous,
fervora.
Zebra,
zebro.
Zenith,
zenito.
Zephyr,
venteto.

Zero, nulo.
Zest, gusto.
Zigzag, zigzago.
Zinc, zinko.
Zinc-worker, zinkisto.
Zodiac, zodiako.
Zone, terzono.
Zoology, zoologio.
Zoophyte, zoofito.
Zouave, zuavo.

Printed in Great Britain
by Amazon